THERE'S
MONEY
WHERE YOUR
MOUTH IS

Third Edition

A Complete Insider's Guide to Earning
Income and Building a Career in Voice-Overs

Elaine A. Clark

ALLWORTH PRESS
NEW YORK

Allworth Press books may be purchased in bulk at special discounts for sales promotion, corporate gifts, fund-raising, or educational purposes. Special editions can also be created to specifications. For details, contact the Special Sales Department, Allworth Press, 307 West 36th Street, 11th Floor, New York, NY 10018 or info@skyhorsepublishing.com.

16   5 4

Published by Allworth Press,
an imprint of Skyhorse Publishing, Inc.
307 West 36th Street, 11th Floor, New York, NY 10018.

Allworth Press® is a registered trademark of Skyhorse Publishing, Inc.®, a Delaware corporation.

www.allworth.com

Cover design by Adam Bozarth

Library of Congress Cataloging-in-Publication Data
Clark, Elaine A.
 There's money where your mouth is : an insider's complete guide for making money and building a career in voice-overs / Elaine A. Clark. -- 3rd ed.
    p. cm.
 Includes bibliographical references and index.
 ISBN 978-1-58115-878-6 (alk. paper)
1. Television announcing--Vocational guidance. 2. Television advertising--Vocational guidance.
3. Voice-overs--Vocational guidance. 4. Voice culture. 5. Radio announcing--Vocational guidance. 6. Radio advertising--Vocational guidance. I. Title.
 PN1992.8.A6C53 2011
 791.4502'8023--dc23
                          2011032422
 ISBN 978-1-58115-878-6

Printed in the United States of America

This book is dedicated to my voice-over students, talent agents, producers and directors, who have shaped and molded my voice-over career, companies that have trusted me to cast and direct their audio projects, and corporate clients who have benefited from the skills in this book and my personal training to enhance their lives and virtual communication skills.

I urge you to take your time while reading this book to practice the exercises and absorb the information. Write in it. Dog-ear the pages. Refer to it often throughout your career. It is dense with valuable information for voice actors of all levels.

What people are saying about the book and Elaine Clark's teaching method:

"Nothing feels more natural than being in front of the camera doing my thing. When it comes time to go into a carpeted room alone and talk to a microphone, that is not so natural. Elaine has a brilliant way of making you feel instantly comfortable, like she was a friend for years. A few minutes later she had me using my hands (as I feel natural doing anyway) to create changes in my voice. Amazing! Her techniques are incredible. Her system is quick and clear. I now look forward to that carpeted room."

Jeffrey Saad, Host of Cooking Channel's *United Tastes of America*

"In today's competitive voice-over market, it's all about specifics. From acting, to analyzing copy, to agents and marketing, *There's Money Where Your Mouth Is* generously outlines and details the business of voice-over."

Bob Bergen, Emmy Award– and Annie Award–nominated voice actor and Porky Pig in Cartoon Network's *The Looney Tunes Show*

"When looking for a text to support the introduction to voice acting class at San Diego Community College, I found *There's Money Where Your Mouth Is* to be the perfect choice. Students are able to test their talent using the many real world examples that cover the gamut of the business and figure out if they have what it takes to make it. With the business changing so fast, having a new edition with up-to-date business and marketing chapters will continue to make this a must-have book for anyone wanting to know more about the business and where they might fit."

Connie Terwilliger, full-time voice actor and voice-over instructor

"There are countless books about voice-over with suspiciously similar titles to *There's Money Where Your Mouth Is,* and at least one of them significantly plagiarized it. Why? Because this book — from the moment it was first published — firmly established itself as the Bible of our industry and Elaine Clark as the ultimate authority. Now, at last, she's giving us a new, up-to-date version of the best book on the business. Let's just say it's the New Testament!"

Harlan Hogan, voice actor and author of *Voice Actor's Guide to Recording at Home and on the Road* with Jeffrey Fisher and *VO: Tales and Techniques of a Voice-Over Actor*

Contents

DEDICATION		III
CONTENTS		V
ACKNOWLEDGMENTS		XI
INTRODUCTION		XII
WHERE ARE PROFESSIONAL VOICE-OVERS USED?		XII
HOW BUSINESSES USE VOICE-OVERS		XIII
THE FOUR LEVELS OF LEARNING		XIII
I. BUILDING A FOUNDATION		1
Chapter 1	GETTING STARTED	3
	YOUR VOICE	3
	WHO GETS THE WORK?	4
	BEGINNING YOUR CAREER	4
	UNION VS. NON-UNION	6
	ACTING & IMPROV CLASSES	7
	PRACTICING AT HOME	8
	HOME RECORDING	9
	STUDIO NEEDS AND OPTIONS	10
	OPTION 1: INEXPENSIVE	11
	OPTION 2: MOBILE DEVICE	12
	OPTION 3: MODERATE PRICE	12
	OPTION 4: INTERMEDIATE PRICE	12

OPTION 5: PROFESSIONAL LEVEL   13

TECH TALK   14

   WAV, AIFF, & MP3   14

   MP3 CONVERSION CHOICES   14

Chapter 2   VOICE-OVER AEROBICS, CARE, & HEALTH   15

BODY WARM-UPS   15

FACIAL WARM-UPS   16

VOCAL WARM-UPS   17

   RESONANCE   17

   ARTICULATION   19

   BREATHING   23

A PROFESSIONAL UNDERSTANDING OF THE VOICE   24

Chapter 3   COPY BASICS   30

IDENTIFY THE PRODUCT   31

SLOGANS   31

COPY POINTS   32

THE MESSAGE   34

COMPARISONS   35

NUMBERS, DOLLARS, & PERCENTAGES   36

PATTERNS & LISTS   37

   PATTERNS   38

   LISTS   39

SCRIPT CONSTRUCTION: SET-UP, BODY, RESOLVE   42

COLORING THE ADJECTIVES   45

THE AUDIENCE   45

Chapter 4   HIDING "THE SELL"   47

CREATING A DIALOGUE WITH THE LISTENER   47

	EXERCISES	48
	TIME TO PRACTICE	49
	BUILDING A CHARACTER	51
	WHO ARE YOU?	51
	WHERE ARE YOU?	53
	WHAT ARE YOU DOING?	55
	WHEN IS THE ACTION TAKING PLACE?	57
	WHY ARE YOU THERE?	58
Chapter 5	MAKING IT M.I.N.E.™	60
	WHAT DOES MAKING IT M.I.N.E. MEAN?	61
	MOTIVATION	62
	INTENTIONS	64
	NEED	65
	EMOTIONS	67
	PUTTING IT ALL TOGETHER	69
	SCRIPT ANALYSIS	70
	HIDING THE SELL	70
	M.I.N.E.	71
	SUMMARY AND SELF-EVALUATION	71
Chapter 6	MELODY & TEMPO	72
	MODULATION	75
	MELODY	76
	RHYTHM	77
	TEMPO	77
	UNDERCUTTING	78
	HOOK	79
	POP-UP WORDS	79

ARROW UP & DOWN   80

TRANSITIONS & BEATS   80

USE OF BREATH TO CREATE REALITY   81

WORD EMPHASIS CHART   81

    TIME TO PRACTICE   82

Chapter 7 COPYWRITER'S INTENTION: DIRECTING
TALENT & YOURSELF   83

INSIDER VIEW OF THE INDUSTRY   84

THE WRITER'S JOB   85

    TIME TO PRACTICE   86

Chapter 8 LAYERING TECHNIQUES   88

HAL RINEY INTERVIEW   88

TIPS FOR LIFTING THE WORDS OFF THE PAGE   90

    THE SCRIPT   90

    PERFORMANCE CHOICES   90

    ATTITUDE CHOICES   90

    BODY LANGUAGE   90

    VOICE QUALITY   91

THE PYRAMID SCHEME   92

Chapter 9 BELIEVING WHAT YOU SAY   95

FINDING THE TRUTH   96

FINAL THOUGHTS   97

    WARM UP YOUR VOICE AND BODY   97

    EMBRACE YOUR SOUND   97

    ACT WITH PERSONALITY   97

    UNDERSTAND THE COPY   97

    IDENTIFY THE PROBLEM AND SOLVE IT 97

    BELIEVE EVERYTHING YOU SAY   98

COMMIT TO YOUR CHOICES 98

DON'T MAKE EXCUSES 98

DON'T PUSH 98

REMEMBER WHERE YOU ARE 98

HAVE FUN 98

II. PUTTING IT TO PRACTICE 99

Chapter 10 TAGS, DONUTS, PROMOS, & TRAILERS 100

Chapter 11 ANNOUNCER 111

Chapter 12 SPOKESPERSON 126

Chapter 13 REAL PERSON 138

Chapter 14 COMMERCIAL CHARACTERS 150

Chapter 15 MULTIPLES 161

Chapter 16 CORPORATE NARRATION & DOCUMENTARIES 171

Chapter 17 AUDIOBOOKS 192

INSIDE THE AUDIOBOOK INDUSTRY 193

Chapter 18 ANIMATION, VIDEO GAMES, & TOYS 204

INSIDE THE ANIMATION WORLD 210

III. GETTING THE WORK 227

Chapter 19 THE DEMO 228

TYPES OF DEMOS 228

WHAT DO YOU PUT ON A DEMO? 229

SHOULD YOU PRODUCE IT YOURSELF? 230

BRANDING YOURSELF: FINDING YOUR NICHE 230

WHAT DO YOU DO WITH A DEMO? 231

UPDATING DEMOS 232

Chapter 20 GETTING AN AGENT LOCALLY & BEYOND 233

WHERE ARE THEY? 233

REQUESTING REPRESENTATION 234

SIGNING WITH AN AGENT 234

AUDITIONS 235

UNDERSTANDING AGENTS 235

Chapter 21 MARKETING YOUR TALENT 244

SOCIAL NETWORKS 244

BRANDING 245

AWARENESS CAMPAIGN 255

MARKETING STRATEGIES 256

WEBSITES 259

BUILDING A CLIENT LIST 259

Chapter 22 STAYING ON TOP OF THE BUSINESS 261

THE BOOKING 261

MOVING FORWARD 263

FOLLOW UP 264

THE BUSINESS 264

UNION 264

NON-UNION 266

Chapter 23 EPILOGUE: THE PEP TALK 268

SUMMARY TIPS 268

GLOSSARY 270

INDEX 278

Acknowledgments

A special thanks to my good friend Harlan Hogan for connecting me with Tad Crawford. For my parents, students at Voice One, Connie Terwilliger, and other voice-over instructors around the world who use my book as a text for staying on my case to write a third edition. For Joseph Schmitz, who supplied much-needed help, support, and suggestions. To the contributors, Bob Bergen, Simon Vance, John Erlendson, Vanessa Gilbert, Joan Spangler, Eugene O'Reilly, Ned Lott, Ian Price, John Crane, Robyn Stecher, and Mark Evanier. For all my Voice One students in San Francisco and beyond, whom I've enjoyed teaching for over a quarter of a century. And most of all to my wonderful daughters Emily, Laura, and Lizzie, and husband, Rob, who have supported, scolded, made fun of, and loved me while I was stuck to the chair writing this book and not doing fun things with them. May all you readers benefit from the information so you too can say: There's money where *my* mouth is. Enjoy the learning.

INTRODUCTION

Merriam-Webster Dictionary defines voice-overs as:

1 a: *the voice of an unseen narrator speaking (as in a motion picture or television commercial)*
   b: *the voice of a visible character (as in a motion picture) expressing unspoken thoughts*
2 a: *a recording of a voice-over*
First known use of Voice-Over: circa 1947

The way I define voice-over is: *the art of bringing life to written words.*

There are various and specific objectives in voice-overs:
   1 **Commercials:** to motivate the listener to feel and take action
   2 **Narration:** to inform or educate
   3 **Film, Animation, Games, and Toys:** to entertain
   4 **Voice Mail:** to greet and direct customers
   5 **Audiobooks:** to inspire imaginative thought

WHERE ARE PROFESSIONAL VOICE-OVERS USED?

Radio, TV, and Web commercials; Infomercials; Promos for TV shows, entertainment, and sporting events; Trailers for upcoming movies; Documentaries; Corporate narration for websites, e-learning, software, products, kiosks, and presentations; Film and games: Looping background voices, ADR (Automated Dialogue Replacement) matching on-screen lip flap with new dialogue, and Walla, creating a wall of sound in large crowd scenes; Cartoons; Voice Mail systems; and audio guides for museums, tourist sites, and visitor centers.

HOW BUSINESSES USE VOICE-OVERS

Phone sales and support, presentations, conference calls, tutorials, websites, e-learning modules, talking products, and events.

A speaker's primary issue when reading aloud is that it usually sounds like it's being read. Sentences start strong and taper off at the end. They lose volume and energy with every word. Commas, periods, and other forms of punctuation are either heard by the listener or disregarded by the reader. The message doesn't sound believable, real, and spontaneous. It sounds like individual words rather than complete thoughts.

The purpose of this book is to provide professional communication skills. Whether you are reading a commercial, voicing a video game, or making a presentation to a client, the techniques described in this book are guaranteed to improve your reading and speaking skills. It teaches the power of suggestion, rather than demand; the empowerment of letting the listener think the message you just delivered was his or her own idea, not yours; and the creative use of emotions to make the listener feel a certain way and want to take action.

Speaking is more than a mouth and tongue movement. Physical actions affect the tone, pitch, and emotion of the voice. A toe wiggle, head nod, shoulder shrug, clenched fist, and other physical body movements impact speech. Learning to play this instrument we call a body is what makes the words come alive. Action is in the movement. Emotions are in the breath. Being consciously aware of our unconscious behavior and using these techniques when speaking helps the message come alive.

As you learn the numerous techniques provided in this book, cut yourself some slack. Some days you will be amazing. Other days, the gears will move slowly. Analyze your understanding of each concept using this simple yet complex system of understanding ourselves:

THE FOUR LEVELS OF LEARNING

1. Unconsciously Incompetent — You're a bad communicator and don't know it.
2. Consciously Incompetent — You know you're a poor communicator and don't know how to fix it.
3. Consciously Competent — If you think about it, you can deliver the message, but it sounds a little pushed.
4. Unconsciously Competent — You pick up any script and it sounds natural and believable, like you're talking.

This book is dense with information. It is not meant to be read in one sitting. Each chapter contains a full lesson that takes time to absorb. Write in it. Read it through several times. Practice aloud. Record yourself and listen back. Finely tune your ears to the subtle nuances of the voice. Coordinate your body movements with the words. Learn to trust and use your emotions.

Dive in and let the learning begin!

I. BUILDING A FOUNDATION

Chapter 1

Getting Started

Thomas Edison is credited with saying, "Genius is one percent inspiration and 99 percent perspiration." So, wipe your brow, folks. You've got some work to do.

YOUR VOICE

Having a good voice is a gift. Knowing what to do with it is the challenge. Delivering a message properly requires *eye-brain-mouth* coordination. There is no room for multitasking. Full concentration is required. Distractions, insecurities, nervousness, and other mental blocks result in a proverbial train wreck as words are transposed, emotions are lost, and pronunciations and phrasings become garbled.

So, how is your voice? Most people's voices are fine. Some have texture, some are smooth, some are high, and some are low. Whatever voice you have, it's you! Common issues or complaints people have often include sibilance (a hissing "s" sound); accents, regionalisms, and dialects (which may be an asset in one area of the business and a detriment in another); lisps and enunciation issues; upswings at the end of sentences and phrases that imply a question rather than a statement; thin/quiet voices that need strength and air support; and high voices (unless used to perform children's voices). With some practice, many of these issues can be improved. Other issues involved in the recording process, including mouth noises, plosives from p's, t's, k's, and other articulators, volume inconsistencies, and spit on f's and other fricative and aspirated sounds, add additional challenges. These, too, can be worked on, minimized, or edited out in the recording session.

WHO GETS THE WORK?

When I started my voice-over career in the Stone Age year of 1980, 90 percent of the work went to men and 10 percent went to women. Over the next thirty-plus years, the division of labor has become a bit more balanced as women claim 30–40 percent of the market. As more women become CEOs of large companies and hold high-level political positions, the market share of voice-over work reflects that change. The gender of who gets the work is not only the result of a good audition or demo but also a direct result of the times we live in. Historically, the style of work changes with each new political and economic climate. In times of war, deep, authoritative voices are in demand. When the economy is good, humorous spots are more in vogue and lean towards younger voices layered with sarcasm and irony. As the large baby boomer population ages, older voices selling pharmaceuticals are needed. If a tragic event occurs in the country, compassionate voices are the norm. When the economy hovers in the middle, it's fair game for anyone, as no tried-and-true rules apply. The best way to keep up with these trends is to listen. Your ears are the most important assets in voice-over work.

Also, as the world becomes more globally connected, accents and regionalisms are accepted by the general public and desired by many who hire talent. Actors who were told they would never book work because of their foreign accent are in demand for jobs targeted to a broader global market.

Bottom line is that when it comes to a choice between a believable delivery and a vocal quality, good acting always wins out.

BEGINNING YOUR CAREER

The once perceived closed field of voice-overs has broken wide open with the prolific use of free, inexpensive, easy-to-use audio recording software and inexpensive microphones. Pay-to-play websites like Voices.com and Voice123.com make it accessible to just about anyone who wants to hang up a voice-over shingle. Landing a talent agent for more lucrative jobs takes a bit more effort. Acquiring additional representation in numerous cities all across the country and world is yet an additional goal for many people pursuing this business. Audition scripts are emailed; the voice actor records it at home and either emails, posts, or uploads the mp3. Actors, especially when they are first signed with a talent agent, often have the option to go into the agent's office to audition. This allows face time to get to know the agent and the benefit of another person's direction and feedback.

While once a very social business, voice acting has become a home-based business with a lot of solitude. Some actors work at home and never venture into a professional recording studio. Numerous others don't have agency representation or go into their offices. When a voice-over gathering occurs, it's a treat to connect with fellow actors. It's an even better opportunity to mingle with directors and producers who hire talent. When these gatherings occurs, the actor should remember these Networking Golden Rules:

1. Thou shall not brag or be a talking résumé.
2. Thou shall not descend on directors, agents, and producers and talk shop or ask for a job unless they initiate the topic.
3. Thou shall get to know people in the business as human beings and not as a prey to be trapped and cornered.
4. Thou shall remember that people like to work with friends and colleagues whom they trust and enjoy being around.
5. Thou shall remember that human qualities that connect one person with another make for a lasting relationship.
6. Thou shall remember that you are not your job but what you do when you are not recording.
7. Thou shall not write about auditions and jobs on social networking sites until the job has aired or permission to print or air the information has been granted.
8. Thou shall refer colleagues to jobs and they shall repay the favor.
9. Thou shall not write extremely long emails. The longer the email, the slower the response.
10. Thou shall always leave a positive impression and follow up in an appropriate manner during business hours.

The truth is no one needs another voice actor. There are plenty in the business. But, like a good restaurant, if the offerings are tasty, clients will be there to sample the goods. You just need to make sure your talents are ready to compete when you enter the market. Get good, solid training. Take time to learn the craft. There is no way anyone can learn all there is to know about voice acting in one short class. It takes time to learn the nuances and expectations of each style of work. When you're ready, put together a demo that plays to your strong suits. Each talent agent in each city has slightly different expectations for demos. Ask them first what style they prefer. If not represented, go to the talent agency's website or to Voicebank.net and listen to the numerous demos that are posted. Odds improve for casting recognition on pay-to-play sites like Voice123 when individual audio clips are uploaded and named in a manner that appeals to global talent searches. Instead of listing the job title or name of the client, list the style of delivery: warm, quirky, intelligent, etc.

UNION VS. NON-UNION

There are two performing arts unions that represent voice talent: Screen Actors Guild and American Federation of Talent and Radio Actors. Prior to the digital age, the difference between the two unions was simple. SAG represented actors on film; AFTRA represented actors on tape. Now that everything is digital, the definition is less clear. Radio commercials, industrial narrations, TV shows, newscasts, and local TV commercials are typically under the AFTRA umbrella. National TV commercials and film are in SAG's domain. Video games and web ads are just two areas where the two unions have cross over jurisdiction.

The two unions are also different in the joining process. AFTRA has an open-door policy; anyone can join if willing to pay the one-time initiation fee and bi-yearly dues. SAG requires that the actor be hired by a union producer first before consideration. This requires additional Taft-Hartley paperwork on the producer's part to prove that no union actor possessed the skills, look, or sound needed for the job and fill out a special request. When the request is granted and the actor is hired for the first union job, that actor can benefit from residuals (additional income for usage as stipulated by the union) without having to pay the initiation fee. Another term used to describe the first hired actor for a union job is a "Must Pay." A thirty-day grace period to work union or non-union jobs is granted the actor. For any union job the actor accepts after day thirty-one, the actor must pay the initiation fee and join the union.

As most people are born non-union, that's the obvious place to start. There is a lot of non-union work out there. The advantage is a simplified payroll and invoicing system. The disadvantage is lack of governance to insure payment within two weeks, predetermined minimal fee structure, and residuals. All work is a buyout. How non-union actors bid and get paid for jobs is all over the map. Some charge a set fee for the recording time, others add in their editing time in addition to being the voice, others charge on a per-file basis and add in a few dollars for labeling individual files, some have a minimal fee for every job but charge a two-hour minimum. The going rate for non-union work is whatever the market will bear. It'll be higher in robust economic times and lower when budgets are tight.

So, what happens when an actor joins the union and is offered non-union work? Union actors should refuse the job. When that is an option the actor does not want to pursue, he or she may submit a request to become a dues-paying non-member. This is a serious decision that means the actor will be blackballed and not allowed to vote or attend union meetings. Becoming financial core hurts the union and is frowned upon. Keeping the union strong is important to all voice actors, union and non-union. It establishes the rate of pay and work standards for all actors. At the time of this printing, SAG and AFTRA are in negotiations to form one joint union. For more information about this merger, check the SAG and AFTRA websites.

ACTING & IMPROV CLASSES

Most everyone who enters this business gets into it because someone tells him or her they have a beautiful, interesting, deep, resonant, funny, cute, sexy, or amazing voice. Then, the voice actor quickly learns that this business if more than just talking. It's about bringing life to the written word. That means we have to trust our instincts and act truthfully. Rather than reading word-word-word, we have to convey thoughts and feelings. As a trained stage actor, I struggled with my entry into voice acting. I know I could do a good job in a week or two once I absorbed the information and the character formed and came to life within me. Quickly, I learned that process takes too long. Immediacy is what's needed. Being willing to take a chance and change it on a dime is essential. Improvisation is the closest thing to voice acting. It teaches trust, spontaneity, and a willingness to take chances.

Depending on your ultimate career goals, acting and improv classes will move your career to greater heights. There's a part of a voice actor who believes he or she is lying when not an actor. The voice is the primary focus, not the manner in which the listener takes in the information. Therefore, I highly recommend that all voice actors take acting and improvisation classes. Besides having FUN, you'll be able to tap into deeper emotions, gain confidence in yourself, develop a stable of characters, and keep growing as a performer. Musicians practice their instruments every day. Singers sing. Runners run. Actors should act. If you're afraid to take this leap, that's a sign that you should sign up for an acting or improv class

NOW. Don't be afraid. Check out the acting and improv schools and colleges in your community. I guarantee you won't regret it!

PRACTICING AT HOME

Several things are needed to keep your skills moving forward: ears, mouth, heart/gut, mind, and body. Your ears are the most important. Listen to commercials, video games, cartoons, documentaries, and corporate narrations. Figure out what works and what doesn't. You can easily do this every time you turn on the computer, ride in the car, watch TV, or see a film. Listen for patterns, inflections, melody, tempo, and emotional shifts. Figure out where the voice is placed. Check to see if the styles or trends have changed. Mimic what you hear. Develop your own personal style that is current and interesting.

Learn how to use your body for optimum impact. We gesture every day, yet many readers get stiff and don't move when they read. Movement adds personality, emphasis, and ease to the delivery. It also helps with timing. A quick body movement replaces a dead, pregnant pause and creates change in the tone, attitude, and rhythm. Explore how specific movements influence the sound. Using the right hand, left hand, and both hands together give you three different vocal pitches. Jiggling the head, tilting it at an angle, or nodding offers additional nuance to the words. Shrugging the shoulders makes a word or phrase sound effortless. Squeezing the buttocks muscles deepens the voice and adds tension to the read. Opening the eyes wide, squinting, and moving the eyebrows up and down also change the voice. Explore how your movements alter the voice. That's part of learning to play our instrument.

Use your brain to comprehend the message and make script analysis choices. Then, put it on hiatus. Everything you say needs to sound believable and truthful. Connect the message to your heart and gut. If it stays in the brain, the listener will know you're lying. Bring passion, authority, and believability to everything you say. Placing your hands on your heart adds warmth and empathy, putting hands on the hips make a person sound confident and cocky, and arms above the head make a person feel and sound happy. You can use body movements to connect with your emotions and share them with the listener. Visualizing a situation that's important to you is another way to feel and share your emotions. Smiling adds positive impact.

After you've done your homework — understood the message, loosened up the body and opened yourself up emotionally — it's time to speak. Like an athlete or musician, warming up has a direct impact on the final result. Warm up the voice. Open your mouth and let the sound out. Explore the different sounds when you talk straight into the mic, at an angle, looking down, looking up, close to the mic, or several inches away.

HOME RECORDING

I asked several audio engineers what actors should expect when they set up their home recording studios. The answer was unanimous: More and more expensive boxes showing up on your doorstep. Most people start out slowly and inexpensively. Then, as their ability as an actor and audio engineer increases, they develop microphone, preamp, and room isolation envy.

As a guideline, here are a few simple recording dos and don'ts:

DO

1. Find a quiet, carpeted, well-padded place to record. This will minimize unwanted room tone, as the voice bounces off hard surfaces.
2. Buy an external microphone that is suited to your voice and budget.
3. Wear quiet clothes when recording.
4. Use an audio software program that records or saves your voice in wav or aiff formats and is able to convert sound files to mp3.
5. Wear headphones when listening back to your recording. You'll be able to tell if you are on mic and speaking into the mic's diaphragm, have breaths and clicks that need removal, the voice recording clips when it exceeds recording levels, unwanted ambient noise is present, and buzzes or hums persist due to audio digital interference. If you encounter A/D interference, turn off your mobile phone, unplug and replug the cables, and restart the audio recording program. If interference continues, you may have a more serious problem that requires research and advice from authorities on your particular hardware and software.
6. Pay attention to file naming conventions. Type the name of each file correctly as requested.
7. Normalize the sound file to uniformly increase the amplitude. Adding additional gain may also be necessary to increase the volume.

8. Be up-to-date on the latest file delivery options: Dropbox, personal or company ftp sites, third-party large file delivery sites, email, etc.

<u>DO NOT</u>

1. Position your microphone at the end of a long hallway or in a large open space. You will sound like you're in a cave.
2. Use the microphone in your computer to record auditions and jobs. Also, make sure that your recording software is set to the external microphone setting before recording.
3. Wear noisy clothing, have coins in your pocket, adorn yourself with jangling jewelry, or tap or blow into your microphone.
4. Send sound files in unsupported formats that are only readable on your computer. For example, Audacity's free downloadable program saves in an aup format that most other computers can't open. An added step is needed to export files in wav or mp3.
5. Deliver finished recordings without listening. Listening back to what you've recorded is part of quality control. Wearing headphones increases your ability to hear the finer details of the recording quality.
6. Disregard file names. Where sound files are used and located depend on the naming conventions. Type it appropriately and take note of the file format: wav, aiff, mp3, or other specific formats used by some companies.
7. Send sound files that have very low audio levels. They are very hard to hear.
8. Make an attempt to email large files that exceed ten megabytes. Most likely, they will bounce. Or, say you don't know how to deliver sound files. There are many options out there. Just type "upload large files" into your bowser, and numerous free and pay options will be listed. If you want to upload many files quickly and easily onto an ftp site, type in "drag and drop file upload." Select the best option that suits your computer and usability.

STUDIO NEEDS AND OPTIONS

There are simple and inexpensive ways to set up a home recording studio for your auditions, jobs, and podcasts. Free recording software, inexpensive microphones, and ways to minimize room tone keep budgets in check. There are also expensive options for top-level home studios. I've broken the choices into five categories to satisfy price ranges and needs. Feel free to mix, match, and research options that aren't listed. The industry changes quickly and new equipment and software emerge constantly.

Option 1: Inexpensive

Download Audacity at audacity.sourceforge.net or use another free, easy-to-use recording software program that may be preinstalled on your computer. Make sure you have the ability to deliver files in .wav, .aiff, and .mp3. Additional downloads may be necessary to convert and export mp3 files. The Audacity site provides a link to the Lame mp3 encoder. In the Help section of the site are a user manual, a tutorial, and tips to educate you on the recording process.

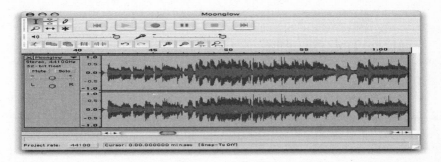

Next, you'll need a microphone. USB microphones are not the best quality but are much better than the microphone in your computer. Here is a list of several condenser mics under $150: Blue Microphones Yeti (better than the Snowflake and Snowball); Audio-Technica AT2020; Samson G-Track, C01U, and C03U; MXL 990; and AKG Perception 120. Some of these mics come with a desktop base, others require an additional purchase of a microphone stand.

To minimize some of the room tone echo, place your microphone in the closet between your clothes, stack pillows around you, talk into a corner of the room draped with heavy fabric, or create your own sound studio by building a box with acoustical sound foam on the inside to put your mic inside. It's not very glamorous when you stick your head inside these areas, but they get the job done.

To listen to your recordings, insert the earplug connector from your cellphone or portable music device into your computer. You'll get a better sound than listening to the recording back through your computer speakers.

Option 2: Mobile Device

Phone and hand held devices like iPhone and iPad offer light, portable, and cheap options for recording and editing your voice. The iAudition app is less than $5. Twisted Wave is around $80 and offers more functionality. The AT2020 and Blue Yeti microphones work well with these audio programs.

Option 3: Moderate Price

Microphones from $200–$500 include the Harlan Hogan Signature Series Voice Over Microphone, Rode NT1-A, SE Electronics USB2200a, and Sure KSM32. Some are complete kits with shock mount, XLR cable, and pop shield. Others need microphone stands, shock mounts, cables, and pop filters like the Royer PS-101 and Avant Electronics PS-1. Two-hundred-dollar recording, mixing, editing, and mastering software programs include Adobe® Soundbooth® and Logic Express.

For non-USB microphones, CEntrance MicPort Pro, Blue Icicle, and MXL Mic Mate Pro are XLR to USB audio interfaces with microphone preamplifiers. To hold your script, consider the Manhasset M48 music stand. Or, connect your iPad to the microphone stand with an iKlip. For recording and playback, Sony, AKG, Shure, and Sennheiser make good studio-quality headphones for around $100. For better acoustics for under $150, the Porta-Booth® is pre-made and ready for you to set on the desk, place your microphone inside, and talk into. You can read scripts off lighted handheld devices like an iPad, Kindle, or smartphone, or add an inexpensive LED book light inside the box to read the printed script.

Option 4: Intermediate Price

Microphones from $500–$1200 include the JZ Microphone BH-2, which has a true, clear sound based on golden drops technology, the Sennheiser shotgun MKH-416, the AT4050 with its good, flat neutral sound, the warm-sounding AKG C414, or the Neumann TLM 103. Recording software in the $350 area includes Adobe® Audition® and Sound Forge™. For acoustical help and ambient noise control in the $350 range, consider the Porta-Booth Pro® or Primacoustic® FlexiBooth 24" x 48" wall-mounted acoustic cupboard. If you have a spare closet that can be turned into a recording booth, Auralex makes studio foam wedge panels that glue to the walls. For actors with clients who want to direct over the phone, add a JK Audio Inlinepatch or Telos Systems One phone patch. For real-time remote sessions that stream uncompressed audio to another location, Source-Connect has a range of choices to fit almost any voice talent's needs.

Option 5: Professional Level

Microphones in the $1500 plus range include the very popular Neumann U87, Microtech Gefell MT 71 S, Telefunken R-F-T AK47, JZ Vintage 47, and JZ BlackHole 1, BH1S and BH3. With the better mic, you should get a better pop filter like the JZ/PF for $140 or the $400 BH/SPK used with the JZ BlackHole 1–3 series mics. You'll also need a good preamp, like the Millennia SST that has EQ and compression in-line to blend solid state and tubes channels to get a warmer tone or the Neve Portico half-rack units. At this point you should definitely upgrade to Monster cables, too. Consider building your own voice-over booth or purchase a sound isolation room from WhisperRoom, Inc. or VocalBooth.com. You'll also need a good pair of speakers, so consider something in the $200–$600 range like the Focal Professional CMS 40, Mackie MR8, or JBL LSR2325P. While you're upgrading equipment and have a need for more recording and editing capabilities, step up to ProTools HD or Logic Pro. To complete the listening experience, upgrade to headphones in the $200–$350 range like the Audio-Technica ATH-M50S, Ultrasone Pro 750, or Sony MDR-7509HD. And if you have clients in other parts of the country, ISDN may be needed, in addition to Source-Connect and a phone patch.

Microphones are very personal. Audio equipment and software change and upgrade frequently. It's hard to make a blanket recommendation of the best ones to buy in each category and I'm sure I've left off someone's favorite. The information listed above is merely a suggestion. Do your research and find out what's best for you. There may be additional pieces of equipment you'll need or want to purchase to complete your home studio.

TECH TALK

These are the most common requests for recording audio out of your home or small office:

WAV, AIFF, & MP3

Sample Format: 16 bit

Sample Rate: 44.1 kilohertz

Record in MONO and deliver the files that way unless a STEREO conversion is requested.

MP3 Conversion Choices

Bit Rate: 128k (approximately 6 to 1 compression) and 192k (nearly 4 to 1 compression) are best for emailing and posting on websites. Smaller bit rates loose a lot of sound quality and are smaller files. Conversely, larger bit rates have better quality and are larger files. Check the preferences menu of your recording software to set your conversion rate.

Chapter 2

VOICE-OVER AEROBICS, CARE, & HEALTH

Two key components of communication are clear, clean, crisp *enunciation* and sustained, supported *breath support*. It requires breathing from your feet all the up to the top of your head and pushing the words out to the end of the sentence and a few seconds beyond. The body and facial muscles need to be warmed up so they are flexible and able to handle sudden changes in emotion and speed, as well as difficult word combinations and stylistic differences.

Tension resides in the muscles, particularly the shoulders and neck. For speech to sound confident, relaxed, and natural it is important for the body to be loose and free of nervous tension. The following is a list of exercises to warm up the body, face and voice.

BODY WARM-UPS

Warming up the body helps liven up the voice, circulate air through the body, and add a sparkle to the read. It is especially important to warm up and engage your muscles when you are tired or have been sitting a long time. Additionally, it helps clear the mind of outside distractions and add focus to the vocal performance.

The following is a list of simple exercises. To hear how these and other static and ballistic stretches effect the voice, record a few lines of a script when the body is cold and then record the same lines after the body is warmed up. You should hear a marked improvement in the second read.

1. Shoulders — Roll the shoulders forward, up, and back several times. Hold each position a few seconds. Next, pull the shoulders up to your ears and hold it in that position for 10 seconds, up and back 10 seconds and then down. Repeat 2–3 times. Now, roll them up, back, and down in a circular motion 5–6 times.
2. Neck — You need to be careful when warming up the neck. Don't push yourself too hard so that it hurts. Gently drop your right ear to your shoulder. Hold it for 5–10 seconds. Repeat on the left side. Then drop your chin to your chest and hold it. You'll feel your back muscles stretching. Repeat if necessary.
3. Arms — Stretch your arms out straight, shoulder high. Make little circles clockwise several times and then counterclockwise. Now make large circles forward and back. Finally, swing your arms across your body and back out to your sides like you're hugging and releasing a person.
4. Upper Body — Put your hands on your waist and rotate right and left a few times. Next, reach your right arm up and over your head as you lean to the left. Hold for a few seconds and repeat on the other side. Finally, clasp your hands behind your back and lift them up as high as you can comfortably. Release and shake your hands out 10–20 times.
5. Lower Body — If you're able, stretch out your thigh muscles by bending your knee and pulling your foot up behind your back. Hold it for fifteen seconds or so before releasing and repeating on the other leg. Next, spread your legs apart, lean over, and touch your toes, ankles, or legs (whichever you can reach).
6. Put it all together — Shake out your wrists and then your arms. Raise one foot and shake that out before repeating on the other leg. Gently bounce up and down and shake out the rest of the body.

FACIAL WARM-UPS

Many people barely open their mouths when they speak. In this business, we need to have a rubber face. That means using more face, tongue, and neck muscles. The wider and more open the mouth, the prettier the sound will be as it's projected through the microphone and into the recording.

Facial warm-ups are especially necessary when reading trailers, promos, retail, and highly technical copy. It's another way of protecting the voice when performing a character for cartoons, games, and toys.

Some of these exercises can be used to create new voices when you lock your face in that position and speak with clarity. Yes, it's hard. But that frozen position locks a voice in place and changes the rhythm of the words and the vocal quality.

As you warm up your voice, return to a neutral position between exercises.

1. Open your mouth as wide as it can go. After you feel that stretch, open and close your mouth in a chewing motion. Do this five or six times, like a cow chewing its cud. If you like, make some noise while you're doing this.
2. Pucker your lips and stick them out in an extreme kissing position. You should be able to see your lips. Twist your lips to the right and hold. Then repeat to the left.
3. Open the mouth wide again and drop the jaw so that it forms an "O." Pull the lips inward and wrap them around the tops of your teeth.
4. Open your mouth and stick out your tongue. Try to make it touch your chin. Hold it for a few seconds until you feel the muscles in the back of the tongue start to relax.
5. Like a bulldog, place your bottom teeth on your upper lip. While in this overbite position, lift the chin up slightly and gently stretch your neck muscles.
6. Open your mouth and eyes wide and then scrunch it together. Repeat this open and closed facial position a few times.
7. Yawn and add an "ahhhh" sound on the exhale.

VOCAL WARM-UPS

This section is focused on resonance, articulation, and breathing. If you haven't already done so, warm up the body and face first before practicing these exercises.

RESONANCE

Voice resonance is the result of vibrations in the facial bones, mouth cavity, teeth, and hard palate. It is what separates a thin, light, wispy voice from a tonally full, rich, commanding voice. Some people are blessed with natural resonance; others must learn to create it. When speaking, vibrations should resonate from the forehead, between the eyes, back of the nose, sinus area below the cheeks, under the jawbones, and sides of the throat.

As you practice the following exercises, use your fingertips to feel for vibrations in these areas.

1. Grab a good breath and say, "hum." Hold onto the final "m" sound until the lips vibrate. Move your lips around until you find the most buzzing sensation. Sustain the "m" sound for ten to fifteen seconds. Feel the vibrations in the lips, nose, jaw, cheeks, sinus, and sides of the throat.

2. Make an "n" sound by opening the mouth and touching the tip of the tongue behind the upper front teeth. As the tongue vibrates on the back of the front teeth and the palate, a vibration should be felt in the nose bone, maxillary sinus area, jaw, and sides of the throat. Move the tongue along the roof of the mouth, from behind the front teeth to the middle of the palate, without losing connection or the vibration.

3. In a similar fashion, make an "l" sound. Note that the tongue is curled slightly and placed a little further back than the "n" position. Move the tongue back and forth along the roof of the mouth without losing contact.

4. Alternate between the "m," "n," and "l" sounds. The "m" sound stimulates the front of the face; the "n" sound moves the focus backward, away from the lips; and the "l" sound is more open and has an upward movement. Now, say the word, "mental." *(Funny, I know, but it has the right sounds in it.)*

5. Place your top teeth on your bottom lip and make a "v" sound. Move your bottom lip out and back while keeping a constant vibration.

6. Pull your lips back, as if it's in a wide smile, and make a "z" sound. Create different "z" sounds by moving the tongue back and forth and puckering and releasing the lips.

7. Open the mouth, breathe in and release the air as you verbalize an extended "ah" sound. Feel the vocal chord vibrations in the front of the throat as the sound reverberates in the larynx. Repeat the exercise several times. Each time, drop the musical pitch one or two notes lower until you reach your lowest register. This exercise is very effective when it's necessary to relax the voice or speak in a lower pitch.

8. Open your mouth in a wide oval position and make an "ah" sound. Engage your lip muscles and stretch your lips forward until they form a small "o" shape and make an "oh" sound. Repeat the process, moving back and forth between a wide "ah" sound and a small "oh." Listen to how the sounds in the

mouth cavity change as it adjusts to the shape of the lips and mouth.

9. Breathe in and make a long "e" sound. Hold the "e" until you feel the vibrations in the jawbone, sides of the throat, and sinuses.

10. Breathe in and create a chant starting with an "ah," going to an "m," and ending with an "o." Repeat three or four times, trying to sustain one continuous sound for thirty seconds.

11. Awaken your vocal cords by singing your favorite tune a cappella or along with the song. Forget whether or not you are a good singer. Sing loudly and with gusto!

ARTICULATION

One aspect of a voice actor's job is to be able to clearly pronounce difficult word combinations. Words and phrases such as "mileage may vary according to road conditions and driving habits," "regularly priced," "February" (with the middle "r" pronounced), and "cubic foot frost-free refrigerator-freezer" can tongue-tie even the most seasoned voice actor.

Whether you're playing a quick-talking game show host, soft-spoken real person, booming "voice of God," or smiley retail announcer, you need to be prepared. The following exercises will help combat sibilance, plosives, lazy tongue, and mouth problems.

• Sibilance

Sibilance is the result of an exaggerated "s" sound. It is reminiscent of a leaky radiator, slithering snake, or radio station as it loses its signal. Minor sibilance distortions can be corrected in the studio by using a "de-esser" during the recording or afterwards in post. This high frequency sound is created when someone has dental problems (like missing teeth or loose dentures); the *s*, *sh*, and *z* sounds are not differentiated but all are spoken as an *s*; sustaining the *s* sound too long; or having too many sibilant words in a single sentence.

There are a few ways to minimize sibilance:

1. Smile on the *s* sound. This pulls the *s* backwards as the lips are separated, spread apart, and pulled back.

2. Drop the jaw quickly every time you say an *s*. This breaks the continuous sound.

3.   Place *s* words at different musical pitches to separate the sounds.

4.   When sibilance can't be fixed using one of these techniques, point your index finger upward and position it in the center of your mouth. It won't fix the pitch, but it will help prevent the air from hitting the microphone and amplifying the problem.

Exercises:

1.   Say the word "yes." Hold onto the final consonant and put your hand in front of your mouth. If the *s* is properly formed, you should not feel a rush of air. If you do feel air, adjust the mouth placement. Repeat the *s* sound eight to ten times, making sure that each sound is short, crisp, and concise. Using this succinct *s* technique, say the following phrase:

I kissed the silly salesperson that sold me this mattress for seventeen cents.

2.   The *sh* sound cuts through the air like wind through a car window. The tongue accepts a neutral position and the lips protrude slightly forward, as evidenced in the words "hush" and "shush." Say the words and feel the placement of the lips on the final *sh* sound as a steady flow of air rushes out. Now, repeat it eight to ten times so that it creates a short burst of sound. Notice how the lips protrude and retract at each verbalization. Using pronounced lip movements, read the following sentence aloud. Note that not all *sh* sounds are spelled the same way, like in the word "surely."

Josh, I surely wish you wouldn't push people when you rush to pay cash for Shirley's new plush dishtowel.

3.   People are often lazy when they pronounce a *z* because it requires more effort to execute than an *s*. The tongue needs to be awakened to the buzzing sensation. To form a proper *z*, place the tongue in the s position, then arch the tip of the tongue and move it slightly backward on the roof of the mouth. Hold the *z* until a strong vibration can be felt in the tongue and teeth areas. Say the word "zebra," holding onto the opening *z* sound until a strong vibration is felt. Using shorter spurts of sound, practice saying the *z* sound eight to ten times, ensuring that each *z* has a vibration. Then read the following sentence

two or three times, first slowly and then at normal speed. Feel each *z* buzz. Note that sometimes a word with an *s* is actually a *z* sound.

These sizzling hot sales days are yours and ours because winning a prize is always a breeze at Joe's Trailer Zone.

4. To ensure differentiation between the *s*, *sh*, and *z* sounds, practice saying the popular tongue twister, "She sells sea shells by the sea shore." Remember the phonetics: SHe SellZ Sea SHellZ by the Sea Shore. Now try a more apropos tongue twister:

Voiceovers are sheer joy when the s's sound sexy.
VoiSeoverZ are Sheer joy when the Esses Sound Sexy.

5. Finally, read the sentence below using the drop jaw, smile, and melodic pitch change options to minimize the *s* sound. Focus on the vowel nearest the s rather than lingering on the *s*.

Since sibilance is a disaster it is essential to simplify and shorten the *s* sound.

• Plosives

A plosive is a sudden explosion of air as it hits the microphone's diaphragm. The result is an undesirable loud pop or distortion in the recording. Hard consonants such as *b*, *k*, *p*, and *t* are the usual culprits. If you place your hand in front of your mouth as you say these letters, you will feel a sharp rush of air as it hits your hand. Microphone pop filters and windscreens help alleviate some of the problem.

The following is a list of solutions to minimize or eliminate the plosive:

1. Change position on the microphone and talk across the microphone at an angle to its diaphragm.
2. Smile so your lips are spread rather than protruding.
3. Shift focus away from the consonant and onto an accompanying vowel sound.
4. As a last resort, put one finger pointing up in front of the mouth when voicing the plosive word. Remove the finger from that position as soon as that word is voiced.

• Vowels and Consonants

Words strung together in a sentence form a melody with a distinct tempo and rhythm. Articulated consonants add rhythm. Resonating vowels and consonants behave like string instruments. Vowels hold the tune together.

The following are some exercises to help you warm up your musical notes.

1. Quickly repeat each letter of the alphabet four to ten times, starting with the letter *a*. Listen to where the sound originates, how it is formed, and the location, and speed at which the air is released. Note the specific functions of the tongue, lips, and teeth.

2. Say the alphabet again, this time elongating each letter. Open and close the mouth and lip opening to find optimal resonance. Notice how consonants like *b, c, d, g, p, t, v* and *z* end in a final "e" sound, *j* and *k* form a long "a," and *q* and *w* become a "u" sound.

3. Read the following script three ways. Once quickly tapping the consonants, a second time elongating all the vowels, and a third time mixing it up so you only elongate the key words like *movie, new giant-screen TV, Dynovision*, etc. Notice the difference of how you play these "notes" creates a different "tune."

> Okay, all you movie fanatics. Here's your chance to own your own movie theatre! Don't believe it? It's the affordable new giant-screen TV by Dynovision. You heard it right. Dynovision, the leader in video technology. Check out the six-foot diagonal screen. The resolution and sound are so superior you'll swear I'm standing right in your living room. The new giant screen TV by Dynovision makes you feel like you're in the movies. The only difference is *you* have to pop the popcorn.

• Verbal Weight Training

"Verbal weight training" is to the mouth what ankle weights are to a runner. When weight or resistance is removed, the targeted area feels light and easily maneuverable.

Begin the training by putting your front teeth together. Without separating your teeth, recite the following tongue twister four times as clearly and distinctly as possible. Start out slowly, making sure you voice all the sounds. Then you can speed up. The tongue and lips will have to work harder to compensate for the lack of jaw movement.

How much curry can a great chef add if the kitchen is all out of curry?
Not enough curry to satisfy the chef who must have curry in a hurry.

Now, separate your teeth and say it again. With full mobility the mouth should spring open, and the words should sound round and clear. This resistance technique is useful on disclaimers and other pieces of copy where speed and clarity are extremely important.

BREATHING

Breath support and control can either make or break a read. To find out if you have proper breath support, see if you can read this entire retail ad in one breath. Don't tense up. Stay relaxed, breathe in, hold the air in for a split second to let it settle, and read the script aloud.

Twenty-percent savings on lawn chairs, barbeque grills, patio furniture, sun umbrellas, birdbaths, gazebos, fountains, above-ground swimming pools, sun decks, spas, swing sets, planters, garden tools, pink flamingos, and outdoor sprinkler and lighting systems.

Did you make it? If you did so without turning blue or sounding strained, pat yourself on the back. If not, you need to develop your lung capacity and breath support.

Without proper breath support, somewhere in the middle of the copy, the actor's breath becomes strained, runs out, and stops. Reading a lot of words in one breath requires the same focus, relaxation, and air intake as a swimmer preparing to swim the length of the pool underwater. Without a thorough cleansing breath to expel the old air and a deep intake, the swimmer sputters to the surface gasping for air only seconds after diving into the water.

Getting a good breath does not involve moving the shoulders up and down or puffing the chest out unnaturally. Proper breathing engages the diaphragm and rib cage. Place your hands just above your waist with your fingers on the back and your thumbs on your stomach. Open your mouth, relax the throat, and gently inhale. You should feel a sideways expansion of the ribs.

A PROFESSIONAL UNDERSTANDING OF THE VOICE

A voice-over actor who is also a nationally certified Speech-Language Pathologist (SLP) attended one of my classes at Voice One in San Francisco. He noticed parallels in the techniques I use with traditional clinical procedures he's routinely utilized during his thirty years as a SLP. Although the intended outcome of our teaching and assisting of others is different, the rationale is the same. Here are some of his clinical insights.

Eugene O'Reilly, M. A., C. C. C.-SLP, Speech-Language Pathologist Certified by the American Speech-Language Hearing Association California Speech-Language Pathology License, located in San Francisco.

An important aspect of Elaine's teaching technique is the use of movement and gestures to accompany speaking. In helping patients with coordinating speech movements, hand/arm gestures are often used to help facilitate movements of the mouth, jaw, etc. Gestures and body movements used in the way Elaine teaches add super fortification of coordinated speech to someone reading copy for voice-over. Elaine's facilitating techniques help speed up learning and provide a great foundation of physical memories and methods for the voice-over artist. This is because voice-over artists are essentially unlearning the normal everyday way of speaking and newly learning the very specialized way of speaking involved in voice-over.

Elaine graciously invited me to include information/ techniques from my background for this section of her book.

Top to Bottom Guidelines for Safe and Healthy Voice Usage

1. **Importance of Hydration for Voice Health:**
    Don't let yourself become thirsty!
    When we drink liquid, our vocal cords do not get wet. If they did, we would drown. Normal Swallowing prevents food and liquid from going into our lungs (aspiration). Breathing and vocal cord vibrations happen in the "front pipe" of the throat and swallowing food and liquids happens in the "back pipe" of the throat.

    Your vocal cords need a thin layer of specialized mucus coating them in order to vibrate and produce sound properly. It takes an hour for water we drink to travel through the body and change into that specialized mucus.

A general guideline for producing the specialized mucus for the vocal cords would be to drink two glasses of water at each meal and one hour before using your voice.

If you have a dry mouth and there is no water available, gently bite your tongue to produce saliva. Avoid lozenges, hard candy, gum, or anything similar, because they use up saliva (dehydrate), which takes time for the body to replace. Caffeine or any other diuretic will also dehydrate us. We lose 10 percent of our body water each day, simply by breathing. Other conditions that cause dehydration can be alleviated by drinking water often throughout the day.

If you have persistent thick or excessive mucus, chronic dry mouth, or related symptoms, schedule an examination with your doctor to determine the cause. Persistent (chronic) problems with dry mouth, difficulty with swallowing, or excessive mucus should also be addressed and treated by your physician or an Ear Nose and Throat Specialist (Otolaryngologist).

2. Few Comments about Excessive Throat Clearing

Throat clearing is normal for moving unwanted mucus/objects out of the windpipe. The problem arises when an individual has repeated colds or persistent upper respiratory conditions such as allergies. During those conditions they inevitably clear their throat because of excess mucus and begin to memorize throat clearing for relief.

The problem arises when they continue to clear their throat when it's no longer needed because it became a memorized habit. To overcome this is a matter of conscious control. Don't clear your throat unless you have to, and avoid throat clearing by swallowing or sipping water.

Persistent or chronic problems with throat clearing should once again be addressed by your physician and or an Ear Nose and Throat Specialist (Otolaryngologist).

3. Overview of Articulation (Pronunciation)

The structures of the face, mouth (teeth, tongue, soft and hard palate, etc.) are unique to each individual and give us each a unique voice and manner of speaking. Our body's complex speaking equipment consists of various kinds of specialized tissue, an intricate array of muscles in the tongue and face, throat, and chest, and a proper balance of fluids/mucus in the mouth and throat.

Coordination and combining of tongue movements with jaw movements and soft palate movements while simultaneously coordinated with breathing and vocal cord vibration are the minimum requirements for speaking. Every speech sound we make when talking is produced with a particular posture of the aforementioned structures. It's difficult to say "ahh" with your lips puckered. It's difficult to say "oo" with your mouth wide open to say "ahh." That is once again because every speech sound has a corresponding posture of the mouth, lips, tongue, etc.

For precise articulation, learn the "oral postures" of the individual speech sounds you wish to produce. Once again, it is recommended to learn proper Speech Articulation from a certified Speech-Language Pathologist.

4. Lisping & Related Speech Sounds

Lisping and saying the sound of "r" incorrectly are the most common Speech errors of school-aged children. They often persist into adulthood without treatment.

Swallowing is done all day, every day. The development of swallowing, chewing, and eating in children coincides with the development of their speech and language skills.

In early infancy with no teeth and a liquid diet, an infant's speech is limited to imprecise sounds. As our teeth develop and we begin chewing, the muscles of the mouth and tongue grow stronger and get ready for speaking. How an infant is postured while they eat will determine the shape of their teeth and clarity of their speech as they get older. A straight posture, i.e., "sitting up straight" (*not flat on their back*) while feeding an infant will help develop a normal swallow pattern. This essentially means that the tongue will go from front to back of the mouth not toward the front teeth while swallowing.

Children who have weak tongue muscles and a reversed swallow pattern commonly develop a lisp and have overall imprecise speech. Children with a reverse swallow often develop a dental overbite, frequently have middle ear infections, and have trouble with reading. With or without speech therapy all of these conditions often affect adult life communication skills.

For adults with a persistent lisp, imprecise speech sounds, or any difficulty speaking or swallowing, an evaluation by a certified Speech-Language Pathologist is recommended. Contact the American Speech Language and Hearing Association to find a qualified professional in your area.

5. Breathing and Vocal Quality

Our vocal cords have been labeled "the queen of wind instruments." They work the same way as the reed on a saxophone or clarinet. Air must flow through them at a certain pressure to make them vibrate and produce sound. With no airflow the vocal cords will not vibrate. Too much air pressure and our voices will be too loud or not work smoothly. Voice sound is produced via air flowing through the vocal cords. No air, no sound. The greater the air pressure, the louder the sound.

Breathing is a body function that goes on without our thinking about it, but it can also be consciously controlled and trained for different purposes in human endeavors. We can also learn to breathe for precise and healthy voice usage.

Basic Guidelines for Efficient Breathing:

1. Learn to breathe in the lower part of your body.
2. Resist breathing in the area of your collarbone and upper chest. Allow your shoulders and upper chest to remain like a coat on a hanger (not moving).
3. Learn to inhale and speak with the lower part of your body. It is common for most people to raise their chest and move it up and down when they inhale/exhale. This manner of breathing works against using the voice properly. They also speak trying to use the upper chest muscles and throat, which is once again counterproductive.
4. Avoid holding your breath as this pushes your vocal cords up into your throat, which you don't want.
5. Without going into detail here, professional voice users should learn to inhale with the diaphragm and to exhale (and to speak) with the abdominal and lower back muscles. Essentially use the lower torso for inhaling and speaking. A simple directive for breathing in the lower part of your body would be "Breathe through your Feet!"

It is recommended to seek professional help in learning to use breathing to control voice loudness and pitch and properly use breathing for a long-lasting healthy and consistent vocal quality. Any problems with breathing or breath control should once again be addressed by your physician or qualified specialist.

6. Common Voice Disorders and What to Do about Them

There are two kinds of voice disorders. One type is caused by the person abusing or misusing their voice, and the other is caused by disease of some kind (virus, cancer, etc.).

Voice abuse/misuse disorders (caused by excessive yelling, overuse of the voice, and other lifestyle behaviors that damage the vocal cords) can often be remedied with voice treatment by a qualified SLP working in conjunction with ENT. Left untreated, abuse/misuse voice disorders such as vocal nodules may eventually require more serious intervention such as surgical removal.

In a limited way I will present a very general overview of common symptoms that would warrant a visit to your physician and/or an otolaryngologist:

a. Chronic Hoarseness—this is often overlooked as aesthetically pleasing in show business. It is one of the most common symptoms related to voice disorders such as vocal nodules (a callous on the vocal cords caused by abuse or misuse of the voice).

b. Loss of Voice or Voice Fatigue — Your voice should last up to nine hours without tiring. If your voice becomes tired quickly or if you have lost your voice or lose your voice often see your doctor and/or an otolaryngologist.

c. Need for Constant Throat Clearing or a Chronic Cough — especially without the presence of the cold, flu, or other respiratory ailment, should be addressed by your doctor or an otolaryngologist.

d. Acid Reflux Disease — Or any condition that allows stomach secretions to move up into the throat (e.g. *bulimia*) can cause burns on the vocal cords and the above listed symptoms. These conditions should once again be addressed by your doctor or an otolaryngologist.

For persistent problems, schedule an appointment with an otolaryngologist who specializes in care of the voice for an endoscopic vocal cord examination. If a serious vocal issue exists, you should be assessed and treated by qualified personnel. Contact the American Speech-Language and Hearing Association to find out about qualified personnel in your area. Non-Member: 800-638-8255; Fax: 301-296-8580; TTY (Text Telephone Communication Device): 301-296-5650; Email: actioncenter@asha.org; website: asha.org (There is a "find a professional" section on this website). National Office: 2200 Research Boulevard, Rockville, MD 20850-3289; USA Local: 301-296-5700.

7. Oral Resonance

Oral Resonance is the way the mouth and throat create a resonating chamber by movement and positioning of the tongue and jaw. Together they amplify and add different tones to one's voice while speaking.

Three Tips for Improving Oral Resonance:

1. Lower your jaw for all vowel sounds. This will add a little chamber for your voice to be amplified.
2. Avoid pulling back your face muscles (corners of your mouth and cheeks) while speaking. This tends to pull the vocal cords into a position too high in the throat, which works against good voicing.
3. Resist pulling your tongue to the back of your mouth while speaking. Bring it toward the lower gum ridge of your front teeth as often as possible while speaking to improve the resonating sound chamber of your mouth.

8. Accented Speech

Foreign accents and regional dialects deserve mention. They can help a voice actor authentically speak in those specific ways when the audition/work calls for it. An accent creates a niche for the voice actor, but it can also become a limiting specialty by "type casting" them.

Neutralizing an accent to speak with "Standard American Dialect" and or learning to speak in various accents or dialects can be useful. However, it is a challenging learning process.

Elaine provides classes for voice actors to learn to speak with authentic accents and dialects to expand their repertoire of skills and increase the variety of auditions they get. In my work, I perform the reverse process by clarifying authentic accents that are difficult to understand or are drawing negative attention to the person.

Difficulty being understood in everyday conversation or receiving a low employee evaluation score due to a difficult accent in the workplace can be addressed by Speech-Language Pathologists who specialize in helping adults with communication skills. Speech-Language Pathology techniques applied to persons with difficult-to-understand accented speech is a quality and effective service available from SLPs certified by ASHA.

I thank Eugene O'Reilly, certified Speech-Language Pathologist for his professional guidance and tips.

Chapter 3

COPY BASICS

Winston Churchill said, "Personally I'm always ready to learn, although I do not always like being taught."

Learning how to read words for maximum impact and receive direction from outside sources can take a toll on a person's ego. Natural tendency is to defend our choices and disregard suggestions. The simpler and faster way to deliver the goods is to let go of preconceived ideas, accept direction, make adjustments, and trust the new vocal delivery. There's more to communication than opening the mouth. Word stress, tempo, melody, timing, emotion, pitch, and subtext contribute to the message's impact. There is a beginning, middle, and end to each story. There are words that require more or less stress. There is information that a client knows that you will never be privy to unless told. So, accept, accept, accept, and you will go far in this business. (This the basis of improvisation. . . another reason why you should take improv classes!)

This chapter provides the technical foundation. Styles change, but this information remains constant. If you were a tree, it would be the trunk that holds the limbs and leaves in place. Master this chapter, and you'll find it easy to pick up any script and know what to do with it. So, spend a lot of time on this chapter. Read, reread, practice, record, and listen. Here's a quick checklist for you to remember and keep next to you at the job or audition:

1. Identify the Product
2. Check for Slogans
3. Locate Copy Points
4. Define the Message

5. Identify Competitive Product Comparisons
6. Emphasize Numbers
7. Add Tempo Changes to Lists
8. Discover Patterns
9. Honor the Structure: Set-Up, Body, Resolve
10. Define the Audience

IDENTIFY THE PRODUCT

Read the script and find out what is being sold, introduced, or promoted. Highlight, circle, or underline the client's name. This is what's called the "money" word, since that company will pay you if you book the job. Make sure you know how to pronounce it. Your audition will never be submitted to the client if you get it wrong, and it will never air if it is incorrect. Go online, ask around, or call the company to hear its outgoing message if you have any doubt about its pronunciation.

Your job is to help the listener remember the client's name and make their bank account increase. You should shape the client's name in an effective, memorable, and motivating manner. Gesturing, smiling, stretching it out, and adding pride on the company's name will help it stand out. Adding a short millisecond pause before and after the client's name draws focus and allows time for the listener to retain the information.

SLOGANS

Check to see if there is a phrase, sentence, or series of words that defines the company. Highlight, underline, or circle this information. If you like highlighters, you may want to use a different color highlighter than you used for the company's name. Then read the slogan with an attitude that reflects that company's philosophy. A furniture store with the slogan "Exotic hardwood is our business," might want it to sound serious and adventuresome; a retail store that's pitching a particular sale like "No Sales Tax Day," may want it to sound effortless and free-spirited; and a toy company that uses short descriptive words, "Play. Laugh. Imagine." may desire a lighthearted, fun delivery.

COPY POINTS

Copy points are the essential elements that need to stand out and be remembered. They include the client's name, key phrases, slogans, sales items, times, locations, and other crucial client information that prompted the need for presenting the information to the public. The essence of the script's success lies in the listener's ability to remember the copy points and the actor's ability to make them stand out in a manner that is stylistically appropriate. Here is a simple copy point checklist:

Who is the hero client?
What is the client selling?
Why does the consumer need the product?
When do customers use the product and/or when can the product be purchased?
Where is the product or client located?
How is the product used?
Is there a slogan?

For practice purposes, highlight or underline the copy points.

J-19
TV / 30 seconds
Visual and SFX of a preschool class filled with kids playing and making messes.

Welcome to Kiddie School, where the walls get messy quick! Now J-19 has a wall cleaner that handles the challenge. *New* J-19 Wall & Window Cleaner. J-19 dissolves crayon marks, messy handprints, and sticky built-in food goo. In fact, it's three times as effective on slimy messes as the top-rated wall cleaner. Even tougher than little Herbert here. When it comes to dirty handprints, J-19 is the best. *New* J-19 Wall & Window Cleaner. Available at grocery and drug stores in cities where four-and-five-year olds live.

The copywriter chose a children's setting to illustrate the power and necessity of the product and targets parents of small children. Following the Who, What, Why, Where, and How analysis, this is how the script breaks out:

Who is the client?   J-19 — *The name is mentioned 5 times.*

What is the product?	Wall & Window Cleaner — "Wall" is listed 4 times.
Why is it necessary?	Walls get dirty, especially when small children are around.
When should the consumer use it?	When the walls are messy, sticky, and dirty.
Where can it be purchased?	Grocery and drug stores.
How does it work?	Spray or wipe on; product dissolves dirt.
Why is it good?	It is three times more effective than the top competitive product.
What makes it special?	It's New — *Repeated 2 times.*
Is there a slogan?	"Handles the challenge."

One way to check if you've selected the right copy points is to read them. If we list the highlighted words, it reads:

Walls get messy.
J-19 wall cleaner handles the challenge.
New **J-19 Wall & Window Cleaner.**
J-19 dissolves messy sticky.
Three times as effective wall cleaner.
Dirty handprints, J-19 best.
New **J-19 Wall & Window Cleaner.**
Grocery drug stores.

Although the message using the copy points is more cryptic than the original commercial, the directive is still clear. In contrast, if the non-bolded words become the focus of the read, this would be the announcement as it switches from dirt ratification to the origination of the grime:

Welcome to Kiddie School, where the quick!
Now has a that.
Crayon marks, handprints, and built-in food goo.
In fact, it's on slimy messes as the top-rated.
Even tougher than little Herbert here.
When it comes to is the.
Available at in cities where four-and five-year-olds live.

THE MESSAGE

The message is based on copy points, music, sound effects (SFX), and script specifications. It is not a summary of the script. Instead, it is the underlying message. It may be an awareness campaign to draw focus to a new product; an escape script to prompt the listener to take action and visit their location or use their product; or a challenge script that defies you to do something different and try their product. Rarely does the copywriter define the message this simply. It's embedded in the script, and they expect you to see it! They also use punctuation, spaces, and line placement to tell you when there are attitudinal shifts. Short of reading the script for you, this is the best they can do to help you understand the message they intend to be conveyed.

The message is often explained at the end of the copy. Take a look at the following script and decide what message the copywriter and client wanted conveyed. Then read the script using that choice.

Bobby Socks Diner
Radio / 60 seconds
Specs: Carefree, fun, and nostalgic
SFX: Nostalgic upbeat dance music from the 1950s.

There was a time when bobby socks were keen and circle skirts had poodles on them. When going to the hop on Saturday night was a way of life.
Boys carried girls' books home from school.
(And no one ever locked their door.)

A lot has changed since then, but one thing hasn't: Bobby Socks Diner. The jukebox cranks out the classic tunes from the '50s.
Burgers and shakes are made the old-fashioned way.
And everyone who works there is neat!

So grease your hair back, or pull it up in a ponytail, and hop on down to Bobby Socks Diner for delicious burgers, fries, and milkshakes.

Relive the past at Bobby Socks while you enjoy the present.
(Just lock your front door on the way out.)

Bobby Socks Diner. Located at 5th and Grant, across from the Tower Building.
(Who says you can't go back again.)

If you defined the message as an "escape" script, you'd be right. It tells the listener that things are dangerous today and the only way to feel safe and happy is to eat out at this nostalgic burger joint. The reminder is in the door lock references at the beginning and end of the spot. Other choices that could be used in the reading are a need for simplicity, fun, nostalgia, or a new dining experience. Try recording the script five different ways, using one of these choices per read. Then listen back to see if you can hear the distinct differences. Your attitude and word stresses should change based on the "story."

COMPARISONS

Comparing products is advertising's way of waging war. Millions of dollars are spent each year claiming one soft drink is better than another. Car rental companies vie for the right to claim the number one position. Fast food chains duke it out over who has the best-tasting, most nutritious, or lowest-priced items on their menu. For legal reasons, nothing negative can be said about the competition unless there is substantiating evidence to prove this point beyond a reasonable doubt. Instead, attitude defines the good from the bad as you compare products using the *smile* vs. *no smile* technique.

When saying anything about our hero product or service, we need to smile, show pride, or possess a positive attitude. In contrast, any information about the competitive product or service should be said in a neutral way with no smile. Add to that a timing differential. Slow down when you say the positive information. Speed up when you say the neutral information. Psychologically, the listener hears and retains the positive information and not the neutral.

Try reading this short retail ad. Remember to slow down and smile on the client's information and not smile, speed up, and "throw away" the competition's information. To make your job easier, the positive copy points have been italicized.

> *Half-Price Clothing Store brings you the latest fashions for half the price.* **Brand A Store has the** *same fashions* **but sells them for a whole lot more. Why spend more at Brand A,** *when you can get the same quality at half the price? Half-Price Clothing Store. Where looking great* **doesn't have to cost an arm and a leg.**

Did you notice that the words "same fashions" appear in the middle of the competition's information? Our hero company sells the latest fashions, so those words need to be positive. Otherwise, we negate our company, too! That requires that the speaker make a quick, precise positive adjustment to the read in the middle of the competitor's information. To help with the tempo and attitude switch on the last line, tap the "t" in "great." The tongue placement on the roof of the mouth is an upward movement that will keep the phrase positive, add a natural articulation pause, pitch the remaining negative comparison information downward, and speed it up. By reading it this way, we support the philosophy that slow positive information is retained and fast neutral statements are forgotten.

Making fast facial gyrations as you smile and drop the smile may feel strange and unnatural at first. Get used to it. Effective voice work often requires the adeptness of a rubber face.

NUMBERS, DOLLARS, & PERCENTAGES

With the exception of local car dealerships and going-out-of-business sales where the price is loud and slow, most companies prefer that the price sound small and insignificant. This is easily achieved by saying the amount quickly and matter-of-factly. Subconsciously, the listener comprehends the financial investment as positive and reasonable. Often the words "only" and "just" precede the dollar amount, lending further credibility. Conversely, when comparing prices with our hero's product, the competitor's prices should be read slower and be devoid of emotion. This makes their price seem unreasonably high.

In this next practice example, shrug your shoulders and smile when you say our hero product's price. Then, in the second sentence, drop your smile when you mention the competition's dollar amount. Don't forget to balance out the sentence with the comparison of "our product" versus "theirs."

Our product is only $9.95. Theirs is $9.97.

Of course, advertisers typically base their sales strategy on more than a two-cent price difference. The main issue is that the reader shares a positive and negative opinion about the price for the listener to absorb and appreciate.

Another question people have about money is when to say "dollars" and "cents." As a general rule, the word "dollars" is used more often when the money is an even amount, as with $15 (fifteen dollars). Very rarely is the word "cents" used. Besides taking up valuable airtime, the listener comprehends that the subject matter pertains to money and doesn't need to be reminded. Also, omitting these words softens the sticker shock. A car that sells for $23,500 likes the amount read as "twenty-three five."

Contrary to dollar amounts that are read in a manner that makes them sound small, percentages are expected to sound large. Five percent savings, when read slowly with authoritative pride, can sound like a huge savings. It's not until the words are seen in writing that the actual small percentage amount sinks in.

Read this short retail script below. Smile and stretch out the first percentage amount and make it sound fabulous. Then, drop the smile and speed through the latter half of the second sentence where it contains the competitor's measly percentage savings.

Save 40 percent on brand-name tires. Grand Tires saves you more dollars every day than the 2 percent savings advertised by our competitors.

Note that in addition to the percentages, there are word equivalents to numbers. "More" and "every" in this script should also be stretched out. They define our hero's company's superior financial policy over the competitions. *All, each, additional, added, extra, another,* and *less* are a few other number modifiers that should stand out when spotted in a script.

PATTERNS & LISTS

There are patterns in basic sentence structure and lists. A sentence typically contains a subject, verb, and object. This SVO pattern can be short sentences: "I love you." *I* is the subject, *love* is the verb, and *you* is the object. Or longer, more complex SVO sentences like "Johnny, the maître d' at the restaurant, ordered the cleaners to use bleach on the napkins." In this case, *Johnny* is the subject, *ordered* is the verb, and *cleaners* is the object. Depending on the message, one word has longer stress and more nuance than the others. The word of medium importance is read at a medium speed and stress. The word with the least importance is read faster. These slow, medium, and fast speed variables draw focus to what's important. And, it's what we do in natural speech. In the script analysis, is it essential that the noun, *Johnny,* ordered the cleaners to do something? That Johnny took action and *ordered* the cleaners around? Or is it more important that Johnny define *who* should clean the napkins, the *cleaners?*

Years ago, English classes taught students to diagram sentences. There was a straight line that contained the SVOs. All other words and phrases dropped off the line in a series of angles. As a general rule, words that fall off the line are read faster. These would include prepositional phrases that tell us when, where or why like *under the chair, behind the tree, without a doubt, during breakfast.* Conversely, modifiers are often stressed or "pop up" to clarify the message. Adverbs modify verbs, other adverbs, and adjectives and answer how, when, and where questions. Adjectives modify nouns, pronouns, and noun phrases and clarify what kind, which one, and how many.

PATTERNS

Changing reading patterns to reflect our natural speech patterns requires that the brain be reprogrammed to accept and deliver these changes in pace and word stress. Spend a lot of time on this section. It's not as easy as you think. Once you recognize these recurring patterns, cold-reading scripts will become much easier. Figure out what phrase or sentence is the slowest, medium speed, and fastest (thrown away), and if a modifier should be stressed.

> **The perfect getaway. Pleasant Pacific Cruise Line, for the time of your life.**

Answer: Client's name is the slowest. Perfect tells us why our getaway is better than others. It's the middle speed. The last phrase is the fastest because it's easy to have a good time.

[handwritten: reason for shopping]

> **It's time to enjoy the great outdoors, and what better place to get equipped than Marine Outdoors.**

[handwritten: shrug]

Answer: Once again, the client's name in the phrase "than Marine Outdoors" is slowest. The first phrase has two stress options: enjoy or great outdoors. Either way should be read at medium speed. The middle phrase should be read the fastest. By doing so, it tells the listener that it's easy to quickly find the equipment that you need.

[handwritten: where you are,]

> **I'm the manager / of a Yellow Belly Catfish Restaurant. / It's my job to make sure all the seafood served / at Yellow Belly / is fresh and prepared to your liking.**

Answer: This script is a little more complex, so slashes have been placed to define the five phrases. Before you begin, remember that no one cares about you and your job as a manager when you read this. Instead, they're interested in the quality of the food and the friendliness of the staff. Since real people don't sell, and this is written in the first person, do not oversell the restaurant. You'll still stretch out the second phrase that includes the client's name, you just need to make it sound natural and not like an announcer. "All" is the modifier that either defends their food or tells the listener why their restaurant is better than the competition's. "All the seafood," "fresh," and "prepared to your liking" are all copy points that should be read at medium speed. It's not necessary to stretch out the second Yellow Belly because it will sound too sell-y. So, in these situations, it's okay to read the client's name faster. "I'm the manager" and "It's my job to make sure" should be read at the quickest pace because they tell us nothing about the product.

A general note: No matter what speed you read the phrases and sentences, every word should have meaning, attitude, and nuance. It's just that some information is downplayed more than others. If you emphasize too many words, the listener goes on overload and retains little or no information.

LISTS

Scripts often contain lists. They may include single words, a series of phrases, or several sentences. All these lists, no matter how long or how short, need variety. Each item on the list should sound different from the preceding item. Musically, you need to stair step each list item up, down, or zigzag the notes in the musical scale as tension is built up and released. There are four musical choices: stair step up (C-D-E), stair step down (E-D-C), start low-go high-and split the difference with the middle note (C-E-D), or start high-go low-and finish with the note in the middle (E-C-D). By delivering each part of the list on a different note, the reader can move more quickly through the information because a pause is no longer needed, and the listener can retain the information more easily.

Listing three things is the most common list format as it follows the "Rule of Three."

In the following examples, decide which melodic stair-stepping method is best. When asked to deliver an ABC read (three variations of the same copy), you can use three of the four musical choices to vary each read.

What comes in *chocolate chip, macadamia nut, and oatmeal?* **Mr. Garland's cookies, of course! They're baked fresh every day.**

Answer: (C-D-E) By musically stepping each cookie ingredient up the musical scale, it poses the question. Then it requires that the client's name be dropped in pitch to separate it from the last item in the list.

"Of course" should be thrown away (read more quickly) and end on a lower note than "Mr. Garland's cookies" in order to establish authority and insight in the company. The third sentence starts low, rises to its highest point at "fresh," and drops back down the musical scale on the final two words to give a definitive ending to the message.

(E-D-C) Stair-stepping the list down creates a different attitudinal dynamic, as the delivery must shift to a more teasing, knowledgeable, authoritative style. "Mr. Garland's cookies" rises in pitch and "of course" goes even higher as it is thrown away. The final line arrows down the musical scale.

Zigzagging the list so that "oatmeal" ends on the middle note means that all the other information needs to jump up and down the scale as well. If "Mr. Garland's cookies" arrows up, then "of course" does the opposite and arrows down. "They're baked fresh" requires a knowing attitude to sustain the single note delivery before the switch on "every day" to musically end the commercial down. The opposite musical variation occurs when the sentence following the list arrows down, rather than up. This creates a more relaxed, matter-of-fact delivery.

Sometimes the product benefits determine the best way to read the list. Decide whether this list should be read up, down, or zigzagged.

For a *deep, rich, golden tan,* buy Miami Tan.

Answer: If you answered up, that would imply that the tan would leave your skin. Zigzagging the list is an adequate choice, and can work when read with the right attitude. Stair-stepping the list down is the best choice because it implies that the tan is going into the skin. One word that should be read quicker or "swallowed" so the listener hardly hears it is "buy." By emphasizing that someone has to spend money, it will negate the sale and the benefits of a sexy tan.

Often, lists come in a series of sentences or questions. Because of the length of the sentences, zigzagging the list is the best choice. Decide which note, high or low, is best to start the list. Also decide what word or words per sentence should be emphasized.

Are your muscles sagging? Does your body look like a carton of cottage cheese? Does putting on a bathing suit make you burst into tears? Maybe it's time to shape up at Buffo Health Club.

Answer: Starting the commercial on a higher note makes it more difficult to create empathy. By beginning on a lower note, the listener can hear and relate to the pain points more easily. Then, the shift to the hero client suggestion is able to be more upbeat.

In deciding which words to emphasize, say them aloud to see if they tell a story. If you said "sagging, cottage cheese, tears" you realize it's a pretty ridiculous story. Selecting "muscles, body, bathing suit" to emphasize creates a more visceral response. Note also that "Maybe it's time to shape up" should be a suggestion and not a demand. It should sound as if the weight falls off and the toning begins by simply walking into Buffo Health Club. How you say the client's name tells the listener a lot about the types of people who work there. Since the ad is targeted to out of shape people, a warm and sympathetic tone would be most desirable.

At times, the Rule of Three will be bent when four or more items are listed. Stair-stepping more than three items up the musical scale results in a strained, high ending pitch when the last item is reached. Conversely, stair-stepping all the items downward bottoms out the voice at the end. The style is either to zigzag the whole list (C-E-D-F), stair-step the first three items up and drop the last item down (C-D-E-D), or stair-step the first three items down and lift the pitch up on the final item (E-D-C-D). Decide which way you'd like to read the spot and why that's the best choice. Should you emphasize the verbs or the objects?

Tony's Tune-Up will *rotate your tires, tune up your engine, change your oil,* and *smog-check your vehicle.*

Answer: Once again, "tires, engine, oil, vehicle" convey less of a message than the active choices of "rotate, tune up, change and smog-check." When going to a car mechanic, customers know that tires rotate, not engines. Therefore, there's no need to draw focus to the objects. When read, the verbs should have movement and action.

When should you emphasize the conjunctive word "and" and when should you not? The simple rule is that it is not an important word unless you want to draw focus to the most important final item in the list or it's a very long sentence (common in corporate narrations) that alerts the listener that the thought is finally coming to an end. In that case, "and" is the magic word and should be stretched out.

Five or more list items are considered a *laundry list*. Stair-stepping the notes up the scale, for most people, is out of the question. Instead, randomly place each item on a different note in the musical scale. It is most effective if you use your hands to gesture on each item. Place your hands at different locations on each item, similar to a choral director, to insure that notes are not repeated. Alternate each item from one hand to the other, move your fingers, shoulders, and arms. Give it a try. Figure out how to make the list quicker and slower.

> **It's time** for the **May Madness Sale** at **Latimer's** on *socks, slips, panties, boxer shorts, cotton briefs, T-shirts, pajamas, pants, dresses, dress shirts, skirts, blouses, belts, wallets,purses, shoes, sheets, towels,* and *more.*

> *Answer: The tighter and smaller the motions are to the body, the faster you can read the words. If you need to slow the list down, make broader gestures. Remember, the rule of thumb with lists is variety! If all the items are read continuously on the same musical note, the listener only hears one item. Additionally, if two items in the list of three are read side-by-side on the same musical note, it sounds like only two items. Be sure to coordinate your movements with the words so you're not flailing away aimlessly.*

SCRIPT CONSTRUCTION: Set-Up, Body, Resolve

Commercials follow a specific formulaic pattern. Recognizing and honoring the script construction helps you deliver the words more effectively. The three main components are the: SET-UP, BODY, and RESOLVE. On occasion, there is an additional short element at the end, usually for comedic value, called a BUTTON. This will either be scripted or improvised.

SET-UP — The opening section is designed to grab the listener's attention and identify a pain point, the problem. It could be lack of time, energy, romance, excitement, etc.

BODY — The middle of the copy provides a solution to the problem as the client's information is mentioned. It answers important who, what, why, when, and how questions implied or posed in the set-up.

RESOLVE — This is the call-to-action for the listener to go into a store, call, or go online to make a purchase.

BUTTON — Its function is to add personality and complete the story. Descriptive copy information is generally not given. A button can be a very short responsive sound, word, or sentence that adds cleverness, humor, or finality to the end of the spot.

The following spokesperson spot is selling romance in the form of synthetic firewood. When you read the copy, make sure there is a definite transition between the three sections. One way to ensure a change is to shift weight from one foot to the other without moving the mouth from its position on mic or lifting the feet off the ground. The voice and emotions will change slightly with each new position. Another option is to cock your head in different positions or gesture with your right hand, left hand, and two hands together.

BURN-A-LOG
TV / 30 seconds
The visual starts outside a house in winter then cuts to the inside of the home. The woman has just completed her winterizing tasks. The man puts a log on the fire. The couple sits down together and get cozy.

SET-UP
It's that time of year again. You guessed it, winter. Time to drag out the warm clothes, clean out the furnace, and cozy up with a loved one by a roaring fire. What better way to take the chill off of winter than with Burn-A-Log.
BODY
Burn-A-Log is the fast, clean easy way to have a fire. Just place Burn-A-Log in your fireplace and light it. There's no messy starter fluid or kindling. One match is all it takes to start Burn-A-Log.
RESOLVE
So the next time you want a romantic evening, or could use a fire to stay warm on those cold winter nights, try Burn-A-Log. Guaranteed to start with only one match.

Script analysis:
Problem = a chill in the relationship and in the weather.
Lists: Drag out, clean out, and cozy up; fast, clean, easy; want a romantic evening, could use a fire, try Burn-A-Log.
Numbers: One match.
Comparatives: Messy starter fluid or kindling versus one match.
Resolve: The romance and the fire were started with one match.

KENO LOTTERY
Radio / 60 seconds
SFX: Water sounds and people talking on a cruise ship.

SET-UP
Let me have your attention for a minute. How'd you like a chance to win $200,000? $200,000 you must be saying to yourself. Of course I want $200,000! Who wouldn't? I could buy a new house, new car. . . heck, a fleet of new cars, college for the kids, vacations, all kinds of stuff for the house.

BODY
Well, that's exactly what you could win if you enter the Keno Lottery. Just pick three numbers out of 49 and the average top prize is over $200,000. That's right, $200,000! Spend a buck, win a chance at $200,000. Look at me, I won and now I'm enjoying a luxury cruise around the world. Best of all, you don't have to be present to win. The Keno Lottery people find you and give you the cash, no matter where you are. . . on the high seas, or in your living room with that tattered furniture. Right now I'm waiting to see if my latest three-number pick wins. There's no limit to the amount of times you could win. So why stop?

RESOLVE
The Keno Lottery. It's a chance to make your dreams come true. So, cruise on down to your local Mom and Pop shop, plop down some cash, and enter your winning three numbers. It's the easiest 200,000 bucks you could ever make.

BUTTON
Say, pass me that suntan lotion, will ya?

Script analysis:
Problem = Not having enough money to do or have the things you want.
Lists: The second sentence through "Who wouldn't?" The next sentence is a laundry list.
The $200,000 sentences in the body section. " Cruise on down, plop down, and enter" section of the resolve.
Numbers: The money keeps repeating. In this case, it's important to stretch it out rather than hide it because someone is winning, not spending that amount. Also, "3 numbers out of 49" and "three-number pick" contain numbers.
Comparatives: "In your living room with that tattered furniture" identifies the target audience.
Resolve: It's easy to win.
Button: Ties back into the leisurely cruise ship theme.

COLORING THE ADJECTIVES

Every word in a piece of copy has been carefully selected and scrutinized. Whisking right past the adjectives without adding a little bit of color or shading to them is an insult to the copywriter. Have fun with them! They bring additional life to the script. Be careful, though, not to overly elongate or unduly emphasize the adjectives so that they overshadow the copy points. The balance is delicate and should be quick and efficient, without losing perspective of the overall copy intention. Drawing a squiggly line underneath the word or phrase is a good mental reminder to play with these words. Pick up your pencil and practice this marking technique on the following script.

TOFFEE BAR DELIGHTS
Web Ad / 15 seconds

Visual: An animation of a Brit morphing into an American after eating the candy bar.

> We Brits love our bonbons, chocolates, and caramels. But there is one thing you Americans have that we don't. . . Toffee Bar Delights.

> Toffee Bar is a delicious vanilla ice cream bar, covered in mouth-watering toffee and drenched in real milk chocolate.

> When I bite into a Toffee Bar Delight, I fell like. . . well *(SFX: crunch)*, a Yank!

Script analysis:
Adjectives: Delicious, mouthwatering, real (milk chocolate)
Problem = Jealousy regarding the American chocolate
Lists: Bonbons, chocolates, and caramels. Delicious vanilla ice cream bar, covered in mouthwatering toffee and drenched in real milk chocolate.
Comparatives: Brits versus Yanks.
Resolve: It's okay to change to the other side if they have a better candy bar.

THE AUDIENCE

Advertising is targeted to specific genders and age demographics. The general buyer breakdown is 18–24, 24–36, 25–49, 49–65, and 65+. Household cleaning products are pitched during daytime TV programs and soap operas target a female audience — thus the name "soap" opera. Beer is touted primarily to males during sports programs. Toys are pitched primarily during Saturday morning cartoons to impressionable youths.

Understanding the product's intended audience helps the actor make effective choices. Vocal placement, proximity to the microphone, and attitude all need to be taken into account. You'll know which voice to pull out of your verbal "bag of tricks" when you know *who* you are talking to. If the client is pitching bubble gum, the ad is probably intended for a young audience, and the freedom to be wacky, crazy, and fun takes precedence. The same approach does not work for a gum ad that claims to not stick to dentures. This older demographic dictates a more natural and sensible interpretive approach. When you want to take a gamble, reading "against type" can result in a job or the client scratching their head wondering why you made such a diametrically wrong choice.

Industrial narrations are also targeted to specific audiences. There is a different sound for scripts that appeal to CEOs versus first-year employees. A choice must be made on the audience's level of product knowledge, business acumen, and education. Business-specific acronyms, product names, and buzzwords should sound second nature and roll off the tongue. Even if you don't know what you're saying, the listener does, and they expect you to be an authority on the subject. When a product is first introduced, it may be read more slowly. After a brief time, that approach is no longer necessary as the information is known company-wide.

Video games have varying demographics and rating scales.

EC = Early Childhood, with content appropriate for children ages 3 and older.
E is for Everyone ages 6 and older.
E10+ is appropriately titled for ages 10 and older.
T is for Teen.
M is rated Mature.
AO is for Adults Only and may include intense violence, nudity, and/or sexual content.
RP means that the Rating is Pending.

Games geared toward teenage boys often contain heavy monster voices that can scare away a young child who prefers light, friendly, goofy voices. The more mature the audience, the more realistic the voice choices.

Bottom line, if it's not clear who the information is intended to reach, ask the director or make a strong choice based on the copy, title, and script specifications.

Chapter 4

HIDING "THE SELL"

Radio is often referred to as "theatre of the mind" because the audio, rather than the picture, creates the visual image. The underlying message brings the picture to life, adds color, clarity, and depth. Voiceovers, regardless of whether they are commercials, corporate narrations, video games, or cartoons, need to stimulate ideas inside the targeted listener's mind. An active listener is engaged in the message, absorbs it, and retains the information.

Hiding the sell means that you bring your own life experiences, feelings, and opinions into someone else's words. This requires a certain amount of acting ability. The more you understand about yourself and your emotional life, the better your performance. That's why actors are often told, "The words aren't important!" *How* something is said is much more important than *what* is said. It's a matter of showing who you are and how you feel. It's the business of show, *show business*.

CREATING A DIALOGUE WITH THE LISTENER

All scripts should be approached as a dialogue. The person to share this information with should be someone you know, not an imaginary person or group of people. Selecting someone you know opens you up emotionally. This adds attitude and option to your message. It could be a parent, spouse, sibling, coworker, best friend, boss, lover, child, or even a movie star about whom you've fantasized. Thinking about this person should open up your heart and make you emotionally alive and accessible. If you are really "present" and "in-the-moment" you will be aware of this new emotional life. Breathing pattern, pulse, voice, and body position should alter as you react to that person's image. You become a *whole* person that someone can relate to, rather than a stick figure delivering words without any feelings.

Choosing a substitution may be difficult at first. The tendency is to look at the copy and say, "I'm going to talk to a person in a store who is wearing a blue shirt because that shirt is mentioned in the copy." Or, "I'm going to use a friend's experience because I do not have one of my own that involves a professional pizza chef cutting up meats and veggies." Or better yet, "I'm going to talk to a bunch of guys standing on the corner wearing cowboy boots and ten-gallon hats because that would be different and interesting." All may intellectually be the "right" choice but do not stimulate truthful emotional reactions. Generic stories do not work. You must evoke *genuine* feelings.

EXERCISES:

1. **GROUND YOURSELF** — Place one or both of your hands on your heart. Feel it pumping blood through your body. Don't think but *feel* as you listen to your body and reconnect with yourself. Are you feeling happy or sad, nervous or calm, or nurtured and loved? Breathe in and out a few times and let out a long, soft, audible *sigh*. The soothing rhythm and the release of tension from the breath should relax and ground you. Let this hand-on-heart exercise minimize outside interferences and elevate awareness of your current emotional state. If you do not feel anything at this moment, you have "checked out" temporarily because you are living in your head and not your heart. Repeat the process until you feel relaxed, happy, grounded, and connected with your pulse, breath, and body.

2. **PERSONALIZE YOUR MESSAGE** — Image a person in your life either doing or telling you something at a specific moment or place. See the location in your mind, hear the sounds around you, and smell the air. That person's words or actions should elicit a body movement and an emotional response. It may make you roll your eyes, shake your head, smile, jerk your head back, or shift your weight. These little movements help connect you to that person and deliver the words more realistically. If you wait until that natural response is over and compose yourself, it's a wasted exercise. Acting is *reacting*.

3. **ENERGIZE YOUR VOICE** — Before recording, warm up your body, jump up and down, shake out your hands, and laugh. This will put a twinkle in your eye, oxygenate your blood, and make

your voice sound energized. One producer I worked with called it, "Spraying some chrome on the voice." You'll be pleasantly surprised how it makes the voice sparkle.

4. **USE YOUR BODY** — Some scripts require a strong, tense read while others necessitate a more relaxed delivery. How we use our muscles is reflected in our voice. When reading something that requires a lot of energy, tense specific parts of your body or every muscle from head to toe. Practice reading a script three different ways: (1) your fists clenched, (2) buttocks and thigh muscles tightened, and (3) palms of your hands pressed firmly against each other. Read the same script three more times, this go-round with fingers relaxed, bottom wiggling, and arms waving in the air. Every move we make creates a new and unique sound. Learn how to use your body, rather than your brain, to create the desired sound. No matter how much you think you're doing something, if your body hasn't gotten the message. . . no one is going to hear your fabulous idea.

5. **ANSWER A QUESTION** — Directorially, we are required to emphasize specific words or phrases. In order to justify this, we need to know what question has been posed. Imagining a question and using the script to answer it helps jumpstart the read. The example below will add some illumination.

TIME TO PRACTICE

The following script should be read eight different ways. To begin, start by stressing only the first word, then the second, third, etc., until you get to the final word. Be careful not to emphasize any of the other words in the sentence. Only one key word per reading can draw focus. Each time, before you read, decide what question you are answering.

Because all bread should taste like it's homemade.

Questions:
After you've practiced this on your own, see if you came up with the same questions listed below or better ones.

Because:	*Why?*
All:	*How much bread?*
Bread:	*What do you sell?*
Should:	*What about the competition, do they sell homemade bread, too?*

Taste:	*What's the greatest thing about your bread?*
Like:	*Is the bread really homemade?*
It's:	*Where's the bread. . . is it over there?*
Homemade:	*What makes your bread so special?*

Did you notice the different ways you used your body when you answered each question? You might have gestured or pointed when "bread" was the focus word, or shrugged your shoulders on the word "should." Emotionally and musically, did you notice the shifts when you changed the "tune and tempo" of the delivery to linger on the key word? Also, did you notice that the attention shifts from comparing our product to the competition's in the beginning of the sentence to pride of ownership on the last few words?

As we mature into adulthood, we learn tricks that help us survive and live in society. For some, the brain takes over and guides them on their journey into adulthood. Others are more emotional, wearing their heart on their sleeve. Good actors — unconsciously competent actors — blend a unique understanding and interpretation of the written word with a trust in the body, breath, voice, and heart to give life to the mind's and mouth's interpretation of the words. For the brain-heart transfer to occur, the actor must let go of learned, protective behaviors and allow the moment to naturally unfold. For many, this is difficult. Perhaps a bad moment has crept into your memory that blocks your emotions. Maybe outside pressures prevent you from concentrating. Possibly, you do not trust this process and how it works. There is something preventing you from visualizing and experiencing the moment. Releasing the brain's hold and allowing an organic moment to happen is a scary and incomprehensible concept to someone who has counted on intellect rather than instinct to survive. The key to letting go and being in the moment, is TRUST. Truly believable, real, heartfelt acting is recognized and praised throughout the world, regardless of the medium — stage, television, cinema, or voice-over.

Choosing a personalization automatically affects the emotions placed on the written words. In real life, we speak differently to strangers than we do to friends, and the same is true of how we speak to children versus adults or to someone who is ill as opposed to someone healthy. In voice-over, it is imperative that the space surrounding the mic be replaced by a personalization that evokes the emotional overtones needed to drive the story forward. Due to the speed in which voiceovers need to be recorded and delivered to the client, all personalizations must be easy to access.

Assignment:

Make a list of your personalizations that evoke the strongest attitudes and emotions. They will be your go-to people for most of your scripts. Be specific. Perhaps thinking about an old friend makes you feel young and mischievous, recalling a phone conversation with your grandmother brings up guilty feelings for not visiting often enough, recounting a conversation with a boss may make you feel angry or full of pride, visualizing tucking your child into bed may bring back a flood of warm, loving feelings. Remember, all feelings are legitimate if they are genuine. Feelings are neither right nor wrong, as long as they represent your true emotional state.

Once you have mastered the concept of personalization, there will be a noticeable improvement in your work. Your recordings will possess a greater sense of playfulness, ease, and natural authority.

BUILDING A CHARACTER

There are five basic principles to building a character: *Who are you? Where are you at this moment in time? What are you doing? Why are you there/here? When is the action taking place?* These elements help you develop and create a well-rounded character that is alive, breathing, and real. It may be the friendly next-door-neighbor, pompous boss, concerned friend, or zany character that lives in your refrigerator. You need to recognize if the character is the comedic relief or the voice of reason. Integrating the Five Ws into your work will add depth, believability, and a 3-D effect to the flat words on the page.

Who Are You?

Every time you pick up a script, you need to decide *who* you are: friend, parent, spouse, lover, comic, sales associate, blue-collar worker, doctor, nurse, business owner, etc. There are clues within the copy to help you make that decision. This will influence your proximity to the mic and how you stand, move, think, and relate to the listener. Check for intentional grammatical errors, slang words, colloquialisms, and whether the writing has a casual or formal tone. You should also discern whether the character is shy, uncomfortable, vulnerable, bold, caring, brash, straightforward, or ironic.

Many people spend energy trying to rewrite the copy to have it match their personality rather than gleaning information to create the character the copywriter intended for the job. For example, "ain't" is more blue-collar, "grand" versus "one thousand dollars" is casual and cocky, and "is not" is more formal than "isn't."

There's also a difference between a character for audio only, like a radio commercial, versus one that supports a visual image. Radio characters have more movement and dynamic attitudes than characters for TV, and web ads that have to support the picture and not draw focus to the voice.

Television scripts often contain visual descriptions or storyboards that provide additional clues. Humorous visuals necessitate a more lighthearted character, elegant beaches and tropical scenery require relaxing or exotic character traits, and pharmaceutical ads require a more knowledgeable and caring tone of a doctor or nurse.

Music and sound effects also provide clues about the character. The more up-tempo the music, the lighter and more carefree the character. Conversely, the more dramatic the music, the heavier and more serious the person's nature.

Script specs provide obvious information. Ex. "Male or female, 30–45, witty and intelligent, very 'real,' possible regional accent, should not sound like an announcer or cartoon character."

The client and the script's title, usually located under the client's name, add further illumination. It's easy to decide on the character if you've heard the ads before. However, a large portion of our job is to introduce new products. That means that we have to make a decision about our character that best represents the company. How the script is titled can tell us a lot, too. Ex. "Mistaken Identity," "Fish Out Of Water," "The Boss," and "Smart Shopper" tell completely different stories and require different characters.

In summary, the following information tells us *who* your character is and how to perform it:

1. Client
2. Title
3. Specs
4. Medium — TV, Web, Radio, etc.
5. Music and SFX
6. Visual references
7. Grammar
8. Writing style and tone

We wear different hats throughout the day and take some of these character nuances for granted. Catalog your characters, no matter how slight the differences, so they are second nature. Figure out how they stand, think, gesture, breathe, etc. Decide on the vocal placement. Choose whether a higher head voice, mid-range mask voice, or lower chest voice is best for that particular character and job. Understanding your voice and who you are will help your booking ratio.

Deciding who you are in a given script is like playing a connect-the-dots game. By acknowledging your personality, job and life experiences, uniqueness, and voice quality, you'll then be able to hone your skills and minimize bad choices. It's part of learning how to be *typecast*. Are you known as the class clown, caregiver, idiot, friend, athletic type, sexy person, or genius? Maybe you're all of the above at one time or another. Perhaps you only possess one or two of these traits. Who you are in real life will help you decide whether you want to have a "rubber voice" and do lots of characters or stick with just one "you."

Here's an assignment:

1. Take a piece of paper and draw a line down the middle.
2. On the top left, write "Who I Am."
3. On the top right, write "My Character."
4. Under the left column, list everything that makes you special: voice quality, temperament, knowledge and expertise in certain areas, etc.
5. Under the right column, make a list of character choices required in the script.
6. Draw a line from the right to the left, connecting all your attributes with the ones listed on the right. From there, you'll be able to tell how much more you need to layer onto your script's character.

Doing this exercise allows you to see how many of your own personal, naturally occurring assets can be used to enhance the character. And, you will be able to understand some of your own uniqueness! This is also a great way to be selective about the scripts you want to audition for on pay-to-play sites. The closer the character is to you, the more likely you'll be cast.

Where Are You?

Even though you record in a studio, there needs to be a feeling that you are either watching the "real life" scene unfold in the TV, web, or mobile ad or you are part of the "slice-of-life" portrayed in a radio commercial, corporate industrial, or animation. The sound effects (SFX), environmental establishment bed, and music are your scene partners. Location contributes to an actor's attitude, volume, speed of delivery, and action.

Example: Read this commercial and decide where the action would take place. Use your imagination. Read it three times, each time placing the action in a new location. Record yourself and play it back to see if you can hear the differences.

Healthy Pro Dog Food
TV, Web, & Mobile Ad
15 seconds

> Is your dog bored with the same old dog food? He must not be eating Healthy Pro Dog Food. It's specially formulated to give your dog all the vitamins and minerals he needs to make him happy, healthy, and energetic. Maybe it's time for you to switch to Healthy Pro.

When you pick up a script, you need to create this 3-D image in your mind. Let the body adjust to the scene and emotionally respond. Three ways you might have read it are: (1) In a discouraged family member's home as their lazy dog sniffs the dog food and walks away. Establishment shot of product. Final shot of dog being walked around the neighborhood by the happy owner. (2) Pet owner in a park. He throws a Frisbee for the dog to catch and the dog lies there with sad eyes and doesn't chase it. Another dog in the park runs after the Frisbee and catches it. The lazy dog's owner sees a small bag of the hero product in the energetic dog owner's bag as the Frisbee is returned to its rightful owner. (3) A young child in the backyard of her home, mildly upset that the dog is lazy and won't play. The mother is in the kitchen, having just returned from the grocery store, pours the dog food into a bowl and brings it outside to the dog. The dog sniffs it, gobbles it down, the child is happy, and the final shot is the dog and child rolling around in the grass.

Example: Get even more imaginative in this radio commercial where you are part of the action rather than just commenting on it.

Dine-Style
"Dinner"
Radio / 30 seconds

> My family, they're always on the go. With new Dine-Style menus, we get to share healthy meals together, no matter where we are: the baseball game, swim meet, or at home. All we do is pull the self-heating tab. In minutes, we're ready to eat. Jordan loves the chicken carbonara, Sammy can't get enough of the spare ribs, and Laura loves all the vegetarian options. Me? I like the fast and easy cleanup. The packaging is environmentally safe and comes in an assortment of designer colors. With Dine-Style, I know we're getting quality time together as a family and eating food that's good for us.

The script offers three locations where you can set the action: sitting in the bleachers at a baseball game or swim meet, at home, and your family having a tailgate party before the events. Sound effects are going to support the location choice. If the background noise is loud, the voice talent has to speak a little louder. If it's a home environment, the read can be more subdued and intimate. Just remember that even though you've placed yourself in a specific place, the listener is hearing you in their car, computer, or mobile device.

Take chances on the environment where you place the action. Sometimes you will have the luxury of seeing the picture that you will record to but most times you will not. See more than words on a page, create an environment and live in it!

What Are You Doing?

Now that you know who and where you are, you need to decide *what the heck you are doing!* Just because the scene is set in an office, doesn't necessarily mean you are sitting in a big cushy chair behind a large mahogany desk. In any given situation, there are a dozen actions from which to choose. So dig deep and don't stop at the first or most obvious choice. Explore the full realm of the scene. If outside, decide if the person is jogging, standing, being interviewed by the press, hiding from someone, or chatting with a friend. Creative choices result in more bookings as funnier, unique specificity results in an interesting reality that stands out from the crowd.

Find the clues about what the character is doing and act it out. This is called "playing the action." If your character is ordering coffee, stand, gesture, and speak in an appropriate way. Is your character squinting to read the menu, walking to the front of the line to order after waiting in a long line, or fumbling around to find a wallet? When choosing your action, remember to take note of the character's relationship to the product. The hero product should always be portrayed in a positive manner. If you are portraying the "other guy" character that has not yet used the product, what you are doing may be the opposite of what the product gives people. This illuminates the problem and sets it up for the announcer to offer the solution.

Example: Let's see how creative you can get with this corporate narration scenario.

Koffee Barn
"Hot Coffee"
E-Learning Employee Training

Jamie:	Welcome to Koffee Barn. I'm Jamie, your barista. How may I help you?
Kelsey:	I'd like a large Americano.
Jamie:	Your name?
Kelsey:	Kelsey.
Jamie:	That'll be $3.57.
Kelsey:	Okay. Here you go.

SFX: coffee shop noises

Jamie:	(shouting) Kelsey.
Kelsey:	Yo.
Jamie:	Here's your coffee. Be careful, it's hot.
Kelsey:	Ouch!
Jamie:	The paper sleeves are on your right. That'll help.

In this scene, Jamie has to pick up a cup, write Kelsey's name on it, ring up the order, prepare the coffee, shout out Jamie's name, hand over the coffee, and point to the paper sleeves. Kelsey has less implied action and more unique choices to make. The character may be played in a decisive manner when ordering the coffee or in a way that suggests that the character is trying to make up his or her mind while reading the menu posted on the wall behind the barista. When asked about a name, Kelsey may be distracted while locating the wallet, deciding whether to give out a real or a fake name, or very confident and direct. The money or credit card may be in the pocket, wallet, or bag. After Kelsey's name is called, the character may be reading something and look up, waiting impatiently close to the counter, or talking on the phone in a far corner of the store. The hot coffee grab may be quick, slow, or tentative.

What you do is a big part of the script analysis and a way to show your creativity and imagination. Your "stage" where the action takes place may be confined to a small area in front of you or require more room for broad gesticulations. The scene, job type, and voice connection to your body will dictate the size of the actions. Getting in touch with your movements helps you become "wired for sound."

When is the Action Taking Place?

When the action takes place adds yet another degree of realism to the script. People's actions change throughout the day. Some are grumpy when they wake up, while others are happy and jump out of bed. A person may be more energetic at the beginning of the workday rather than the end. Seasons of the year add another dimension to the actor's performance as it affects the character's gait and attitude. Have you been locked inside for days during a winter snowstorm? Are you lying by the pool on a warm summer day? Have the April rain showers finally cleared and the sun come out?

Example: Try reading this script using seasonal choices: warm, hot, cool, and cold. Read it another time assuming different times of the day: morning, noon, late afternoon, and night. Then, mix and match the time of day and seasonal choices. Remember that you are not the on-camera actor, you are merely commenting on the action.

Greatsport
TV Tag

Discover Greatsport. There's a lot out there.

When the action takes place changes the breath flow and consequently, the sound of the words. Waking up in the morning, relieved that the rain has stopped and the sun has come out, results in an "arrow down, arrow up" read as the breath is expelled on the first sentence and the body gets energized on the second sentence. Another choice is a cold winter day, energized and talking on the breath as you imagine winter ski opportunities.

You're only limited by your imagination. Note how your muscles and breath react to each "when" situation.

Why Are You There?

Knowing *why* you are talking in a given situation is the most important part of the Five Ws. Without a purpose, the character will sound stilted and artificial. Undoubtedly you have heard nonprofessional spots like this on the radio and on local cable channels. Why a character speaks gives it purpose. It's the reason why talent is told that the words are not important and to "throw the words away." If you know why you're saying something, you don't have to push. It will sound more like you do in real life.

When creating a character, remember that there is an arc to the story. For change to be acknowledged by the listener, it must start with a conflict of some kind. As the script progresses, a positive resolution must be achieved. When playing one character in a dialog script, it is very easy to want to become the other person. You must stand firm in your character's reality and belief system. In the beginning, the less your fellow actor gives you what you want, the harder you have to work to get the positive response you want at the end. *Relationship* is key to great acting.

Example: This is an example of a very poorly written script. Good actors who incorporate a "why" into the read are able to bring it to life. Decide whether you want to meet, compliment, or make up with someone who's mad at you. Since this is the final section of the *who, what, why, when* chapter, put it all together and incorporate movement (what), when (time of day), location (where), and your relationship with the other person (who).

CAN-O-MATIC
"Soup"
Radio / 30 seconds

Voice 1:	Boy, that soup smells good. Can I have some?
Voice 2:	Sure, help yourself.
Voice 1:	It tastes great!
Voice 2:	Thank you. I opened the can myself.
Voice 1:	You sure have a way with metal.
Voice 2:	It's the new can opener from Can-O-Matic. And watch! See how easy it is to use?

Voice 1:   It's heavy!
Voice 2:   That's right. It's the heavy metal can opener from Can-O-Matic. The only one with a tiny music pod right in the handle.

There are so many choices to make in this open-ended script. That's why most people freeze and do nothing besides read the words. Instead, think of this script as a license for using your imagination. The situation could be at a display table in a grocery story, inside a ski cabin on a cold winter day, at home on a first date, in the afternoon when the lazy roommate wakes up, etc. Since the script doesn't have a strong ending that completes the "who" scenario, it begs for Voice one to ad lib an ending response. That way the listener knows how the relationship ends: friendship, date, forgiveness, etc.

There is a cause and effect to everything a person does. Eliminating the Who, What, Why, Where, and When realities from the voice results in a flat, two-dimensional character. Leaving even one element out of this list leaves room for another actor to beat you out of the job and to lose your listeners' trust and attention.

Chapter 5

MAKING IT M.I.N.E.™

Truly understanding and perfecting the mental, physical, and vocal aspects of voiceovers is much like learning a second language. "Copy Basics" (chapter 3) offered technical guidance; "Hiding The Sell" (chapter 4) provided advice on imaginatively incorporating the Five Ws (who, what, why, when, and where) into your performance. "Making It M.I.N.E." is my trademark approach to quickly get inside the character and lift the words off the page. This chapter is *how* to make the words uniquely yours and share your personality.

Starting out as a stage actor, I became accustomed to several weeks of rehearsal to find the character once the lines were memorized. When I got into the voice-over business, I found the immediacy of realistic reading to be daunting. Once I learned to recognize the writing patterns, styles, and emotional commitments, I learned to look at a script and within minutes know exactly what was needed. This is my favorite part of script analysis: learning how to boil the script down into a one-word need and treat the copy as the *middle* of the story rather than the whole story.

When you practice the concepts in this chapter, cut yourself some slack. I attended an acting class for three years to learn to access my emotions better. The instructor kept saying he'd give my fellow students and me the answer on how to do it. He never did. Out of frustration, I created this technique on my own. It's a way of quickly blending together Chekhov, Stanislavski, The Method, Meisner, and other acting systems. It means you have to get out of your head and into your body, put the clothing of the character on by standing and moving appropriately, play an organic primal *need* (rather than an objective), overcome and resolve an obstacle, live in an "as if" world, and allow yourself to be emotionally vulnerable and physically active. In seconds, you will blend a character from the outside in and inside out by the way you stand, move, and speak.

In the twenty-five years that I've had Voice One, my voice acting school, I've seen actors struggle with how to have an opinion when they cold read copy. By not having an option, the reader is safe. Unfortunately, the client doesn't want safe. The client wants us to believe that what we're saying is right and good. If you're not an actor already, using this technique will make you one. For those who already are actors, using this process will make you a better VO, film, and stage actor. So, grow a synapse or two in your brain while you study, practice, and incorporate the concepts in this chapter into your work.

WHAT DOES MAKING IT M.I.N.E.™ MEAN?

M.I.N.E. stands for Motivations, Intentions, Need, and Emotions. It is the manner in which an actor becomes "emotionally alive," "present," and "in the moment." Either consciously or subconsciously, the actor's complete, multifaceted persona is transferred into the scripted character's speech. Current moments or past experiences that shaped the reader's life are used to form a strong, positive opinion on specific events and products mentioned in the script. A genuine feeling is shared as a rainbow of human emotional colors are exposed and shared.

Every person has an emotional wound. It is what fuels our actions. Recognizing, tapping into, and revealing those soft spots results in vulnerability. The voice-over business is a very intimate business, as listeners are only inches away from us watching TV, listening on their car radio, working on their computer, or plugged into earplugs connected to their mobile device. Joke-tellers often have a need for attention. Friends who always ask if you like something have a need for approval. People who put others down have a need for power, superiority, or righteousness. Consequently, a person's need justifies his or her actions.

Therefore, the *need* is crucial to driving the story forward. By not committing to the need of the character in the script, the actor conveys a need for protection. In most cases, this is very different from the need required in the copy. To sound real and "whole," we need to share our vulnerability, opinion, and emotions. We need to hear attitude from the reader in order to relate on a personal, gut level. No one likes a perfect person. They make the listener feel inferior. By sharing our opinion, we are saying that we had a problem, got through it, and now want to offer a suggestion on how to break through to the winning side, too.

Finding the true need is not always easy. It's the part of script analysis in which many actors struggle. The script may only require a surface need, like a need for food. Or, a deeper need for revenge, love, or relief. As more work is recorded at home and not with the benefit of a studio director, the actor often replaces the true need of the person in the script with the need for completion, so the actor can move on to another task. This is where we have to check in with ourselves, put the client's need first, and believe what we're saying.

MOTIVATION

Motivation gives an actor a reason, attitude, and action needed for saying the words. It is the prior event that justifies why the present action occurs in a specific manner, gives it a past and present history, and provides logical context for the action. For example, some people are motivated to go to work beyond obvious monetary reasons. The motivation to go to work could stem from enthusiasm, self-satisfaction, power, success, obligation, camaraderie, or some other deep-rooted source. People change jobs, or consider changing jobs, when they lose their motivation.

The actor's motivation is the direct result of a prior experience. Rather than the character's life beginning and ending with the words written in the copy, there should be a feeling that the scene is taken from a "slice" of that person's life. The prior situation that was created by the actor is used to connect the actor to the character and fuel the story.

Motivations give an actor a purpose for saying the words. It starts with a "pre-life" scenario, either scripted or imagined, that gives an actor an aura of past and present history. The prior occurrence is then used as the motivating factor to justify the character's actions. As a result, the words sound logical and purposeful.

The order of events in finding the motivation is as follows:

1. The actor looks at the script to find clues as to how the character should behave. It could be happy, sad, mad, glad, exhausted, energetic, frustrated, bored, determined, anxious, relaxed, etc. From that behavioral choice, the character's mental and physical condition is established.
2. The actor then figures out *why* the character feels that particular way. A simple pre-life scenario is developed that reinforces the

desired feeling in a way that will enhance the story. It gives the actor a reason for being in the room, for speaking at this point in time or in a particular fashion or manner. For instance, if the actor were required to sound frustrated, the actor would then search to understand *why* the character is frustrated. The clues would either be inherent in the script or mentally fabricated. Perhaps the frustration is the result of a confrontation with the professional dry cleaners because they just lost the lucky business suit needed for today's sales meeting.

3. Within the pre-life scenario, the actor checks to see if the character's motivation is connected to his or her own personal feelings. Does thinking about the foul-up at the dry cleaner actually stimulate a real sense of frustration in the actor or is it just a cute story?

4. If the actor does not relate to the imaginary experience on a "gut level," a *new* pre-life situation needs to be selected. This time, the selected pre-life scene should be one that rings "true" to the actor. If the very thought of misplacing the car keys makes palms sweat and breathing shallow, that is a sign of a genuine connection. A natural, physiological change occurs as the body experiences "the moment" without the brain interfering and placing judgment.

5. The pre-life that rings true to the actor is then used to move the story forward. The *motivation* from the scenario creates believable actions within the text. Natural tones within the actor's voice expose the actor's vulnerabilities. The intrigue of human successes and/or failures draws the listener into the scene. Best of all, the actor does not have to "act" anymore. The process of interpreting the copy is simplified when natural instinct takes over. The need to "drive a point home" is replaced by the powerfulness of dynamic subtleties. The actor surrenders to the structure rather than constantly controlling the situation.

To create a motivation, the actor may verbalize or add an action before the scripted words. Rolling the eyes, shaking the head in disbelief, and putting hands on hips are just a few ways that we react to people when they say something we have an opposing opinion about. Answering a question that you've created in your mind is another way to motivate the scene's opening actions. Adding unscripted words like "well," "okay," and "so" are ways to voice your opinion and fuel the action in the written script. Verbal "handles" before the scripted words may be left in when submitting auditions or jobs for radio. In television, web, and other visual ads where the voice supports the picture, you'll need to leave a space between the added sound and the scripted speech so you can edit it out of the recording.

INTENTIONS

Intentions are the tactics used to "meet the need" of the scripted character; this is the way in which an actor's purpose is attained. Within a given script, it is usually necessary to employ numerous intentions. As tactical approaches become worn-out, stagnant, or ineffective, new intentions must be used. Therefore, the *manner* in which the words are portrayed add new and varied *colors* to the actor's performance because the voice quality has to alter in order to adapt to each new intention. Dramatic intention changes are called *transitions*.

Subconsciously throughout our daily lives, we use intentions to try and get exactly what we want. When the current intention no longer works in our favor, we must change our approach. A child who wants a new toy may *flatter* his mother by saying. "I love you. You're the best mommy in the whole world." When the mother responds, "No, you can't have that toy," the child must make a transition. The new choice may be to *impress*. "I'll clean up my room for a week if you let me have that toy!" If the response from the mother is still "no," the child has to decide whether to accept the defeat or choose another intention. This time the decision may be to *humiliate*. "You never get me anything." If the mother still resists buying the coveted toy, the child has to resort to something more drastic. Perhaps the child decides to flop on the floor and have a temper tantrum in hopes of *provoking* the mother into buying the toy. If that intention still doesn't work, the child might cry and kick louder. *Embarrassment* would be the next tactical intention choice.

Therefore, intentions are measures used to insure a "win." Conflict occurs when neither participant backs down, as evidenced in the example of the mother and child. Each party stands their ground in an effort to "win." In the case of the child, even if the mother had refused to buy the child the coveted toy, the child would have made the mother *wish* she had!

For clarity, the actor should define the character's intention in one word. Below is a list of some intentions. Feel free to add to it. As you read each intention out loud, add onomatopoetic meaning so that it sounds like what you are saying. Preface each word with, "I intend to. . ." This adds **action** to what you are saying.

alarm	allure	antagonize
apologize	appease	assert
bait	beckon	beg
calm	challenge	charm
command –	contemplate –	convince –
create	criticize	dazzle
decide	demand	embarrass
empathize	encourage	excite
flatter	flirt	goad
harass	hassle	humble
humiliate	humor	implore
impress	inspire	intellectualize
intimidate	intrigue	irritate
meddle	meditate	moderate
mystify	observe	patronize
persuade –	placate –	plead –
please	promise	provoke
revitalize	romanticize	seduce
scold	sneak	snub
socialize	soothe	tantalize
terrify	tease	titillate
torment	urge	warn

With every punctuation change, a new intention is needed. Take a script and write your intention above each phrase. The more interesting and varied your intentions, the more interesting your read will sound. Many voice actors use the same five to ten intentions over and over again. That's why their reads start out okay but soon sound boring and predictable. Practice incorporating a wide range of intentions into your reads. Intentions lend action to the words. So, don't forget to add gestures and movements to each new intention. You may gesture with your right hand, left hand, then two hands together, shrug your shoulders, raise an eyebrow, wiggle your toes, etc. You'll hear a new action and intention with every movement.

NEED

In contrast to intentions that change, a character's *need* remains constant; **the *need* never changes.** That is because life experiences shape a person in a very specific manner in order to fill a void. The fear of rejection could create a need for acceptance, the fear of not being loved could result in a need for love, or the fear of not being seen or heard could show itself in a need for acknowledgement. This need is subconscious and embedded in the psyche. The need, therefore, becomes the "through line" — or driving force — of a person's life and the actor's read. As an actor, the ability to recognize and use the *need* as a *through line* becomes a valuable tool in personifying the character and giving the scripted lines purpose.

Before you can recognize the need of a person in a written script, you must first acknowledge and embrace your own deepest fear and resulting need. That means searching your past to find out what makes you "tick." This step is important because it adds depth to your performance. Rather than recording your audition or job subconsciously wanting to satisfy your own need or acting out your fear, you recognize and acknowledge the potential "trap" and concentrate on the through-line of the character's need. Understanding your own need serves as a "hook" between you and the character, bridging the gap between what is real and what is fake. It's the part of the character that "speaks to you" and allows you to relate to the character on a basic, fundamental level.

Through careful backtracking, good and bad experiences that shaped and affected your life when growing up will become exposed. It is important that you process these thoughts. If your quest for self-recognition is successful, the subconscious mind will unleash the hidden need inside you and expose the vulnerability to the conscious mind. Then you can use the knowledge of yourself and relate it to the copy, rather than hide from it, hoping *(usually unsuccessfully)* that no one will see it or hear it in your voice.

Multidimensional *need*-driven acting is reflected in the actor's ability to ask probing questions in order to identify the deep-rooted need of the character. By continuing to ask questions like "what?" and "why?" the underlying meaning is eventually divulged. For example, in a commercial that requires an actor to tout a facial cream, the actor might run through a litany of questions something like this:

Why am I here?	To buy the product. *(obviously)*
What will the product give me?	Young-looking skin.
Why do I want to look young?	Because I want to feel good and confident about myself.
Why must I feel good about myself?	Because I want to increase the chance of someone liking me.
What will I get if someone likes me?	*Love.*

The series of questions ends with the recognition of the basic need — *for love*. Now, the copy can be read in a manner that relates to people who have a need to be loved.

The need gives us so much more than cosmetics, clothing, hardware, telephone service, cars, vacations, and other advertised products. It gives us what is missing and needed in our lives: the need for security, recognition, confidence, comfort, power, acceptance, fun, validation, love, approval, understanding, etc.

The NEED = WHAT THE PRODUCT *GIVES* THE PERSON. The opposite of what the person needs is at the beginning of the script, fueled by the motivation. Intentions and emotions color the words in the script and lead to the end result, the character getting his/her need met.

To best use this technique, write the product name at the top of your script and the one-word need next to it with an equal sign between: Product = Need. When using or talking about the need, use the word "for" before it. A need for: love, acceptance, respect, change, etc. Intentions, on the other hand, are prefaced with "to." I intend to: eat, party, sleep, avoid, challenge, etc. The need doesn't get met until after the script is complete. The need provides the continuation of the story, or the "moment after."

EMOTIONS

Emotions occur internally; they are the product of a human "condition." They are neither "right" nor "wrong." Instead, emotions have their own freedom and are capable of instantaneous change. This change is especially evident in small children who have not yet learned the adult art of "hiding emotions." In a matter of seconds, a child can drift from ecstatic leaps of joy to convulsive tears of sadness or from deep depression to forthright love. Adults, on the other hand, often strive for perfection and a supreme sense of order and control. In so doing, a person can lose touch with his or her emotions — the very *essence* of acting. The emotion lets us hear the *arc of the character* as it goes from disbelief to satisfaction, agitation to relief, fear to comfort, hectic to relaxed, etc.

In voice-overs, as in other forms of acting, it is necessary for a voice actor to regain some of that child-like emotional verisimilitude. After all, an actor's *emotion* adds depth and realism to the scripted words. The copy is merely the skeleton to which an actor adds flesh and substance. Because of this, it is necessary for the actor to know how to breathe life into the copywriter's craftily sculpted skeleton.

Twenty-five percent of the success of the copy is in the script; the other 75 percent is in the acting!

Begin by familiarizing yourself with your own emotional life. Take note of how you feel at different moments of the day. Notice how your breath changes and where the different tensions are in your body. Does your body get rigid during an argument? When you are anxious, does your stomach do flip-flops? If someone frightens you, does your breathing become shallow? Do you throw things when you get disgusted, or do you curl up in a ball and start crying? Memorize how you feel at each given moment and try to replicate it. It is one of the steps in becoming consciously aware of your unconscious behavior.

Emotions are the result of a *situation*. The very act of waking up in the morning can be exhilarating to the person who is anxiously anticipating an exciting event or depressing to the person who has to pick up the pieces of the previous day's disaster. As the day progresses, events either enhance or degrade the condition.

Happy and *sad* are the emotional extremes. Between them falls a vast spectrum of emotional conditions. Below is a partial list of emotions to help you get started. When you read them out loud, preface the word with a sound that helps the listener understand and relate to how you are feeling. For instance, if you are angry, add a sound of anguish, like "uuugh," before saying the word. If you are nervous, breathe deeply a couple of times before talking. When surprised, take a quick gasp of air before speaking. This allows you to *unite the emotion with the breath*.

Emotions reside in the breath and have movement. Note which sounds have an upward, downward, outward, inward, and wiggly breath support, movement, and inflection. Read each word in the list below and add the appropriate sound before it. It may be a whimper, sigh, grrrr, gasp, etc.

angry	anxious	ashamed
bored	cautious	confident
confused	depressed	disgusted
ecstatic	embarrassed	enraged
exhausted	frightened	frustrated
guilty	happy	hopeful
hysterical	jealous	lonely
love struck	mischievous	overwhelmed
sad	shocked	shy
smug	surprised	suspicious

By selecting an emotion or series of emotions within a script, the voice-over gains "purpose" because it leads the listener to an emotional response. The audience quickly understands how the character feels about the situation or product and how the listener should respond to the information.

Of course, commercial voice-overs are seldom designed to reflect the truly hideous side of human nature. Whenever a product is sold, it is usually accompanied by an element of fun. The energy has a positive upward motion rather than a negative energy that drags the whole spot down. When the commercial states a problem in the set-up, it is resolved with a feeling of hope and relief at the end. In commercials that involve argumentation, there should always be an element of fun and naïveté. No listener wants to hear a commercial with whining or vicious argumentation. These unpleasant emotions are too real and scary. They can alienate the listener and send the client into bankruptcy.

Some voice actors get tripped up in the belief that all scripts require a huge, smiley delivery referred to as "puking out a spot." That style is rarely used these days. A pleasant attitude needs to be reflected in the hero product and services; there is a whole gamut of emotions at one's disposal. When speaking about the competition or "other product," more emotional latitude is available to poke fun or chastise. Ironic, provocative, and funny approaches are highly successful approaches. Your primary job is to make the listener feel and take action. Unlock your emotions and use them to book jobs!

PUTTING IT ALL TOGETHER

Now it's your time to put it all together using the example script below. Where you see options, make the appropriate changes/gender choices. After the commercial is an example of how to use the three script analysis elements: Copy Basics, Hiding the Sell using the Five Ws, and M.I.N.E.

NUTTY CRISPS
"Bar"
Radio / 60 seconds

I was sitting in a café, drinking a double espresso, when this gorgeous/handsome blonde walked in. My heart skipped three beats. Could I be having a heart attack? No, it must be the sudden influx of caffeine. I let out a quiet sigh of relief as I grabbed a handful of Nutty Crisps. *(crunch)* Mmmm, they sure taste good. *(crunch)* Nutty Crisps, I thought, are the perfect complement to this double espresso. *(crunch)* It was then that I noticed. The gorgeous/handsome blonde sitting in the corner didn't have any Nutty Crisps! She/he would miss out on the delicious crunchy taste of Nutty Crisps. *(crunch)* How unsatisfying! *(crunch)* My hand shaking, I lifted my bowl of Nutty Crisps off the table. Putting one determined foot in front of the other, I walked to her/his table. "Hi," I said. "I noticed you don't have any Nutty Crisps." That's when I noticed. I didn't either. I'd eaten the whole bowl!

ANNOUNCER: Nutty Crisps. The crunchy snack you can't quit eating.

SCRIPT ANALYSIS

COPY BASICS

Client:	Nutty Crisps
Key words:	Taste good, perfect complement, deliciously crunchy taste, really good
Slogan:	The crunchy snack you can't quit eating.
Set-up:	The first four sentences establish the relationship and emotional condition.
Body:	It starts when the product is introduced: *I let out a quiet sigh of relief as I grabbed a handful of Nutty Crisps.* And it ends before the announcer tag.
Resolve:	Announcer tag

HIDING THE SELL

(Note: Some of the choices listed below may differ from yours as they involve personal choices, experiences, and imagination.)

Personalization *(who you are talking to):* It shifts from retelling the story in your head or telling a good friend to talking to the person at the table.

Who Are You? Yourself reliving a date in the past, single, attractive, a bit timid, flirtatious.

Where Are You? In a café.

What Are You Doing: Sipping coffee, eating, walking to the table, placing product on table

Resolve: Announcer tag

M.I.N.E.

(Note: The motivation is personal and will differ from person to person. The one listed below is merely one option.)

Motivation: Friend just asked, "I didn't know you have a boy-friend. How did you meet him?"
Intentions: To understand, to explain, to gain courage, to assert oneself, to defend, to flirt, to encourage
Need = Love
Emotions: Confused, relieved, encouraged, excited, determined, nervous, resigned, embarrassed, hopeful

SUMMARY AND SELF-EVALUATION

Understanding and using M.I.N.E. requires trust and personal exploration. It is only after you come to terms with your own inner character that this subtext is implemented. Take time now to make a list of what you perceive to be your own personal assets and frailties. Make two columns. It may look something like this:

ASSETS	FRAILTIES
Funny *Balanced*	Shy
Creative	Nervous
Good mimic	Lack confidence
Assertive	Transpose words when nervous
Genuine	Talk too fast
Honest	Rely more on intellect than emotions

Holding a mirror up to yourself and examining what lies beneath is very courageous. It allows you to see what works in a script and what doesn't. You might also note that elements from both columns were needed in the example script. If you only shared your assets, the listener wouldn't be able to relate to you. All scripts contain dualities: assets and frailties. Embrace them and improve areas that need improvement. You have the ability to live up to and achieve your full artistic potential. You'll also notice that what you put into your work also seeps into your everyday life.

Chapter 6

MELODY & TEMPO

Written scripts contain music. As voice actors, we must find the precise tune for each script. There are pop-up words that add pitch rises and falls, rhythmic staccato words punctuated by *d*, *t*, *b*, and *k* articulators, round vowels, and mellifluous *m*, *n*, *l* and *v* resonators. Rhythm changes occur as the speaker lingers on key words and breezes through unimportant words and phrases. Some scripts have fast tempos, and other scripts require a slower delivery. Speed is dictated by complexity of information, attitude, target audience, and product value. For example, the more expensive the product, the slower the tempo. Conversely, the less expensive the item, the faster the read.

When diction is sloppy and word endings are dropped, the speaker has a locked jaw and doesn't open the mouth properly, so multiple phrases are treated as one thought, and the music of the message gets muddled. Musical shifts in speech allow phrases to be separated so the listener can take in the message quickly and easily. Using new body movements and gestures every time you see punctuation or a new phrase results in natural musical shifts. Learning to play the instrument — your body — results in fast, easy, and specific musical shifts.

Read and record the following sentence. The first time, don't move your body and just read the words. The second time, gesture with your right hand on the first sentence, left hand on the second, and use both hands together when you gesture on the third sentence. Make sure to keep your right hand out and don't bring it back to your body when you say the second sentence.

Don't stop learning. Keep trying. Put melody in your voice.

Did you hear the three distinct musical pitches? If you did, you realized how easy it is to create musicality by simply using very specific body movements. If you didn't, you probably returned to a neutral body position between sentences. Keeping the body engaged and active results in a balanced sound. The first two sentences are 180 degrees apart as you gesture from right to left. The final sentence splits the difference and brings the two diametrically opposed thoughts together. Practice reading the sentence using other movements like shoulder shrugs, eyebrow lifts, hip wiggles, etc. We're wired for sound. Use it!

Punctuation is the script's road map or musical score. You need to train the body to change every time your eyes see punctuation. This may be confusing as many directors tell actors to throw away or disregard the punctuation. The two directions are actually the same! Many readers pause and breathe every time they see punctuation. For people reading for time, this is a deal breaker. They're also not saying make one long sentence out of the text. Commas (,), dashes (-), colons (:), periods (.), and ellipses (…) are important. They tell us a lot about the rhythm of the words and help define and separate thoughts. What a director is saying when asking talent to disregard punctuation is to get rid of the "ready" quality and make it sound more natural. Learning to use rather than disregard the punctuation is an easier approach to voice acting.

On a random search about word musicality, I came upon this poem:

The Musicality of Words
By ~Deep-Emerald
http://deep-emerald.deviantart.com/art/The-Musicality-of-Words-86726473

Words, I find, must have a rhythm
They ought to be placed with care
Though free verse means there is no need
For rhyme or metric feet
Still words must communicate
Through their musicality.

Words, when they are free
May lose musicalit-ness
They stagg-
er and

cut and
trip
Fall unto themselves
With barely a whiff
Of aforementioned pulse.
However, this is not what I would like to do
I find it does not amuse and entertain the reader — you.

Words ought to have a meaning
When written in free verse
They may be formed
Dif-fer-rent-ly
Than we are used to seeing
But that strange form should still
Communicate a sense
Of what the author means it to.

Words are building blocks
Used by the noble poet
The function of a poet
Seems innately to be play
Play with words, play with sounds
Play that lasts all. . . afternoon

Words can be a sly trap
Ensnaring he who reads
It needn't be the pretty sonnet
Which the Bard favoured so
'Tis not to say, however,
That such forms don't have their place
Simply that each choice
Should be made
With the truest, utmost care.

Words, I find, must have a use
They should not be employed in vain.
Let all your texts reflect this truth
And greatness, you'll attain.

So, embrace the muse and add musicality to your speech. It will
serve you well.

MODULATION

This is a very intimate business. The listener is inches or a few feet away. Actors performing in video games and looping films need to project to cut through the music and sound effects tracks (M&Es). The rest of voice work involves imploding the sound rather than exploding. This imploded energy creates a rumble in the gut that fills the voice with an emotional intensity that makes the eyes twinkle and the voice shimmer. In other words, it makes your voice come alive. Leaning a few millimeters into the mic can draw focus to words while continuing to deliver the message in a consistent volume. When required to shout on mic, think of the sound going up from your toes through the top of your head rather than outward to the back wall.

Practice Exercise: Read the following line three ways.

Hurry! We've got to get out of this place. Go, go, go.

1. **Shouting** — Stand six–eight inches from the microphone. Make a strong, quick arm gesture to the ceiling, using all your muscles, including the tips of your fingers.
2. **Intimate** — "Kiss the mic." This is a term used when you get as close as you can to the mic without creating plosive and breathing distortions.
3. **Real person** — Stand three–five inches from the mic and talk in a normal voice. Thinner, weaker voices may need to be closer while voices with good "cut through" on the mic may need to position themselves an inch or so back.
4. **Real person and Intimate** — Lean into the microphone on the last sentence as you say, "go, go, go."

With modulation changes, you also have to mentally live in a different environment. The shouting read is good for military fighting games where the voice needs to cut through the loud music, explosions, and helicopter sounds. The intimate read requires a lot of pent-up intensity, as the scene would take place in a more confined area like an abandoned warehouse. Reverb room tone effects would be added to increase the reality. This modulation style is also good for trailers and promos. The majority of commercials and narrations are read in the real-person style, a few inches from the microphone. Reading in your normal volume voice allows subtle nuances to shine through. In the final read, when you leaned into the mic on the last sentence, you should have heard the difference between someone talking to you face-to-face and someone leaning into your ear to tell you a secret.

MELODY

TV reads call for a tight melody of only 3–5 notes. Radio reads usually use 7–10 notes on the musical scale. Cartoons, video games, and toys have a broader musical spectrum based on the character portrayed. Our ears are accustomed to hearing these patterns. When they fall out of the proper tessitura (the part of the register where most of the vocal tones should be for a particular character/script), we immediately know that something doesn't sound right. The voice has either gone too high or too low in the musical scale.

I like to think of voices as having three melodic choices.

1. It starts low and rises, but always returns to the low resting note.
2. It starts high and lowers, returning to the high resting note.
3. A middle register voice that goes high and low but rests in the middle note position.

Musicality is one way we can define and separate thoughts. It saves time as spaces between phrases and sentences can be eliminated. Precision is needed to achieve the desired result. Most people have a natural melody when they speak. Then, when given something to read, it goes away. How much melody one uses depends on the medium where it will be played and the character portrayed. You will either broaden or shrink the tessitura.

Practice example: Read the following script following the marked rise in the middle of the sentence and the bended note with the half circle under the client's name.

Shopping is always easy at Megastore.com.

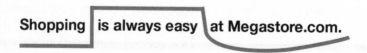

When you read this tag, you should have heard the natural separation between the three sections. Shopping is at a lower pitch, the second section is at a higher pitch, and the final segment has curved sound that goes lower in pitch and returns to the original note where the read started.

RHYTHM

Years ago, legendary radio producer Dick Orkin coined the phrase "radio rhythm." It's a means of lingering on the key words and phrases and speeding through the unimportant words. These distinctive rhythm changes draw focus to the client's key information. Words in sentences alternate between quick and slow rhythms.

Practice Example: The slow sections are capitalized. All other words should be read at a normal, faster rate. Treat the client's name "Rough & Tumble" as one word, assuming a dash between each word.

People that TRAVEL, always carry ROUGH & TUMBLE suitcases.

Rhythmically, it's quick, quick, s-l-o-w, quick, quick, s-l-o-w, quick. Joanie Gerber, successful Los Angeles voice actor and teacher for more than forty years, tells her students to "Gershwinize the words and not John Philip Sousa them." The steady beat of a marching band isn't nearly as surprising as the changing rhythm of a Gershwin tune. If you keep the audience guessing what you're going to say next, you'll hold its attention.

TEMPO

Finding the proper tempo of a script depends on the target audience. Corporate narrations are typically read at a moderate to slow pace due to the complexity of the information and the increasing number of English as a second language employees. Commercials vary their tempo according to picture, music, sound effects, and product type.

Changing the tempo of each sentence is important, too. Each section, subject, verb, object, etc., needs to be spoken at a slightly different tempo to draw focus to the important information and "throw away" the unimportant information. To illustrate this point, we will return to middle school English writing classes.

Practice Examples: Say the **bolded words slower,** *italicized words faster,* and the other words and phrases at a normal pace.
Independent Clause (subject and verb):
    I **got it!**

Dependent Clause (needs the independent clause in addition to the subject, verb):

I **got it**, *as I walked over to the counter.*

Simple Sentence (subject, verb, and independent clause):

I **got it** *and gave it* to a friend.

Compound Sentence (two or more independent clauses joined together by *but, and, yet, or, nor, for, sometimes* conjunctions):

I **got it** *but I knew that.*

Complex Sentence (independent clause and one or more dependent clauses joined by a subordinating conjunction — *when, where, while, before, until, as, since, if, etc.* — or a relative pronoun — *that, which, who, whom, whose):*

I **got it** *when Jane told me* the answer to the question.

Compound-Complex Sentence (two or more independent clauses and one or more dependent clauses):

I **got it on Friday,** and Jane learned it on Saturday, Sunday, and Monday *since there was a lot to learn before the test.*

When given direction to emphasize or linger on a word other than how you spoke it, the entire sentence is impacted by the tempo change. The slow, medium, and fast tempos change to different focal positions. The complex sentence example, changes from "**I got it** *when Jane told me* the answer to the question" to "*I got it* **when Jane told me** the answer to the question" and "I got it *when Jane told me* **the answer to the question.**"

UNDERCUTTING

Vocal variation and interest are given to a sentence by dipping down and throwing away the quick aside, or less important information. The dipping-down action can establish intimacy, add personal insight, attitude, draw focus to a phrase or word, or be used as the punch line to a joke. When the phrase that dips down is said more quickly than the rest of the sentence, the tempo changes. This makes the reading a lot more interesting to listen to and the listener better able to follow the main train of thought. Some speakers talk out of the side of their mouths or under their breath on the lower-pitched, dip-down section.

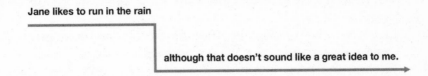

Jane likes to run in the rain although that doesn't sound like a great idea to me.

HOOK

A hook can either be used on one word or a whole phrase. The pitch starts high, dips down, and rises back up. It quickly draws focus away from the previous commercial and into our hero product's information. When used on the opening word, the speaker needs to quickly glide into three notes and flatten out the speech pattern on the remainder of that sentence. The same principle is applied when a vocal hook is used on a phrase, as the three-note variation is spread out over the desired words and flattens out on the remainder of the sentence.

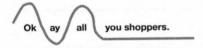

O k ay all you shoppers.

Okay all you shoppers. It's time for the Bargain Sale.

POP-UP WORDS

Key words need to stand out. There are several ways to make that happen.

1. A sharp, finger-pointing gesture results in a quick sound, especially when the selected word ends in a "t."
2. Raising and lowering the shoulders, lifting the eyebrows up and down, and raising and lowering a finger or hand in an

inverted "v" motion lifts the pitch of a single word up and down.

3. Lowering and raising the chin, shoulders, or hand in a "v" motion drops and raises the pitch of a single word.
4. Jiggling the head gently from side to side quickly in small motions, wiggling the fingers or toes, and dropping the voice to the back of the throat to create a scratchy sound on a specific word or phrase results in a shimmery or hazy voice quality that stands out from the rest of the read.
5. Use wide, slow hand or arm gestures to elongate a word or phrase.
6. Quickly cup hands close to the mouth to create parentheses on words or phrases that are meant to be secretive or under-played. (Hands will need to be close to the mouth during the whole reading, otherwise there will be an unnecessary pitch and volume shift.)

ARROW UP & DOWN

Certain phrases and sentences can rise progressively in pitch to set up a problem or situation. Dropping a sentence or phrase down the musical scale answers the set-up and implies a resolution.

Example: Who does insurance best? Genuine Insurance.

The first sentence arrows up. The client's name arrows down.

TRANSITIONS & BEATS

There are three basic transitions: set-up, body, and resolve. They are the equivalent of a play or film's first, second, and third acts. The character and problem are established, a solution is offered to alleviate the problem through the benefits of the hero product or service, and a suggestion is made to the listener to make the change and buy or use the product.

Beats are throughout the copy. They are often shown as blank spaces between sentences on the script. They are single or multiple sentences that are continuations of a single thought.

Example: I need to change banks. The one I'm with has high interest rates. There's got to be something better.

These three sentences are a continuation of the same thought, even though each sentence requires a different emotion. Therefore, they should be read in one breath, similar to the way you would talk to a friend. Continuing the message through the beats, rather than breathing between every line, results in a more believable delivery.

USE OF BREATH TO CREATE REALITY

Reality can be added by using the breath naturally. Breathe out and sigh when relaxed or confused. Take a quick, gasping breath in when surprised or excited. Talk on the breath to cut through the microphone and add stability to the words. Let the words trail off on a thought. Use a glottal stop to temporarily stop the flow of air for a brief moment. Let the emotion live in the breath. It connects the listener with the speaker.

WORD EMPHASIS CHART

The following is a sample of how you might quickly mark your script to change rhythm, tempo, and melody. They draw focus to specific words and designate places to breathe.

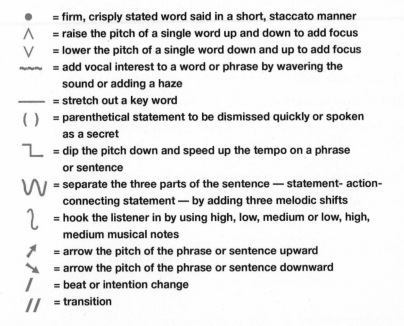

● = firm, crisply stated word said in a short, staccato manner

∧ = raise the pitch of a single word up and down to add focus

∨ = lower the pitch of a single word down and up to add focus

~~~ = add vocal interest to a word or phrase by wavering the sound or adding a haze

—— = stretch out a key word

( ) = parenthetical statement to be dismissed quickly or spoken as a secret

⌐ = dip the pitch down and speed up the tempo on a phrase or sentence

Ⱳ = separate the three parts of the sentence — statement- action-connecting statement — by adding three melodic shifts

ↄ = hook the listener in by using high, low, medium or low, high, medium musical notes

↗ = arrow the pitch of the phrase or sentence upward

↘ = arrow the pitch of the phrase or sentence downward

/ = beat or intention change

// = transition

Time to Practice:

Now it's your turn to learn how to mark a script using the word emphasis chart symbols. The first two lines are marked for you. Complete the rest. Remember to properly mark the key words: EProductsForYou.com, real-time advice, hassle-free shopping, latest advice and products.

EProductionsForYou *+ Assets and Frailities*
Radio / 60 seconds

Okay, you're in the computer store trying to figure out what the latest model with lightning-fast speed can actually do when you look around. Does the store really have salespeople? Whoop! One just dashed by. (At least there's a sign of life.) It's noon, so you figure they're all on lunch break. Right? After all, you are. Maybe interfacing with a human being isn't all it's cracked up to be. So you grab a sandwich and trot back to the office to search the web. You come across EProductsForYou.com. Their prices are competitive, and you can chat with a live salesperson. Sounds like a plan. So, you sign in. Sally appears. She is smart, friendly, shows you the various options available in your price range, and answers all your questions. You get real-time advice while sitting in your chair eating your grilled panini. She doesn't even mind that you squirted tomato juice all over your white shirt. Minutes later, the order is placed. In a moment of excitement you ask Sally what she's doing tonight. She giggles, says your order will arrive the next business day, and signs out. You sit there staring at the computer screen and wonder what else you can order.

TAG: Visit EProductsForYou.com today. Hassle-free shopping with the latest advice and products.

Chapter 7

COPYWRITER'S INTENTION: DIRECTING TALENT & YOURSELF

Before reading a script, we need to get inside the writer's head, connect with the logical and emotional elements, and motivate the listener to take action: place a call, visit a website, order on-line, walk inside a store, etc. We are not privy to client/writer meetings and discussions about why the message needs to be conveyed a certain way. It's our job to make that choice.

Typically, an actor approaches a script from the "I" position, asking questions like: Who am I? What am I doing? How do I relate to the product? Writers come from a slightly different perspective. Their first priority is the client: How can we make our product or service the obvious choice for our target audience? What emotions do we want to tap into to get the desired result? What type of personality or voice would best relate to our customers? For the two worlds to meet, writing elements must be acknowledged and appreciated by the actor.

Almost every piece of writing includes three main rhetorical elements: *ethos, logos,* and *pathos.*

- **Ethos** establishes who we are and why we have the authority to represent our hero client's company.
- **Logos** is the logical information. The product is faster, more convenient, better value, reliable, etc. It describes what the product is and how it works.

- **Pathos** is the emotional link that connects the audience to the message. It conveys how a person feels when he or she uses the product: healthier, sexier, happier, more relaxed, rejuvenated, uplifted, confident, etc.

These three writing elements need to be acknowledged and utilized in the read so that the listener hears the authority in the voice, the logic in the information, and the emotional benefits. Many voice actors spend unnecessary time wanting to rewrite copy because the logic doesn't make sense. That means the focus is wrongfully placed on logos rather than ethos. Our job is to bring life to the written words no matter how poorly written or confusing the information.

Below is an interview with a writer, producer, and director who will help clarify what goes on behind the scenes before you receive a script.

Insider View of the Industry

John Crane, John Crane Films

What parameters does a client give you for creating a commercial or advertising campaign?
Good clients have well-prepared goals and objectives in mind. A client like Charles Schwab knows where it's going. It has a heart and soul and is not afraid to communicate it. That's important because people these days are looking for a company they can relate to and not simply buy a product from.

What influences your decision to write the copy a particular way?
We have to find a way of effectively tapping into an emotion. This is far more powerful than a phrase someone can memorize. Funny is great because it stands out. If done well, humorous commercials work better than feel-good spots because people tend to remember them and use them in conversation.

What tricks do you use to write effectively?
Rhetoric, which is the art of argumentation, plays a huge part in my writing. Advertising is all about persuading someone to take action. After all, the client wants a return on the investment.

What frustrates you when actors read your copy?

I can answer that easily: lack of preparation. The actor has to come in with the ability to analyze the copy — or at least be in the ballpark — with tonality, attitude, and understanding of his or her own voice as an instrument. Otherwise, they've missed the boat. The words are put on the page for a reason. It's a bad joke within the industry to hear an actor ask, "What is my motivation?" Doesn't an actor know it? Use some script analysis and figure it out! If I have to tell you what your motivation is, you're not worth hiring. Also, don't be needy or annoying. It's usually based on insecurity. Even if you're playing a character that is insecure, the actor has to *be secure* about the role. Insecure people waste a director's time. *Bring your tool kit;* have the fundamental tools down so you feel secure in knowing you can do the job well.

How would you describe great acting?
Great acting is a *snapshot of the human experience.* Subtext cannot be conveyed by words alone. Great acting involves body language and emotions. The audience wants and needs to feel. It's the actor's job to fill that void.

THE WRITER'S JOB

To be hired, we need to understand the writer's process.

1. Know your client's competition.
2. Identify what quality separates your client's product or service from the competition.
3. Recognize if your target audience is different from your client's competition.
4. Write copy that capitalizes on the hero client's identifying quality.
5. Choose a voice talent that best suits the product: male, female, young adult, middle-aged, old, or child.
6. Decide on a vocal quality that will stand out from the competition: clear, crisp, hazy, raspy, sandy, comedic, intelligent, warm, sexy, strong, high, low, or mid-range.
7. Request an attitude that reflects the company's heart and soul.
8. Hire someone who's a perfect fit and requires little or no direction.

Auditioning and working from home means that we have to do research on every script we receive. Looking at the advertiser's website or visiting that business tells us a lot about their image, style, attitude, and strengths. Within minutes, you'll glean a lot of valuable information that will help you stand out from the competition: other voice actors!

Time to Practice:

Read this script and analyze the words from the copywriter's perspective. Note that placing spaces between paragraphs is their way of defining emotional beats and where the voice talent should breathe. Also, by writing each sentence on a different line, the copywriter is letting you know that a picture will change to accompany each sentence.

Voice Recognition
TV & Web / 30 seconds

I'm not my job.
I don't have a computer for a brain.
My mouth doesn't spew out documents —
black and white or color.
Although I wish it could.

I don't type ninety words a minute,
and I'm not a good speller.

I'm not the president of the company
or even a VP.
I'm just an employee.
And I don't have time to think about megabytes or RAM.

Because I've got a lot of important projects to finish.

I need a computer that thinks for me.
Or at least understands what I'm saying.

TAG: VoiceRecognition. Smart software for your computer.

Script analysis:

1. The *competition* is standard computers without built-in voice recognition software and several other past and present voice-activated word processing programs.

2. The hero product's ability to think ahead and understand the listener are comments about the *quality* of our client's product as opposed to the competition's less-than-stellar performance history and *size* of the software.

3. The audience is *targeted* to middle- to lower-management employees and everyday people who want to speak to their computer rather than type. The competition's target audience is upper-management business professionals.

4. The copy capitalizes on the hero client's *identifying quality*: Frustrated with the current products available. Needs an intelligent program that saves time and computer space.

5. *Voice talent:* male or female, middle age.

6. *Vocal quality:* clear, ironic, intelligent, mid-range.

7. *Attitude* that reflects the company's heart and soul: relaxed, confident, ironic.

8. Hire someone who's a *perfect fit:* Do you fit these specs or can you make an adjustment to sound like this type of person? If so, you've got a chance of being hired. If not, you should either pass on the audition or keep studying until you can create this type of character.

Ethos of the character is: intelligent, average businessperson, who has an active life outside and inside the office.

Pathos of the character is: frustration, hopeful, content, busy.

Logos: People aren't computers. They want computers to be an extension of them and think like them so they can save time. Knowing that's probably too much to ask, they just want a voice-activated program that works efficiently.

Chapter 8

LAYERING TECHNIQUES

Our job is to create a reality out of words and places that aren't naturally ours. We have to keep up with current trends and implement those styles and attitudes into our reads. Subtle information about our character has to be gleaned from the script from a performance, writer, and client's perspective. Written words need to roll around in our mouths until they sound natural and spontaneous. The purpose of the dialogue needs to be clear. We need to BELIEVE everything we say!

Before legendary advertising giant, Publicis & Hal Riney founder, and Advertising Hall of Fame member Hal Riney passed away, I had the privilege of sitting down with him to ask a few questions about the advertising business. Many people attribute him to the shift in advertising to a more realistic "real person" style. His agency produced some of the most iconic advertising in history. As a voice performer for many of his national clients, his metered, heartfelt reads continue to be copied by many performers. His comments are here to help you understand the selection process from the other side so you can layer your performance more effectively.

Hal Riney Interview

What do you hear on voice actors' auditions?
One of the problems we have with people who aren't directed at auditions is their tendency to oversell and overact. Also, a lot of the voices available are simply too perfect, too polished, too professional. They don't reflect the kind of "reality" we're often looking for. Today's voices are more low-key, natural, and understated than in the past.

Microphones have improved, too, which allows the voice actor to bring down the performance into a more natural and realistic delivery. I know that many of the scripts come with TV and film star suggestions for the voice actor to emulate. Who are your favorite voice actors?

That depends on what you're looking for. John Crawford and Dick Orkin have the best humorous voices for radio. Orson Welles and E. G. Marshall were the best of their time, for richness and authority. Colleen Dewhurst was a fabulous female voice. There are some people who are tremendously successful, such as Percy Rodriguez, whom few people have heard of, but who made an awful lot of money in this business.

What do you think about movie stars voicing commercials? They certainly have added to the demand for journeyman voice actors to be more low-key and natural.

If a movie star's voice is unique, distinctive, and recognizable — and the star has a favorable image — perhaps there is some value in paying some huge amount of money to use that voice. But frequently clients will hire movie or TV stars to do voices despite the fact that few people could identify who's talking. It might be good for the client's ego, or pumping up folks at a sales meeting, but it seems to me to be a terrible waste of money.

Too bad more producers at large advertising agencies don't think that way. Every time you turn on the TV, it seems that another screen star has been hired to voice a national product. What trends do you see in the future?

I see our business continuing to change. Much of our business will exist in the hands of giant global agencies, simply because there will continue to be increasing numbers of giant global companies. The creative activity will become more and more fragmented, with specialists and freelancers doing a substantial portion of the creative work. However, there will continue to be dozens of bright new agencies born each year, as there always have been.

Do you have any encouraging words for voice actors?

It's a great business if you can get enough work. It's the easiest business in the world, doing what you normally do every day... talking.

Tips for Lifting the Words Off the Page

Talking naturally does sound easy. To make it sound effortless and believable, the speaker must consider:

The Script

1. Punctuation
2. Quick asides or inside jokes
3. Specific word usage
4. Performance specifications (specs), sound effects (SFX), music, and visuals cues
5. Number of words on the page, as it defines the speed of delivery

Performance Choices

1. Body position
2. Proximity to the microphone
3. Vocal pitch and range
4. Attitude
5. Acting method and "being in the moment" choices
6. Sense memory
7. Relationship to the product or service
8. Relationship to the microphone as a person's ear
9. Use of breath (talking on it, being out of it, sighing, excited intake, etc.)
10. Emotions

Attitude Choices

Edgy	Skeptical	Warm
Disbelieving	Amazed	Friendly
Excited	Dejected	Weary
Relieved	Snarky	Amused
Ironic	Sarcastic	Surprised
Enthusiastic	Cocky	Wry

Body Language

The way you stand and where you look affects the read.

1. **Keep your eyes on the script.** Only a few seasoned actors are able to look away from the script, keep their mouths consistently

placed on the microphone, and remain in character. For most, looking up at the microphone becomes the equivalent of avoiding eye contact with the listener. It results in a disconnection from the listener as the "need" is changed from the client to yourself. Public speakers look up to make sure people are listening, are engaged, and understand what you're saying. In the recording world, assume that the audience is the paper. It will also minimize timing issues while you find your place on the script again and microphone proximity issues from looking up and down.

2.   **Avoid crossed or limp arms.** When they are crossed tightly in front of the body, you will sound guarded, defensive, and unapproachable. Limp arms result in a lazy and lifeless sound. Putting hands in pockets is also a form of protection. Unless that is the desired end result, relax the arms and allow them to gesture and move freely.

3.   **Ground yourself.** If you don't believe what you're saying, unnecessary movements and tics often develop that detract from the message. You will sound uncomfortable, nervous, and unfocused if you fidget, tap your feet, or step back and forth from the microphone. To sound confident and authoritative, plant both feet firmly on the ground, bend your knees slightly, connect emotionally with the listener, and breathe. This posture will help you sound trustworthy.

4.   **Don't be afraid to show your teeth.** A smiling face with an open grin creates a confident, eager, and pleasant sound. When talking about serious topics, the competition, and logical information, you may drop the smile. This positive and neutral attitude requires flexible facial muscles. So, don't be afraid to have a rubber face.

5.   **Know the size of your character.** The more open your stance — legs open and arms out stretched — the bigger, more powerful, and more confident you'll sound. Standing with feet close together and keeping arm movements small create a smaller, more behind-the-scenes type character. Turning the body at an angle to the microphone results in a mid-size character that has a cocky, confident attitude.

Voice Quality

1.   **High-pitched voices** are great for animated characters. In commercials and narrations, they can sound young, insecure, and inexperienced. The more confident the character, the more you

should try and place your voice lower into the mask or chest areas. Vocal exercises can also help lower the pitch.

2. **Nasal voices** can be annoying, calculating, demanding, and less professional. At least 70 percent of the population believes that. If you have this type of voice, work on moving the resonating sound out of the nasal area and into the mask or chest areas.

3. **The speed at which you speak either gains or loses an audience.** Really slow speech, with numerous multi-second pauses, can easily lose a listener's attention. Conversely, talking too fast is frustrating for listeners because it is hard to comprehend and absorb the information. A voice that is relaxed, in control, and spoken at a medium speed sounds calm and confident. People will trust you and wait to hear what you have to say as they listen in antici…pation.

4. **Gravelly voices** provide texture, command attention, and project an illusion of experience and authority. It is also perceived as young, hip, and cool and is a popular request at auditions and jobs. If you possess this vocal quality and it starts getting more gravelly, be sure to see a doctor. It may be a sign of throat problems such as nodules and other health issues.

5. **A person with a thin, mumbled, or low-volume voice** needs to work on confidence issues, strengthen his or her breath support to talk "on the breath," and practice diction exercises until these issues are overcome. Our job is to be the voice of authority. That means showing our vulnerability and making a strong stance on an issue — the script.

THE PYRAMID SCHEME

There are two parts to this theory. First is the voice-mind-body relationship.

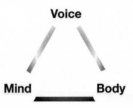

Most jobs only require a person to use one or two of these relationship elements at a time. A voice actor has to focus and use all three. The mind has to decipher the meaning of the script. The body has to trust the mental "homework" and find ways to trust it and not let it show. Then, the eyes have to follow the words on the page so they can be spoken with confidence and clarity.

When the voice is used, it has to make the words sound fresh and real. It has to have purpose and movement. When one of the elements is off, the actor stumbles or has a controlled "ready" quality. One way to break out of that planned, predictable style is to distract the mind with familiar kinesthetic movements. After the script has been properly analyzed, the body needs to trust the message. The actor may need to shake the hands out a few times, jump up and down, laugh, or make some other strong physical movement to move the information from the head to the heart and gut. When the read needs to sound warm, caring, and heartfelt, the actor can stimulate that emotion by placing one or both hands on the heart. A questioning line may be delivered while rubbing the chin. Scratching the head can bring back a feeling of bewilderment. These and many other gestures are performance tricks to immediately create a real emotional moment.

The second part of the pyramid is the commercial's structure to build in intensity and purpose until the very end.

Using the three parts of the copy — set-up, body, and resolve — the commercial has a dynamic build from identifying and relating to the opening problem, sharing a way to fix the problem through information in the body, and resolving the issue by suggesting that the listener take the advice.

Many voice actors have great beginnings because set-ups are typically more interesting to read. When the copy points in the body come in, the actor starts getting bored because the emotional connection with the audience is lost due to disbelief or disconnection with the information. With no investment in the product, the resolve fades away. The result is an inverted triangle where the set-up is big, the body is medium, and the resolve is small. We have to remember that the reason we're there is to give advice and encouragement. This inverted style is unacceptable as it defeats the purpose for speaking.

One way to get used to this build in intensity is to use the body. You might start reading the commercial with your hands close to your body. With each line of copy, gesture outward until the arms are fully outstretched and the shoulder muscles feel tension from the stretch. Don't worry about hitting the stand and microphone. If you start with your hands at waist level below the music stand, they won't be in your way. Once you get used to the additional energy required in the pyramid build — great open, better middle, dynamic ending — you'll no longer need to move the arms in this manner. You will have conditioned yourself to expect the build to occur and muscles to be engaged. Using the M.I.N.E. approach also helps with this build as the speaker's needs gets fulfilled by talking about or using the product/service and then sharing that experience with the listener.

Chapter 9

BELIEVING WHAT YOU SAY

When all the intellectual choices have been made, the performer has to trust the homework: use imagination, load up emotionally before speaking, use the body to connect with the reality of the moment, and fly blind. The brain has to step aside and let the body and voice take over. An emotional build occurs as the actor reflexively offers information to the listener through natural movements one would use with a friend. The actor believes the message, and the listener connects emotionally with the resolution. The product "meets the need" of the consumer. Truth, believability, and reality are achieved.

This is my performance mantra. Use it! It works.

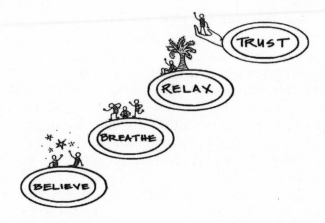

My talent agent for many years explains the processes of finding the truth through right-and left-brain functions.

Finding the Truth

John Erlendson, owner, JE Talent in San Francisco

Voice acting is demanding and immediate. Actors are expected to deliver a performance in five minutes that is 95 percent there. That is the equivalent of five weeks' rehearsal for a stage actor! To get a presentable performance that quickly, there has to be a strong *physical* commitment. The idea is to work from the *body* and not the mind. It's the challenge of finding freedom. There are no judgments, only freeform creation. This is not to deny the acting pedagogy: Stanislavsky, playing objectives, pre-life, given circumstances, etc. It's the concept of breaking through to an unconsciously competent state. It's *active* acting.

Staying in the head immobilizes an actor. The *left* side of the brain is the analytical thinker. It *re-creates* because it is not grounded in truth. The *right* side is abstract and creative, but the intuitive side is afraid of failure. The actor's process is to *find the truth.* When an actor is immobilized by staying in the head, the actor has to break out of that familiarity. The internal work — empowering yourself to break out and direct yourself and feel your way through it — is the vessel of truth. The actor has to go from the outside in to find a "physical reality." Then, when the actor plays a vocal action, the body can physically react. Actions with feelings and feelings with actions have to be wedded together. It's a question of working inside out or outside in.

When the actor moves in truth, there is no denying the rightness of the action. Whether it is appropriate or not to the situation defines whether it is right (truthful) or wrong (untruthful). The choice will not be a bad choice if it is truthful. This process expands the odds of success. When the actor moves in a truthful physical reality, *active* acting from the body occurs. The body physically reacts. The extended realism makes other things — like the product — become important. An actor is able to communicate the truth of his or her feelings to follow the body rather than the mind; feel the action and integrate it into the work.

There are two types of conditioning: *acting* conditioning and *reading* conditioning. Patterns have to be let go. Expect and want a *vicarious* experience from your listening audience. Use your emotions. Come from a feeling. Take action to express that feeling and trust that feeling vocally and physically. Create a "what if" situation. *What if …* "someone asked me to be a farmer?" Begin with, "I feel…" and own the feeling before you start talking (take action). The key is to open with a feeling and stay in the moment.

You have the power to make people feel. Let a sense of "Dis-ease" drive your character forward to ease. Always find the Dis-ease. It's the fire in the furnace. Adjust the heat in the furnace and take action on it. If your character is at ease at the beginning of the commercial or narration, there is no problem to solve! The stakes are low and ultimately there is no feeling to be expressed. Many truthful choices may be wrong to the situation but they will not be bad (untruthful).

FINAL THOUGHTS

Here is a brief recap before you dive into the workout chapters.

Warm up your voice and body

Crisp lips save slips. Be prepared for any situation — pitch variations, tonality shifts, and tough word combinations. Check to see if your body is tired, tense, or stiff. Shake out the hands, warm up the body, and find a way to make your eyes twinkle.

Embrace your sound

Play to your strengths. Match your best voice — head, mask, or chest — to the job. Put the right "hat" on that's appropriate for the script and client.

Act with personality

Bring your whole self to the job. You'll get consistent work when people know who you are and can relate to you. Decide if you are witty, intelligent, smug, cocky, funny, dry, warm, sarcastic, etc. Then, nurture the positive aspects of your personality.

Understand the copy

Don't just read words; convey a message. Turn the script over and improvise the spot to make sure you understand the meaning and your job relating that to the audience.

Identify the problem and solve it

Go beyond the words on the page. Create a moment before that emotionally connects with the problem. This will make the hero product sound like the logical solution. Then, you and the listener will be relieved as you suggest taking this course of action.

Believe everything you say

Rather than searching for the belief in the product, connect with what the product gives you. That is the "universal truth." If necessary, use "love handles" (sounds or words expressed before the actor reads the written words) to kick-start the feelings and actions.

Commit to your choices

Play to win and know you can lose. Don't play the scene down the middle. Boring and safe is bad and results in few bookings. Take strong chances that are appropriate to the script and commit to them.

Don't make excuses

Don't apologize for your perceived shortcomings or go to your "dark side." Believe with all your heart that you are the best person for the job. If you find yourself giving away your power and sending out this message, change your thought process immediately! If you don't believe in yourself, no one else will either. Confidence bleeds through the microphone and results in a thriving career. Everyone wants to work with a winner!

Don't push

Trust yourself and your choices. Don't get overly clever and draw focus to yourself. You'll think yourself out of a job. If you believe what you are saying and commit to how you're saying it, the audience (and person who hires talent) will accept the message as truthful.

Remember where you are

Use the microphone to your best advantage to create a believable 3-D scene where you are talking to one person.

Have fun

If you sound like you are working too hard, you probably are. Always remember to have fun. Don't let life's distractions get in the way. Your job is to take the listeners from their bad situation to a good one. As the authority, you've already experienced that and are now in a good place.

II. PUTTING IT TO PRACTICE

Chapter 10

TAGS, DONUTS, PROMOS, & TRAILERS

These short lines are the bread and butter of voice acting. They also require the most precision. A full story has to be told in a few words that clarify the information presented in the body of the commercial: when, where, why, and how. Union voice actors especially love this genre because the actor is paid a session fee every time the tag is lifted and placed on a new commercial. There are additional opportunities for residual payments. Film trailer announcers are the most lucrative and coveted voice-over jobs out there. They require strong, resonant voices that can linger on the words 10–20 percent longer than most speakers.

- **TAG:** The one or two lines of copy that brand a product at the end of a commercial. Advertising agencies spend months creating and refining the exact words for maximum impact and memorability. The person selected to read the tag line must perfectly match the heart and soul of the company in voice and attitude.
- **DONUT:** Sometimes it is necessary to break up the body of the copy with announcer information. Especially in radio commercials, it is used to stop or advance time. The announcer returns again at the end of the commercial.
- **PROMO:** Ads used to promote a show or event. These ads are time sensitive and require crisp diction and strong breath support. They can be one-time jobs for a TV movie of the week (MOW), concert, or sporting event. Contract positions are available for networks and stations promoting

their shows: "Starting Friday," "Tomorrow," or "Coming up next." "Then" is a very popular word used in many promos.

- **TRAILER:** Distinctive voice used to promote a film. They are played in movie theatres in addition to the usual audio/visual advertising mediums.

Time to Practice:

Each of these scripts teaches a different lesson. Pay attention to the specs (title, medium where it will air, length, and stylistic suggestions). Record and listen back to your recordings. Evaluate your performances and re-record if they don't sound truthful, motivating, and representative of the company.

California Tomatoes
TV & Web / 10 seconds
Music: Light, upbeat
Animated cartoon tomatoes dance on top of a dinner table. One tomato is strong and muscular, another sports a sombrero, and a little cherry tomato wears a diaper. On the word "fresh," they all jump onto a dinner plate and become "real" tomatoes.

Specs: The voice should sound fun and lighthearted. Quirky, raspy, or textured voices are welcome.

Whether your meal calls for a beefsteak tomato, a Mexican style tomato, or a cherry tomato, make it a tomato grown fresh in California.

REVIEW:

Product: California Tomatoes.
Key words: meal, the types of tomatoes, fresh, and California.
Implied problem: Canned or bad, tasteless tomatoes that were picked too early from a state other than California, then shipped and sold in the grocery store.
Technique: Besides "playing with" the key words, stair-step the list so each tomato type is at a different pitch. *Fresh* and *California* are the most important words, so put a spin on them.

Golden Fields Bread
TV & Web / 8 seconds
Music: Warm, melodic
A family sits around the breakfast table as the sun filters through the kitchen window. The mother smiles at her children as she places a tray of hot, buttered toast on the table.

Specs: Warm, caring, low- to mid-range voices.

Tomorrow morning, start your day with Golden Fields Whole Wheat Bread. Golden Fields. What mornings should taste like.

REVIEW:

Product: A special kind of whole wheat bread made by Golden Fields

Key words: Tomorrow, the client's name, and taste

Implied problem: Today the listener messed up; tomorrow they can rectify it by eating this special bread. The arc of the story goes from chaos to peace, as exemplified by the music selection and happy family visuals.

Technique: When the client's name is written twice, right next to each other, it is a strong indicator of a melodic and emotional transition. The best choice is to drop the pitch the second time as the story progresses from chaos to ease, and then to the final sentence, which offers advice. This follows the three-part commercial structure: set-up (problem), body (solution), resolve (active suggestion).

Truform Underwire Bras
Radio / 5 seconds
Music: Typical retail music that matches the adult alternative tempo and style that is currently in vogue
Typical retail copy where good diction and personality are a must!

Specs: Mature voice with a hint of sex appeal, female preferred but would be open to a male voice.

New Truform underwire bras, for the full-figured woman.
Available now in fine department stores everywhere.

REVIEW:

Product: The latest underwire bra from the trusted company Truform.

Key words: New, Truform, underwire bras, full-figured, now, fine department stores, and everywhere

Implied problem: The target audience may have been displeased with the old style or wasn't aware of its improvements, or the product previously wasn't available for full-figured clients.

Technique: Almost every word is important in retail ads. Tempo and musical shifts on each defining bit of information are musts! *New* is a very important word that should not be disregarded. Be sensitive and simply state the target audience: full-figured. No need to sound sexy here, it will be overkill. We know that they will be sold in stores. Therefore, the only words that need attention on the last line are *now* (urgency) and *everywhere* (easily available). Tempo shifts for the three sections of copy are: slow (New Truform underwire bras), medium (for the full-figured woman), fast (last sentence).

more body, more diversity   TAG —

1. slate
2. ABC takes
   - 1-2 sec. of roomtone

Kitty Menu Cat Food

TV & Web/ 10 seconds

Music: Slow classical music with a modern electronic twist

A beautiful longhaired white cat with a diamond-studded collar stands beside her 14-karat gold food bowl. The cat is finicky and looks away. A hand reaches down and replaces it with a crystal bowl full of Kitty Menu. The cat, now happy, eats contentedly and licks her lips after the bowl is empty. Final shot of the cat purring as she rubs against a can of Kitty Menu.

Pet, friend, wiggle wobble Secret

Specs: *Either low, sexy female voice or hip, cool guy.*

Kitty Menu cat food comes in four delicious flavors — chunky chicken, tuna supreme, liver pate, and turkey tetrazzini. Kitty Menu, for your gourmet cat.

Jasmine, Charly, RJ
vet   pet sitter   sick cat

REVIEW:

Product: A gourmet cat food made by Kitty Menu.

Key words: Kitty Menu, cat food, four delicious flavors, gourmet cat.

Implied problem: Cat is finicky and doesn't even eat the best cat foods the owner buys.

Technique: Numbers are important, so emphasize "four." The list is unimportant, is there to show variety, and should be read at a quicker pace. "Gourmet" is the selling point and clarifies the type of cat owner who should buy this product.

HEAVY BED TRUCK
TV, Web, & Radio/ 10 seconds and 5 seconds
Music: Strong, loud with a steady, driving beat
Rugged guy gets in a shiny silver truck, drives it through mud, rocks, and potholes on city streets. Final panoramic shot of him driving into the rugged Arizona wilderness.

Specs: Deep male voice preferred, open to hearing realistic Texas accents.

The new deluxe Heavy Bed Truck. Built to take a beating, on the road or off. Unleash the adventurer in you.

REVIEW:

Product: Heavy Bed, a fully equipped rugged truck
Key words: New, deluxe, Heavy Bed Truck, built, on road or off, adventurer
Implied problem: Don't be confined, every day is an adventure that should be lived to the fullest.
Technique: Breath support and attitude are of primary consideration. This spot should be played close to the mic for maximum impact.

News Center **News Magazine**
TV / 10 seconds and 5 seconds
Music: Eerie and ethereal
Visuals of ghosts and apparitions followed by the station logo and time screen shots.

Specs: Male or Female. Must be suspenseful and authoritative. Read each version (tonight, tomorrow, coming up next) with slightly different intensity levels, increasing as the program gets closer.

Do ghosts exist? We'll talk to people who claim they have ghosts living in their homes. Is it a hoax or is it real? Find out tonight (tomorrow, coming up next) on News Center 13, at 11:00.

Meet a family with ghosts, tonight (tomorrow, coming up next) on News Center 13, at 11:00.

REVIEW:

Product: News Center 13.

Key words: Tonight, tomorrow, coming up next, News Center 13, 11:00.

Implied problem: You may have ghosts in your home.

Technique: Timing is tight to fit the pictures. Phrases are broken up into short bits of information. Diction must be crisp. The "sts" combination in ghosts is difficult for many people to pronounce. Make sure the "t" is voiced. Tap the "ts" in *tonight, tomorrow,* and *next* to make sure the times stand out. Linger on "News Center 13" and give 11:00 (eleven) a strong, firm ending. Your point of view is very present with lots of energy and punch without loud volume. Tight mic placement will give it power.

Reliable Bank
Radio / 10 seconds
Music: Quirky, upbeat music
Specs: Friendly next-door neighbor voice. Male or female.

ReliableBank.com. We handle all your banking needs *on* line, not *in* line. We're even members of FDIC. ReliableBank.com. Another reason not to go inside a bank again.

REVIEW:

Product: ReliableBank.com

Key words: ReliableBank.com, online, bank

Implied problem: Long lines inside the bank

Technique: The set-up is the client's name, the next two sentences constitute the body, and the second time the client's name is mentioned starts the resolve. That takes the listener from frustration to relief. No need to push FDIC, since that's common, legal information. Slow down on *online* and speed up on *in line*. Tapping the "t" in *not* and "k" in *bank* will help those two important words stand out and create better radio rhythm.

Creekside Vino
Radio / 60 Seconds
Dialogue: 40 seconds and 8 seconds
Donut: 8 seconds
Tag: 4 seconds
SFX: Romantic music and restaurant ambiance

Specs: Casting announcer role only. Male or female.

Man:	At last, a night without the kids.
Woman:	The babysitter!
Man:	She has our phone numbers, and I alerted the fire department like you told me.
Woman:	Jamie's diaper! Let's go home.
Man:	Relax. I changed her diaper before I put her to bed.
Woman:	Tommy's homework!
Man:	I gave the sitter explicit instructions.
Waiter:	Can I bring you something to drink?
Man:	A bottle of Creekside Vino, please.
Waiter:	Excellent choice. I'll be right back with your Creekside Vino.
Woman:	We're staying?
Man:	You deserve some time off. The kids will be fine. Besides, I just ordered Creekside Vino.
Woman:	That's quite a treat. I feel like an adult again. Listen to me, I'm talking in sentences longer than three words!
Man:	That calls for a celebration.
ANNCR (Donut):	Creekside Vino is a delicious sparkling wine suitable for any occasion. Even if you're just celebrating a night out without the kids.
Man:	Cheers!
Woman:	I love you … and this Creekside Vino is delicious!
Man:	We should go out more often.
Woman:	I'll reserve the babysitter.
ANNCER:	Make every occasion a special one with Creekside Vino.

REVIEW:

Product: Creekside Vino
Key words: Creekside Vino, sparkling wine, for any occasion, every occasion
Implied problem: Relationship and intimacy issues
Technique: Be sensitive to environment and don't break the mood. The wine = sex. The number equivalents (*any* and *every*) quantify how often you should serve this product.

Minitoys
TV & Web/ 10 seconds
Music: Lighthearted, corporate-sounding children's music followed by children laughing.

Specs: Warm, approachable, authoritative voice. Male or female.

This program was brought to you by the makers of Minitoys. Minitoys. A globally responsible company that has united environmentally conscious children in laughter for the past twenty-five years.

REVIEW:

Product: Minitoys
Key words: Program, Minitoys, globally responsible company, environmentally conscious children, laughter, twenty-five years
Implied problem: Other programs are bad for kids and the environment.
Technique: Should be played close to the mic. Clear diction and proper breath support are also important. The client's name mentioned twice in a row signifies the transition between the set-up and the body. The last sentence is the resolve. Since there are three sentences, each sentence should drop in pitch in order to take the listener from problem to solution. Adding a slight pause after "laughter" allows time for the children laughing sound effect to quickly come up and under before the final phrase is spoken.

Explosion City
TV & Web Trailer / 5 seconds
Music: Heavy, heart-pounding music with a large explosion SFX under.

Specs: Deep, powerful, resonant voice

Explosion City! Coming this Friday to a theatre near you.

REVIEW:

Product: *Explosion City*
Key words: *Explosion City*, Friday, you
Implied problem: Don't have anything to do or need a vicarious adrenaline rush.
Technique: Resonance, breath support, elongation of the words, especially the film's title and the release date. "You" is listed as a key word as a reminder to let the last word linger for 5–10 seconds rather than stopping the airflow and attitude after the last word in the copy is voiced.

MedTix
TV, Web, & Radio Disclaimer / 6 seconds
Music: Ethereal music with gentle ocean waves in the background

Specs: Mature male or female voice.

If you experience nausea, dizziness, chest pain, shortness of breath, unsteadiness, lightheadedness, or weakness after taking MedTix, discontinue use and consult a physician immediately. This may be a sign of a more serious condition.

REVIEW:

Product: MedTix
Key words: MedTix (All the other words are for legal purposes only.)
Implied problem: Your medical problem is solvable with our medication but there are serious, life-threatening side effects.
Technique: With the exception of the client's name, all other words should be spoken quickly in a neutral voice. Stay tight on the mic and don't put a lot of power into it. Release your air sparingly so you can get through these lines without having to

stop or take additional breaths. The musicality on legal copy is very tight and should only use 3–4 notes.

Plug
TV & Web / 10 seconds
Music: Light, upbeat

Specs: Bright, upbeat, youthful 20s–30s voice.

The new Plug. A clean, efficient, battery-operated car that charges in any household outlet. You'll be shocked by the savings!

REVIEW:

Product: Plug battery-operated car
Key words: new, Plug, clean, efficient, battery-operated car, charges in any household outlet, savings
Implied problem: Gasoline powered cars
Technique: This is a new product, so this spot is designed to build product awareness and branding. Therefore, take your time. There's a pun in the final line: *shocked*. That's a place to really let your personality shine. The target audience is new car buyers, so a youthful sounding voice is important.

Latte Express
TV, Web, & Radio / 6 seconds
Music: Light, up-tempo modern sound

Specs: Fun, breezy 20s–30s male or female.

Now's your chance to get an ice-cold latte without breaking the bank. $1.59 at any Latte Express location. Can you say *cha-ching?*

REVIEW:

Product: Ice-cold latte at Latte Express
Key words: Ice-cold latte, $1.59, Latte Express
Implied problem: Overpriced coffee at other locations
Technique: Don't sound sell-y. This should be a light, breezy, cool personality read especially in the financial sections. Item and price are the most important elements.

Voice One

Web & Mobile Device / 5 seconds
Music: Swooshing sound loop followed by a sustained note and light twinkle sounds at the end.

Specs: Friendly, inviting non-announcer read.

Visit VoiceOne.org now to find out how you can become the next voice-over star. Your dream is only a click away.

REVIEW:

Product: VoiceOne.org
Key words: VoiceOne.org, voice-over star, dream
Implied problem: Dissatisfaction with current job and desire for a creative outlet
Technique: This spot is to encourage people to take action. Therefore, specific body movements are necessary. Record yourself reading the copy without hand movements and then read it again using these suggestions. Use one or both hands to gesture toward yourself to invite the listener in, smile on "your dream," and use your finger to click an imaginary object on the word "click."

Biskee Bone

TV & Web / 6 seconds
Music: Superhero music

Specs: Looking for a stylized, humorous voice that could sound like a mock announcer or smart aleck.

The Adventures of Aldo and Dumpkin are brought to you by Biskee Bone. It cleans your dog's teeth and keeps him happy.

REVIEW:

Product: Biskee Bone
Key words: *The Adventures of Aldo and Dumpkin* (this sets up an advertising campaign, which translates to regular work for the talent), Biskee Bone, cleans your dog's teeth, keeps him happy
Implied problem: Bored dog and owner
Technique: Don't be afraid to use your big announcer voice but with the tongue firmly planted in cheek. Every phrase is important, so make sure each one stands out in its own unique way. The final mix will have a lot of reverb added to the voice.

Chapter 11

ANNOUNCER

Announcer copy is the most traditional style of commercial. There is no clever dialogue to fool listeners into believing they are overhearing a real, slice-of-life conversation. Nor is there a feeling that the person speaking is associated in any way with the company. The announcer is hired, without pretense, to sell the product. All pertinent information is spelled out directly, efficiently, and candidly. They contain a relentless list of *who, what, why, when*, and *where facts*. There are very few extraneous words. Energy needs to surge up from your toes and out through your fingers. For some styles, it may be necessary to keep your hands close to your mouth and gesture with your fingers to help get the script in on time and the words properly articulated.

This category comprises most of our voice-over work. The delivery styles are varied and include:

- **Traditional** — Vocal quality and technical precision are primary factors in the hiring process. This style is also referred to as *straight announce.*
- **Real Person** — A very popular request, this just means that they want someone to take words that no one would ever say and make them sound conversational. Personality is more important than voice quality.
- **Mock** — This is a tongue-in-cheek vocal placement and attitude choice that makes fun of old-fashioned announcer styles and parodies the delivery. There is a slight wink at the audience as this omnipotent sound from above cuts through the advertising clutter.
- **Stylized** — This takes the mock announcer a step further. It is overly dramatic and requires a singular personality trait that

impacts the voice in a unique and memorable way. Audio engineers like to add reverb on these type reads.

- **Comedic** — The casting requests are usually for comedians and improvisers because of their unique timing and view of the world. The funnier the script, the more comfortable the announcer needs to be in his or her own comedic look at the world so the words aren't pushed but are naturally funny. Unique vocal qualities are also requested for this type announcer.

- **Storyteller** — Another popular request that requires a person with great visualization skills and an engaging delivery that takes the listener on a journey. They want the listener to dive into the message and live in that world.

- **Image** — Rather than focusing on item and price, this style appeals to the listener's lifestyle and what the product gives a person. Voice talent finesses the modifiers rather than the nouns.

- **Awareness** — Whenever you introduce a product or see *NEW* written in the copy, your job is to make listeners aware of the product and why it's better than the competition. Nouns and verbs are stressed, as the product and what it does are the client's primary concern.

- **Branding** — Advertisers spend months deciding the best approach to make their product memorable. Voice talent selected to brand a business need to represent all the attributes of the company. More script analysis is needed to read between the lines in order to connect with the heart and soul of the company.

- **Station Imaging** — Vocal quality and style are of primary interest to TV and radio stations when selecting the best voice to represent their stations.

- **Retail** — Personality and technical precision on the item and price elements are of primary concern. This is good bread-and-butter work for voice actors since sales change constantly and require new recordings every week or so.

With all these styles of announcer copy, one single factor dictates this writing style. There are no personal pronouns like *I, me, we,* or *us* that allude to a closeness or personal connection with the company. The voice talent is hired to perform a duty. Styles change according to politics and economics. In times of war or recession, voices are heavier and more heartfelt. When the country is doing well and the economy is strong, voices get lighter and more flippant. Therefore, listen to the current styles and stay on top of the changes. It will help your longevity in the business.

Time to Practice:

As you rehearse the announcer commercials in this chapter, incorporate style choice, targeted audience, and company image. Voices selling upscale products are usually slower and more luxurious sounding than the quicker paced, lighter voiced inexpensive items. Urgency is a factor when voicing retail ads. Food items should make your mouth water. And, don't forget to keep current market trends.

Goldwater
Radio / 30 seconds
Music: Typical nondescript retail music

Specs: Read this retail ad two ways: once as a traditional announce and the other as a real person.

This weekend Goldwater is having a Midnight Madness Sale to make room for fall. Choose from furniture and accents, carpets and rugs, bed and bath linens, electronics, and home entertainment systems. All at prices reduced as much as 50 percent. Plus, with the Goldwater "Friends and Family" card, you get an additional 10 percent savings. Goldwater is open 'til midnight this Friday, Saturday, and Sunday. The Midnight Madness Sale at Goldwater, Twenty-fourth and Auburn Street in Camden.

REVIEW:

Product: Goldwater's Midnight Madness Sale
Key words: This weekend, Goldwater, Midnight Madness Sale, reduced 50 percent, "Friends and Family" card, additional 10 percent savings, open 'til midnight, Friday, Saturday, and Sunday
Implied problem: The store needs to get rid of its summer merchandise.
Technique: Each key word or phrase needs to be quickly placed at a different musical pitch so it will stand out. The laundry list should be read at a faster pace and have movement as it describes the range of merchandise and/or physical location in the store. Numbers and percentages, including "all," should be

slower. "Friends and Family" should stand out. Midnight is a special time. Friday, Saturday, and Sunday is a list and should be read faster. Three speeds are needed on the final sentence: the type of sale (medium), client (slow), and location (fast).

Color Care Bleach
TV & Web / 30 seconds
Music: Nostalgic, gentle, sweet

Specs: Real and not too announcer. Emotional but not sappy. Tender and caring. Gentle. Soft. Women 30–40 preferred.

He has grass stains on his pants.
She has chocolate on her shirt.
And both need cleaning without losing their real color.

Introducing Color Care.

It's powerful enough to remove stains.
And gentle enough to keep clothes looking new.

New Color Care.
A gentle bleach for colors.
A clean made specifically for kids.

REVIEW:

Product: Color Care Bleach
Key words: grass stains, chocolate, cleaning, color(s), introducing, remove stains, gentle, new, kids
Implied problem: Kids get dirty and their clothes are hard to clean.
Technique: The picture is going to do most of the selling. This has a slow, poetic pace that allows time for the visuals and gentle, loving emotional overtones. The sentences are well balanced: grass stains-pants, chocolate-shirt, powerful-remove, gentle-colors, clean-for kids. "Introducing" and "New" are strong indicators that this is an awareness campaign. It's a new product that people should use to solve their stain problems. Another reason why the pace is slow.

Colorado Golden
Radio / 30 seconds
Music: Slow, sad music at the beginning and a shift to uplifting, energetic music at the end

Specs: Need a good storyteller in either an ironic mock announcer or real person style.

It's a day like any other day. Wake up. Go to work. Go home. What makes this day different is only an errand away: a stop at the store, a walk to the beer section, and a purchase of Colorado Golden.

Colorado Golden isn't any beer. It's a beer that makes even the worst day better. Cold. Crisp. Delicious.

Colorado Golden. It's a party waiting to happen.

REVIEW:

Product: Colorado Golden beer
Key words: Colorado Golden, beer, cold, crisp, delicious, party waiting to happen
Implied problem: Dull dreary life
Technique: Take your time to tell the story and imagine each situation. If you don't see it, the listener doesn't either. Three lists follow the Rule of Three; twice in the first paragraph and once in the second. Note that the script is divided into three sections to show the reader the set-up, body, and resolve. Also, the music shifts from the set-up (problem) to the solution (body). Therefore, the second half of the commercial will be more uplifting.

Baloney's Banquet
TV & Web / 30 seconds
Music: High energy, wacky, and fun, with many loud sound effects layered into the mix

Specs: This needs a unique sounding, stylized voice to cut through the music and sound effects (SFX). Don't be afraid to go too far.

Jumpin' Jack! Highway Baloney is back, bigger, and better than ever. Now he's in Baloney's Banquet, the ultimate food fight of the century. Smashing things hasn't been this much fun since Highway

Baloney ran over furry animals in Baloney's Road Kill. *(SFX: squish)* Duck flying tomatoes. *(SFX: splat)* Avoid pies in the face. *(SFX: plop)* And watch out for the killer garbage disposal. *(SFX: grinding noise)* Highway Baloney is at it again in Baloney's Banquet from Zippo *(SFX: Zippo echoes four times)* Simply outrageous!

REVIEW:

Product: Zippo (client), Baloney's Banquet (latest game in the Highway Baloney franchise)

Key words: Highway Baloney, bigger and better, Baloney's Banquet, ultimate, Zippo, and Simply outrageous (the company's branding phrase)

Implied problem: The older games were small and audiences wanted more action.

Technique: This requires lots of energy, movement, mic technique and attitude. Change the action and mic placement on each of the action words: *duck, avoid,* and *watch out.* At the end, slow down and milk the company name and slogan.

Precious Darling
TV / 30 seconds
Music: Light, cute music that would appeal to a small child

Specs: Warm, sincere, real "mommy" voice that can be slightly stylized to maximize the childhood appeal.

Who's the cutest girl in town? It's Precious Darling, that's who. She's adorable. She's huggable. She's so real you won't want to put her down. Press her heart and she talks. *(Cut to doll saying, I love you.)* Pat her back and she burps. *(Girl burps doll.)* Put her on her knees and she crawls. *(Doll crawls; girl picks her up and hugs her.)* Precious Darling by Semko. Batteries not included.

REVIEW:

Product: Precious Darling

Key words: Precious Darling, adorable, huggable, real, and Semko

Implied problem: Other dolls aren't cute and don't have realistic movements or sounds.

Technique: In the old days, this huge smiling delivery style was called "puking out a spot." Adorable, huggable, and real define how this doll is better than the competition. The verbs press, pat, and put describe how she works. The last time the doll is mentioned, it should sound cute and loving (just like the doll). Be proud of the client, Semko. Read the final disclaimer quickly with a slight smile.

Skizzer
TV / 60 seconds
Infomercial
Music: Fast-paced

Specs: Traditional straight announce.

It's the amazing Skizzer from Cutterby. Tired of scissors that don't cut? Fed up with dull, chipped blades? Don't get upset. Now there's the amazing Skizzer! It's the only kitchen scissor that never requires sharpening.

At long last, a scissor that works time and time again and never gets dull. Don't believe it? Watch how easy Skizzer is to use. It effortlessly cuts through chicken bones. Smoothly slices this metal coat hanger in two. Crisply chops this piece of celery. Ordinary scissors would dull and chip. Not Skizzer! It even passes the paper-cutting test. Yes! Skizzer works every time.

No kitchen should be without one. Avoid the headaches, throw out the old scissors, and get Skizzer!

To order your amazing Skizzer call 1-800-S-K-I-Z-Z-E-R. Operators are standing by. And if you order in the next fifteen minutes, shipping is free! Plus, you'll get a free origami kit. Don't delay. Call or go to skizzer.com today!

REVIEW:

Product: Skizzer (product) and Cutterby (company)
Key words: Amazing (a repetitive word), Skizzer, Cutterby, scissor(s), cuts, slices, chops, order, phone and email address, free, today

Implied problem: Frustration with old, unreliable kitchen scissors.

Technique: Fill up with energy to the brink of exploding, and then hold it back. This creates intensity and anticipation. There are many lists that either need to build or zigzag. So the voice doesn't top out, make sure to breathe and drop the pitch between paragraphs (where there is white space). On the last paragraph, get closer to the microphone and hold back your intensity even more. The final word should be punched to add immediacy.

Love and Country
Movie Trailer
Music: Loud, high-energy music with layers of artillery firing SFX and explosions

Specs: Deep, resonant, restrained, confident, and powerful.

In times of war,
Who thought two people could fall in love?
Especially when they fought on opposite sides.
Love versus Country.
Who will win?
Love and Country.
In theatres this Friday.

REVIEW:

Product: The war film, *Love and Country*

Key words: War, love, opposite sides, Love versus Country, *Love and Country*, Friday (We assume it will be in theatres but Friday tells us when.)

Implied problem: By adding love into the war theme, it is targeted to attract both male and female audiences. It's a modern-day version of Romeo and Juliet.

Technique: Close to mic, milking the words 10–20 percent more than usual, with lots of authority, allowing lots of time for each phrase to breathe. The first three lines are the set up, the fourth and fifth lines are the body, and the final two lines are the call to action that identify the movie title and when it will be released.

Z-Top
TV & Web / 30 seconds
Music: Slow, sexy, and powerful with a steady, driving beat

Specs: Don't rush. The words should have a little space between them to allow for pictures. Voice can be male or female, 30–50. Confident but not arrogant, as if sharing firsthand information.

It's more than a car.
It's more than a feeling.
It's freedom.
Power.
Performance.
And confidence.
The new Z-Top convertible.
Driving will never be the same.

REVIEW:

Product: Z-Top
Key words: Car, feeling, freedom, power, performance, confidence, new, Z-Top convertible, and the slogan: *Driving will never be the same.*
Implied problem: Dull driving experience
Technique: The first two lines acknowledge the problem. The four items in the list constitute the body of the commercial, and the last two lines are the resolve. It should be played close to the microphone, very naturally and not pushed at all.

Burger Heaven
TV / 30 seconds
SFX: Grocery store. The voice will sound like it's coming from the store's PA speakers.
Visual: We see a guy pushing a cart down the frozen food section of the grocery store. He is confused when a voice calls to him. He locates the voice and opens the freezer door. The package talks. He picks it up, smiles, and puts the box in his grocery cart.

Specs: Looking for a mock announcer. Must have irony, sarcasm, and good comedic timing.

Hello, burger eater. Not up there, over here in the frozen food section. Tired of wimpy quarter-or half-pound patties? Have no fear, Burger Heaven is here. Come closer. Open the freezer door. That's right, a man's meal awaits. *(Guy picks up talking box.)* Hee, hee, hee. Hey, that tickles. No funny business, only top Grade-A sirloin beef in huge, man-size patties. *(Guy looks at box and puts it in shopping cart.)* Way to take control big guy. Now, go ahead. Pick up some arugula. That's manly, too. Right?

REVIEW:

Product: Burger Heaven
Key words: Burger, frozen food section, Burger Heaven, man's meal, top Grade-A sirloin beef, huge, man-size patties
Implied problem: Hungry and not satisfied by wimpy-sized burgers
Technique: Take time to milk the words and enjoy playing with the listener's mind. The shift from the set-up to the body starts on the third sentence. The final shift occurs when the announcer makes fun of the man and challenges him to pick up a light, leafy green used in salads.

PSA
TV / 30 seconds
This Public Service Announcement contains strong visual images and a variety of music and sound effects.

Specs: Compassionate, authoritative, real.

SFX: Crowd cheers
He was at the top of his class.
Captain of the football team.
Popular.
SFX: lighter and breathing
Then he discovered meth.
He thought it was fun.
Then it wasn't.
SFX: funeral music
Meth takes everything away.
SFX: uplifting music
Don't let it happen.
Support a Drug-Free America.

REVIEW:

Product: Drug-Free America
Key words: Meth, Drug-Free America
Implied problem: Very clearly, this is about the harmful, deadly effects of the drug on young people.
Technique: PSAs are often depressing, using shock value to send a strong emotional message. The person described was either in high school or college. Therefore, the target audience is teens and young adults. Nothing should be pushed or over-emphasized. It needs a real, compassionate voice to state a realistic problem and support the strong visuals, music, and sound effects.

Radio Imaging
Radio / 10 seconds
Music: High-intensity, driving music with heavy reverb and echo on the voice

Specs: No "real person" sounding folks, we want "in your face" DJ voices or talent with a strong, bold straight announcer voice.

Z98FM. Jam-packed with music all day long. Easy on the talk. Heavy on the music. Z98 has all the hits. Z-Z-Z-Z-Z-Z (repeated and faded out)

REVIEW:

Product: The station
Key words: The station
Implied problem: None; just listen to the station.
Technique: No subtle word finesse, just a big, bold, over-the-top sound. The end product is highly over-produced and layered with sweeping SFXs and echoes. Since this is all about the voice, it is usually not categorized in the freelance voice-over genre. It is, however, a legitimate way to make a living using your voice if you line up a lot of stations.

Obed's Carpets
Radio and TV / 30 seconds
Retail
Music: Persian

Specs: Would love to hire talent with an authentic accent from one of the carpet countries listed in the ad. Not too hard sell. Inviting and real.

Looking for that perfect rug to spice up a room? Come to Obed's Carpets this Thursday through Sunday for Obed's Half Yearly Sale.

Find new and used handmade rugs, imported from Persia, India, Turkey, China, Nepal, and Pakistan. Obed's "no pressure" sales team will help find the perfect rug to complement any room: dining, living, bedroom, or entryway.

The Middle East and Central Asia have produced vibrant decorative pile carpets and kilims for centuries. Own one today, at Obed's.

REVIEW:

Product: Obed's Carpets
Key words: Perfect rug, Obed's Carpets, Thursday through Sunday, Half Yearly Sale, new and used handmade rugs, vibrant decorative pile carpets and kilims, own one, today, Obed's
Implied problem: Have a room that needs improvement or own a rug but need to upgrade
Technique: When accents are requested, read the spot in your natural voice unless you can authentically deliver the lines or are from that country. The client may change its mind about the accent request if it likes your audition. The three sections of the copy are divided up for you, so there's no excuse for not making the necessary emotional shifts.

Lot-O Scratch
Radio / 30 seconds
Music: Light and up and under in the background

*Specs: We can go a lot of different directions in this ad: real, mock announcer,
stylized, ironic, sarcastic, omnipotent, etc. Be creative.*

SFX: laughter
What's that sound? It's the sound of someone who just won ten
million dollars.
SFX: car starting and driving off
And that sound? The new car they bought with some of their winnings.
SFX: ocean, birds, waves followed by people laughing in the distance
And that? The vacation the winner bought for the whole family, even
Aunt Hilda and Uncle Morty.
SFX: scratching
And that? That's the sound of the next big winner.
Lot-O-Scratch. A Lot-O fun, for only a buck.
SFX: laughter
Lot-O Scratch. Play to Win.

REVIEW:

> **Product:** Lot-O Scratch
> **Key words:** Won, winnings, winner, Lot-O-Scratch, Play to Win
> **Implied problem:** You don't have enough money to have fun.
> **Technique:** Leave breathing room for the sound effects; they're
> your dialogue partner. Personality is more important than vocal
> quality.

Super T
TV & Web / 30 seconds
Music: Superhero music in the open and close

*Specs: Looking for a big, fun, comedic actor. The voice should be stylized to
represent a superhero inside the toilet. The recording will have reverb added
in post to simulate the inside of a toilet bowl.*

Open: It's time for another adventure in "Toilet Cleaning." Brought
to you by Super T, the toilet bowl cleaner with superhuman cleaning
powers.

Donut: Stand aside; let Super T go to work.

Close: Ahhh . . . Fresh and clean. Super T does it again!

REVIEW:

Product: Super T
Key words: Toilet Cleaning, Super T, toilet bowl cleaner, super human cleaning powers, fresh and clean
Implied problem: Dirty, stinky toilet
Technique: Use the higher and lower register of the voice so it's not all loud and shouting. Think of it like an old fashioned announcer from the 30s and 40s. Overdo the bravado and linger on *Super T* and *super human cleaning powers.* You might want to position the mic higher and talk up into it since your character is inside the toilet looking up.

DeptMent Store
TV / 30 seconds
Retail
Music: Typical upbeat retail music

Specs: Friendly, approachable, non-announcer (even though it is obviously announcer copy).

SFX: Clock ticking
Set your clock . . .
SFX: Alarm
For DeptMent's Spring Savings Sale.
SFX: Stampeding crowd
The lowest prices of the season are here!
SFX: Music up and under
Pants, shirts, shoes, and coats.
Appliances and cookware.
Jewelry and perfume.
For men, women, and children.
DeptMent's Spring Savings Sale.
Don't miss it!

REVIEW:

Product: DeptMent's Spring Savings Sale
Key words: DeptMent's Spring Savings Sale, lowest prices of the season, and the laundry list of sales items for men, women, and children
Implied problem: People pay too much for or can't afford nice things.
Technique: This ad is riddled with s's and can easily sound too sibilant. Placing *DeptMent's* and *Sale* on one musical note and raising the pitch on *Spring Savings* will help get rid of some of the s sounds. Leaning into the mic on the last line will add a bit more urgency.

Peruvian Blend
TV & Web/ 15 seconds
Music: Light, ethereal

Specs: Intimate, real, not pushed, sexy, soothing, with a hint of humor on "People just can't seem to get enough of it."

Coffee.
The aroma. The taste. It's captivating.
Especially when it's Peruvian Blend.
People just can't seem to get enough of it.
Peruvian Blend. Coffee that tastes as rich as it smells.

REVIEW:

Product: Peruvian Blend
Key words: Coffee, aroma, taste, captivating, Peruvian Blend, tastes, rich as it smells
Implied problem: Needing to go to work but wanting to linger longer with a good cup o' joe
Technique: Don't rush, let the sentences breathe. Stair-step each sentence down in pitch to complete the story. Balance the first and last part of the final sentence by taking a slight pause after "tastes."

Chapter 12

SPOKESPERSON

A spokesperson is a perfect blend of announcer and real person. Scripts are written with *us, we, you, your,* or *our* references to imply that the speaker is part of the company. How you approach the script and relate to the audience is directly attributed to your position with, or relationship to, the company.

The three levels of expertise are:

- **Owner** — You relate to the listener from a higher authority position. The voice looms over the listener in a more formal fashion, as if saying: "Trust us. We've worked hard to create the best, most reliable, and most enjoyable product or service on the market. Everyone knows that our company, product, and employees are the best."
- **Employee** — You offer inside information from a slightly elevated "helper" position. Customer-to-customer approach implies: "Take it from me, your friend. I've shopped around and found that this product is the best one."
- **Customer** — As a fellow friend and consumer, you relate to the listener as an equal. Employee-to-customer style is about taking personal pride in the job. They admire the company and feel honored to help. The underlying message is: "You came to the right place. Our company and product are the best. Relax, we'll help you make the right decision."

Try to infuse your own personality and style into the spots.

Time to Practice:

Choose your perspective: owner, employee, or avid consumer. Record each script three different ways to hear the difference in perspective.

Sofa Connection — Employee to RJ
Radio / 60 seconds
Music: Comedic, uplifting

Specs: Find the humor and add a comedic element to the read. Quirky or stylized voices would be interesting. what's the deal here?

This could be your big chance to win. So listen carefully. First, hurry down to Sofa Connection and try out their huge assortment of love seats, sectionals, futons, and sofa beds. From traditional to modern, contemporary to classic, and fluffy to firm, Sofa Connection is sure to have a sofa that's right for you. Then, enter the Sofa Connection Big-Seat Sweepstakes. If your name is selected in the Big-Seat drawing on June 1st, you'll receive a thirty-inch flat-screen TV. That's right, a new TV to watch while you're sitting on a comfortable new sofa from the Sofa Connection. All you have to do is fill out the sweepstakes form when you come to any Sofa Connection. And you don't have to be present to win. But time is running out. Don't delay. Stop by Sofa Connection today and enter the Big-Seat Sweepstakes. After all, doesn't your seat deserve a little extra padding?

REVIEW:

> **Product:** Sofa Connection's Big-Seat Sweepstakes
> **Key words:** Win, Sofa Connection, huge selection, sofa, Big-Seat Sweepstakes, Big-Seat drawing, new TV, new sofa
> **Implied problem:** Limited time offer to win a TV, and more importantly, get a new comfortable sofa. It also implies that the listener's past losing ways may turn to a win if he or she comes in today to enter the contest. The biggest problem of all is the listener's tired bum from sitting on hard or lumpy furniture.
> **Technique:** This script contains lists within lists. To keep the flow, emphasize *First, hurry down; Then, enter; All you have to do.* A shorter list appears at the end: *Don't delay, Stop by, Enter.* The last line is tongue-in-cheek and should be read quickly with a lot of personality, only emphasizing the key word — *seat.*

Steak Wagon
Radio / 30 seconds
Music: Light country with a rugged edge.

Specs: Deep, rugged, resonant voice with a hint of a Texas accent. Must be real.

How do you like your steaks? Red and juicy on the inside or dark and crispy on the outside? Some restaurants have a hard time delivering what you really want.

Fortunately, the chefs at Steak Wagon understand how to cook steaks. First, they hand select the best cuts of beef. Then, they marinate them over night in their special sauce. Finally, they cook them right at your table. Just say, "when," and the steaks are taken off the grill and placed in front of you, sizzling hot. Steak Wagon steaks are always thick and delicious. That's what brings the customers back for more!

Enjoy a steak cooked your way at the Steak Wagon.

REVIEW:

> **Product:** Steak Wagon
> **Key words:** Steaks, Steak Wagon, best, special, right at your table, sizzling hot, thick and delicious, your way
> **Implied problem:** Other restaurants don't know how to cook steaks properly.
> **Technique:** Food commercials need to be read in a manner that guides the audience to taste and smell. Note the Rule of Three: three sentences in the set-up and three descriptive sentences in the body that start with "First," "Then," and "Just." Words like *best, special, right at your table,* and *sizzling hot* should stand out because they define this restaurant as being better than the competition. The story arc is from hunger to satisfaction.

Heartbeat Way
TV & Web/ 10 seconds
Music: Heartfelt, slow, melodic

Specs: Kind, warm, caring voice that gently suggests the viewer takes action to help those in need.

A gift to Heartbeat Way can make a difference. Why not touch the lives of people around you? Give part of yourself. Give the Heartbeat Way.

REVIEW:

> **Product:** Heartbeat Way
> **Key words:** Gift, Heartbeat Way, give
> **Implied problem:** Donations don't matter; the problem remains.

Technique: Balance the opening sentence by making a break between the client's name and the remainder of the sentence. On the last line, pause after saying the word "Gift." Then, close the message by gently smiling on the final client name.

Wonder Insurance
Radio / 30 seconds
Music: Whimsical and upbeat

Specs: There's a twist in the spot from the seriousness of the first sentence to the smiling, confident delivery thereafter. Should sound like a friendly next-door neighbor lending advice. After the first sentence, it should be very light and airy. Smiling on the key words will add confidence and pride to the read.

You insure your car, your house, your life, and your health. Do you have smile insurance? Your teeth will last a lifetime with good habits and regular dental care. Smile Insurance, from Wonder Insurance, helps you maintain that gleam. That's because Wonder Insurance takes the pain out of seeing a dentist with low monthly premiums. This keeps Wonder Insurance clients smiling. So stop putting off that visit to the dentist. Protect those pearly whites. Get smile insurance. It's something new from your friends at Wonder Insurance.

REVIEW:

Product: Smile Insurance from Wonder Insurance
Key words: Smile Insurance, teeth, dental care, Wonder Insurance, gleam, low monthly premiums, smiling, new
Implied problem: Painful and expensive dentist visits that lead to oral-care neglect
Technique: This is an awareness campaign. The opening list confirms normal checklist items. The second sentence adds a new item to our necessity list. There's a negative and positive comparison in the middle that acknowledges people's discomfort in seeing a dentist and confidence after getting the insurance and seeing one. The call to action has another Rule of Three list: *Stop, Protect, Get*. On the final line, lean into the mic and say "new" to draw focus and add additional client awareness.

Fly High Airlines
Radio / 30 seconds
Music: Traditional Mexican music with a modern twist
Specs: Male or female, 30–50, fun, easygoing read, no hard sell, a bit of a tease, sexy even.

Fly High Airlines now has low fares to Mexico. Visit Los Cabos, Guadalajara, Puerto Vallarta, and Mazatlán. And Fly High Airlines has complete vacation packages that are affordable, too. Reservations are easy. Go to one eight hundred Fly High dot com. That's 1-800-F-L-Y-H-I-G-H. Shouldn't your next vacation be to Mexico? Click Fly High Airlines today, and fly high with us.

REVIEW:

> **Product:** Fly High Airlines
> **Key words:** Fly High Airlines, low fares, Mexico, complete vacation packages, affordable, easy, vacation
> **Implied problem:** Exotic trips to Mexico are expensive and time-consuming to organize. And, in the past, our airline's rates were expensive, too.
> **Technique:** Each city in the list should reflect its trademark style: fun, relaxing, party place, or adventurous. The upsell is on "complete" vacation packages. On the slogan, "fly high with us," take a slight pause before saying the last two words so the client's name will stand out again.

Sparkle Ease
TV & Web / 30 seconds
Music: Quirky, humorous, light, upbeat

Specs: Looking for a good storyteller with crisp diction. Not in-your-face, just a casual observer. Quirky or stylized reads are okay, too.

This is the story of John and Sue.
They had a toilet that always smelled P-U.
They'd scrub all day with cheap detergent.
Nothing worked, even though the need was urgent.
Then one day they discovered Sparkle Ease.
They poured it in
And sure as you please
The smell went away.

For them it was a red-letter day.
And that is the story of John and Sue.
An ordinary couple from Yippidedoo
Who discovered the joy of Sparkle Ease
And lived happily ever after,
No longer on bended knees.

REVIEW:

Product: Sparkle Ease
Key words: Toilet, Sparkle Ease, poured it in, joy, happily ever after
Implied problem: Stinky toilets that wouldn't get clean
Technique: Tap the consonants and elongate the vowels. Share your opinion about the couple, their cleaning issues, and their relief. The last phrase is a warning line that should connect with the listener.

Club Sonora
Radio / 30 seconds

Specs: Deep

If you could design your own resort, you'd probably want a beautiful desert situated by a cool bay. You'd have an Olympic-size pool for swimming and a shallow pool for volleyball. You'd have water skiing and windsurfing at no extra charge. Tennis courts with tanned instructors. Great food and dancing. Entertainment and cozy companionship. Guess what. You're in luck. Club Sonora's designed for you. As close to perfection as a resort can be. Club Sonora. Coconut Bay.

REVIEW:

Product: Club Sonora
Key words: Design, resort, Club Sonora, Coconut Bay
Implied problem: Someone who has been dissatisfied with previous resort experiences or has high expectations and is very demanding
Technique: In the beginning, pretend that you're reading some-one's mind. Follow that with the discoveries you've made about a perfect vacation. Finally, vicariously take that person with you to the resort.

Movie Express
Radio / 30 seconds
Music: Quirky, lighthearted music with music beds from the movies mixed in
Specs: Cocky, ironic, and playful.

Downloading movies just got easier at MovieExpress.com. *Teenage Mutants From Outer Space, Blockade, Beef & Sizzle. Romances like Gee Wiz It's You, Heart Beaters, and Zoinkers.* Cartoon classics. Even the latest Indy flicks.

Just set up your MovieExpress account, select the movies you want or add them to your queue. They're yours in seconds.

MovieExpress.com. Entertainment when and where you need it: phone, computer, TV, the latest gadget.

Join millions of people who use Movie Express today and enjoy the first month free.

REVIEW:

Product: Movie Express
Key words: Downloading, movies, easier, MovieExpress.com, seconds, today, free
Implied problem: Movie Express's old system and some of the other movie download and delivery websites are cumbersome and slow or have some other limitation.
Technique: Pause one or two seconds after each movie listing to allow time for the film clips. Land confidently on the final word: *free.*

Lofton's
TV / 20 seconds
Music: Classical, slow, melodic

Specs: Older, friendly, sophisticated voice. Should sound like they own expensive furniture.

Times are changing and so is your home. That's why Lofton's offers the finest in contemporary home furnishings. Whether you're looking for a dining room set, living room furniture, bedroom suite, or household accessories, Lofton's has all the right selections. Update your home in style with furnishings from Lofton's.

REVIEW:

Product: Lofton's
Key words: home, Lofton's, finest contemporary home furnishings, dining room set, living room furniture, bedroom suite, household accessories, *all* the right selections, in style, furnishings
Implied problem: Your furniture looks old and dated.
Technique: Start with concern and then switch to casual confidence when our client is mentioned. Take a one or two second pause between each of the items in the list so a picture or two can be viewed.

Country Oak
TV & Web / 30 seconds
Music: Light, upbeat music with sound effects of the various activities layered in

Specs: Wholesome, friendly, casual, slightly sarcastic.

It's summer again, when all the summer rituals begin. Swimming. Playing ball in the park. Friends gathering in someone's backyard. And of course, cookouts. It's a weekend ritual. Hot dogs and hamburgers served right off the back yard grill. As always, Country Oak Mesquite-Style Charcoal is there. You can't beat the smoky mesquite flavor of Country Oak. Anything else just wouldn't be summer.

REVIEW:

Product: Country Oak Mesquite-Style Charcoal
Key words: summer, cookouts, grill, Country Oak Mesquite-Style Charcoal, smoky mesquite flavor
Implied problem: A competitor's brand isn't the right charcoal to use, especially in summer, because the food won't taste familiar.
Technique: This spot really needs movement and strong visualization. Imagine yourself talking to a friend in your huge back-

yard while flipping burgers. You can see the kids swimming, another group playing ball, and your adult friends mingling. There will be a close-up of a friend taking a bite of a burger and smiling when you deliver the line about the smoky mesquite flavor. Set up the first two words of the last line and then think for a minute about how to describe it best before saying, "just wouldn't be summer."

Spectacles
Radio / 15 seconds
Music: Typical medium-tempo retail music

Specs: Casual, friendly, easy going.

At Spectacles, we do more than correct your vision. We help you select the right frame to add style and elegance to your appearance. We have hundreds of designer frames to choose from. Spectacles even makes soft contact lenses in less than an hour.

REVIEW:

Product: Spectacles
Key words: Spectacles, more than correct, vision, help, right frame, add style and elegance, hundreds, designer frames, soft contacts, less than an hour
Implied problem: The last store sold you ugly frames and the salespeople didn't help you. Also, you had to go to another location to get your contacts prescription filled.
Technique: The store is branded with being *more* than the competition, being helpful, having variety, and quickly providing additional contact lenses services.

Google Eyes
Radio / 15 seconds
Music: Fast tempo

Specs: Google Eyes is the brand of eye glasses sold in Spectacles stores. Using co-op advertising dollars, this ad will be piggybacked onto Spectacles' ad to make it a thirty-second commercial. There's a bit more urgency to this copy since the sale is for a limited time.

Right now, Google Eyes has two glasses for the price of one. Stop by any Spectacles location. Buy one Google Eyes frame and get the second one absolutely free! That means you get two distinctly different Google Eyes looks for one low price. Google Eyes at Spectacles. A clear choice.

REVIEW:

Product: Google Eyes at Spectacles
Key words: Google Eyes, two glasses, price of one, Spectacles, one frame, second one free, two looks, one low price, a clear choice
Implied problem: Limited time offer to get two glasses for one low price
Technique: Add a little urgency and understated excitement. Parallel the numbers: *two* versus *one*. Smile on the word *free*. Add an ironic or playful twist to the tagline: *A clear choice.*

Viberstate
TV / 30 seconds
Music: It starts with a few ominous, sustained tones and chords, then switches to a more confident and caring tune

Specs: A mature voice that can speak from experience about healthcare issues. Could sound like a doctor or nurse. Should be powerful yet friendly.

It is a fact. People over sixty-five and some over fifty often find it hard to get health insurance. Viberstate Health Insurance understands this concern. We believe everyone should have good health coverage, regardless of age or health care history. In fact, Viberstate does not require any pre-insurance physicals. No one is ever turned down. Find out more at 4Vibers.com, or call 1-800-4-VIBERS today. It'll put your mind at ease.

REVIEW:

Product: Viberstate Health Insurance
Key words: Sixty-five, fifty, health insurance, Viberstate Health Insurance, good health coverage, 4Vibers.com, 1-800-4-VIBERS
Implied problem: Not having or losing health insurance coverage.
Technique: This is a fear spot, designed to draw awareness to a serious health and safety problem. Therefore, age fifty should have a more serious tone than age sixty-five. Viberstate should

sound welcoming and inviting, a stress relief to the problem. The lines about not requiring physicals and not getting turned down should be read straight and logically. No smile is necessary. Sound relieved and happy on the final sentence.

Recliner Heaven
TV & Web/ 30 seconds
Music: Comical

Specs: Humorous, comedic read without trying to sound funny. Irony, sarcasm, snarky deliveries are okay. Quirky or unique voices are preferred. Stylized or mock announcers would also work here.

You've been waiting for the big game all week. Your wife's out of town visiting that person you call a mother-in-law. So, you turn on the big-screen TV, amp up the volume, open a huge bag of onion chips, and twist open your favorite cold ones. There's only one thing missing: a recliner from Recliner Heaven's Year-end Clearance Sale. For a limited time only, you can choose from hundreds of styles of recliners at Recliner Heaven and really enjoy the big game. Recliner Heaven. Because life should be comfortable.

REVIEW:

Product: Recliners from Recliner Heaven's Year-end Clearance Sale
Key words: Big game, recliner, Recliner Heaven's Year-end Clearance Sale, hundreds of styles, life should be comfortable
Implied problem: You want to watch your favorite sporting event and don't have a comfortable chair to relax in.
Technique: Read the opening line at a medium pace. Speed up on the list of personal issues and slow down when you announce your discovery of needing a new chair. Numbers are important, so stretch out the word "hundreds." On the final two lines of the resolve, pretend that you're sitting down on a very comfy recliner. At the end of the spot, the onscreen guy picks up the remote and turns on the TV.

Bodywise
Infomercial / 60 seconds
Music: Opens with a quick beat and then relaxes into a mellow tune when the client's solution is introduced

Specs: Should sound knowledgeable and not talk down or sound condescending. Very helpful, encouraging, and kind.

Are you shopping-impaired? Do your eyes glaze over every time you enter a department store? Do your palms sweat at the thought of buying lingerie in public?

Relax. Now there's Bodywise, the easy way to shop.

All you do is log in to Bodywise.com, create an account, and click the items you wish to buy. It's fast, easy, and fun!

For over ten years we've helped clients like you overcome your shopping fears.

Here's how it works. Answer a few questions about style, size, color, and budget. Click the photo icon and snap, we create an avatar that looks just like you wearing each item. A simple touch of the screen and we add it to your shopping cart.

Need to buy for someone else? Upload a recent photo and answer a few questions. You're ready to shop for that person, too!

Unsure what to purchase? We offer suggestions. Whether you're going on a cruise, traveling the world, visiting relatives, going on a date, or just lounging around at home, Bodywise shows you exactly what to buy.

Personalized, convenient shopping at Bodywise.com. We take the guesswork and fear out of shopping.

REVIEW:

Product: Bodywise
Key words: Shopping, Bodywise, fast, easy and fun, personalized, convenient, the rest of the information logically explains how it works
Implied problem: Not implied here. It's clearly defined as a fear of shopping, or at least, spending money wisely.
Technique: The copy addresses many shopping issues. Each is identified in separate paragraphs. While staying on mic, shift the body slightly or use different gestures to bring out new emotions and attitudes every time you see a paragraph break.

Chapter 13

REAL PERSON

Ø selling in Real Person

When copy has "I," "me," or a person's name in it whom you're to portray, your job is to personalize the message and sound sincere. Real people do *not* sell! This style of script reveals a person's love of the product or pride in ownership and uses that emotion to share thoughts and options that motivate the listener to buy. It should sound as if a microphone magically captured this moment. Another indicator is that, unlike announcer and spokesperson copy, real person scripts are written to be more casual, realistic, and natural sounding. It taps into that side of us that likes to brag about our savings, new purchases, or dreams of ownership.

Hollywood stars voicing national commercials have really upped the ante for honest, believable, sincere reads. To compete, we have to match their gentleness, confidence, and vulnerability. If your job is to be the "before" person who hasn't used the product, your job is to demonstrate your ignorance, humor and lack of understanding. Here are just a few of the real person characters you'll be asked to portray:

- Warm and sincere
- Quirky and offbeat
- The "other guy" who doesn't know anything about the product yet
- Confident and proud
- Knowledgeable and professional
- Nurturing and kind

Real person scripts require more depth and character arc. They will often be more confused before being relieved, more agitated before becoming calm, or more bored before finding excitement. Your acting skills will also be tested more in this section. You will need to use the M.I.N.E. (Motivation, Intentions, Need, and Emotions), Five Ws (who, what, why, when, where), Hiding The Sell, and other techniques mentioned in earlier chapters to achieve believable realism and let your personality and opinion shine through.

Time to Practice:

The key to good acting is asking yourself enough *why* questions until you get to the root of the problem. You are the expert because you experienced the same problem the listener has and found a solution. Your authority comes from you being on the other side of the issue and needing to share your insights with a friend or loved one. Rather than selling a product, you are fulfilling a basic, fundamental *need*. If you recognize what the product gives you and boil it down into one word, then you'll know what the script is all about and how your character feels about it. The common thread of all commercials is that the end result, after discovering and using the product, is always good. Also, don't draw focus to yourself by landing on the personal pronouns. The story is about how the product helps the listener and not about *you*.

One final thought: Real people set up situations. Announcers tie up the loose ends. In the following scripts (as in the real world), assume there will be an added announcer, so don't try to do both parts — being real and illuminating an issue *and* playing the announcer that pushes copy points. Just be you. Don't sell!

Flowers
Radio / 12 seconds
Music: Peaceful, melodic, slow

Specs: Heartfelt, warm, and caring.

It was my birthday, and I didn't think anyone would remember. Then I got flowers from my college roommate. Can you imagine, flowers. Makes growing older that much easier.

REVIEW:

> **Product:** Flowers
> **Key words:** Flowers
> **Implied problem:** You can make anyone's day better if you give him flowers.
> **Technique:** Who would you tell this story to and why? What's

your point? Assume that someone asked you a question like: "Those are pretty flowers. Where did you get them?"

Zippy Running Shoes

Radio / 25 seconds
SFX: City ambiance, cars driving past, running

Specs: Pretend that you're running and talking to a friend. Breathing sounds and awkward pauses are good ways to create authenticity.

Like many people, I run to keep fit, but my feet sure take a pounding. I shopped around and decided my feet deserve the best. That's why I wear Zippy running shoes. They're designed just for me based on my weight and body frame. So it's the perfect running shoe to help me run faster, farther, and avoid injury. With the new lightweight design, my feet feel so much better, I could run a marathon.

REVIEW:

Product: Zippy running shoes
Key words: Feet, Zippy running shoes, new lightweight design, better
Implied problem: Injury and lack of endurance
Technique: Decide why you would tell this story. Did the person you're running with ask you: "Are those new shoes?" or "You're not complaining today, why's that?" This ad has a lot of copy points and information, so toss them off as if it's no big deal. Your goal is run and stay fit. At the end, continue the story by running off mic and continue breathing like a runner.

City Zoo

Radio / 30 seconds
Music: Whimsical

Specs: Looking for a unique voice and personality that is ironic, offbeat, and quirky. Must have good comedic timing.

Okay, I'm here to tell you that you should *not* go to the City Zoo. No, it's not because of the manure smell, which I kind of like, or the frequent stops to buy peanuts. It's because a new baby elephant just arrived by stork or something — it is a zoo after all. And as you know, babies cry. Or maybe that was me when I saw it. So cute and cuddly, only 120 pounds with a long trunk and big floppy ears. Adorable. It took her momma 22 months to make her. She needs some rest! And so does the baby. So stay away. Do not go to the zoo and see the new baby elephant. Unless you happen to have some extra peanuts you don't know what to do with.

REVIEW:

Product: Baby elephant at the City Zoo
Key words: City Zoo, new baby elephant, zoo, babies, baby, zoo
Implied problem: Reverse psychology to keep patrons away so the speaker can have the whole zoo to himself
Technique: Tap the "t" in "not" each time so your point is clearly made. Internalize your issues and comments about how you feel. It's written that way for comedic value. If you make it important, it draws focus away from the client and onto you.

Jiffy Lite Dinners
Radio / 25 seconds
SFX: Kids in the background, a tuba playing in the distance, microwave

Specs: The tuba quits playing at the transition after "ten minutes it's dinnertime." The person is relieved.

I knew when I had three kids I was going to be busy, but not this busy. With Ronnie on the baseball team, Suzie taking ballet lessons, and Erin in the school band, there's never a dull moment. Between working and running Mom's/Dad's "shuttle service," I don't have a lot of time to cook. Thank goodness for Jiffy Lite Dinners. I just pop them in the microwave, and in less than ten minutes it's dinnertime. Jiffy Lite Dinners. They're the easiest part of my day.

REVIEW:

Product: Jiffy Lite Dinners
Key words: Busy, Jiffy Lite Dinners, microwave, ten minutes, easiest
Implied problem: Busy and don't have time
Technique: You're not selling a frozen meal. You're selling time. Figure out what someone asked you. It could be something like: "You look relaxed, what's up?" To personalize it for yourself, think of a specific person and what question that person would ask you that would prompt this response.

Proposition Q
Radio / 30 seconds
SFX: Large thud as a bundle of cash and change I dropped on a table. And, a sound of a rubber stamp certifying legal papers after "Don't let them fool you."

Specs: Should sound like a concerned citizen. Intelligent. Sarcastic. Authoritative.

The proponents of Proposition Q want you to believe that spending more money will solve our city's problems. Come on. Are we supposed to believe that? Of course it's not true. Taxpayers like you and I need better city management not higher taxes. Don't let 'em fool you. Vote NO on Proposition Q. It's a vote for better management, not bigger spending. Vote NO on Proposition Q.

REVIEW:

> **Product:** NO on Q
> **Key words:** Better city management, Vote NO, Q
> **Implied problem:** More money solves the city's problems.
> **Technique:** This is a comparative spot. NO is good. YES is bad. Linger on the good information and connect with the listener. Speed up on the negative YES info and "throw it away." *[Don't draw focus to it.]*

Anti-Smoking PSA
Radio / 15 seconds
SFX: Young kids playing in the background. Cigarette intake and exhale between the last two sentences.

Specs: Sincere, as if sharing to a very close friend. The first part is lighthearted and whimsical. It doesn't get serious until, "Why do you smoke?"

We send mixed signals to our kids. My wife/husband says "yes," I say "no." One day Billy said, "Dad/Mom, do you wanna die?" I said, "Of course not." So Billy asked, "Why do you smoke?"

REVIEW:

> **Product:** Anti-Smoking Campaign
> **Key words:** Die, smoke
> **Implied problem:** Death and loss of a child's respect

Technique: Don't play the ending by being serious all the way through. It's about kids saying the *darnedest* things and surprising us with their clarity. You might want to chuckle at the beginning when you retell this crazy story.

City Fare
Radio / 30 seconds
SFX: Calculator, papers, computer keyboard, and a bus honk at the end

Specs: This is a revenge spot with a twist. The person is on a mission to prove to the "honey" that the car is economical. After adding up the data, the reality is clear. As irrational as it may sound, the person "wins" in the end by finding a logical solution to the economics issue: riding the bus for eight years.

Let's see. $120 a month for parking. $5 a day for gas. Insurance is $1500 a year. Can't forget the tune-ups and repairs. And there's the car payment, $350 a month. And the annual registration fee, $180. Okay, near as I can figure, that's eight grand a year! Honey, you're right, I'm trading in that money guzzler. For what I spend on my car in one year, I could buy a City Fare bus pass for about eight years.

REVIEW:

Product: City Fare bus pass card
Key words: City Fare bus pass
Implied problem: Cars are too expensive.
Technique: Like organizing expenses at tax time, imagine the room and the location of the information. Is it in files, on the computer, already on the desk, in your memory, etc.? Imagine your honey being in another room of the house and shout out, slightly off mic, "I'm trading in that money guzzler." Then, let us hear the wheels turning in your head when you come to the conclusion on the last line. Also, parallel the numbers: one versus eight.

Creamy Delite
Radio / 30 seconds
Music: Quirky, comedic, and up-tempo

Specs: Confidential, like sharing a deep, dark secret. A bit snarky.

I've got a problem. I think I'm becoming an ice cream snob. But I ask you, who cares about those franchise flavors like granola peanut supreme and Hungarian chocolate when you can buy a Creamy Delite bar. You don't just eat a Creamy Delite. You savor it. If you haven't experienced a Creamy Delite you wouldn't understand. So what are you waiting for? Pick up a Creamy Delite bar and become and ice cream connoisseur like me!

REVIEW:

> **Product:** Creamy Delite
> **Key words:** ice cream, Creamy Delite bar, savor, Creamy Delite
> **Implied problem:** Not wanting to share or being very particular about what kind of ice cream you eat
> **Technique:** Use the first two sentences to set up the problem then knock it down when you defend your position. Your job is to make people hungry and jealous. Speed up on the list of franchise flavors, that's a negative comparison to our hero product.

Brewsky Spud
Radio / 45 seconds

Specs: This should sound natural, like you're introducing an out of town friend to your favorite sports bar. You should comfortable in the environment, like you just walked in and sat on a barstool.

SFX: Bar ambiance
After a long day, I like to stop by my neighborhood sports bar and root for the home team.
SFX: Crowd cheer
Go get 'em! Yeah! Football and Brewsky Spud. They go together, right gang?
SFX: Crowd agrees
Brewsky Spud is home brewed, right here in the U.S. of A. No fancy imports for me.
SFX: Crowd cheer
Yes! Great granddad Brewsky started making Spud a 150 years ago.
And Brewsky Spud is still brewed the same way to seal in the flavor. Some big brewing companies say it's old fashioned. Me? I just know it tastes great.
SFX: Crowd roars
Touchdown! Yep, Brewsky Spud and football. Nothing could be better. Right, gang?
SFX: Crowd agrees

REVIEW:

Product: Brewsky Spud

Key words: Brewsky Spud, home brewed, 150 years, brewed the same way, tastes great

Implied problem: Need a way to relax after work

Technique: This spot requires a complete 3-D image of the room: the bar, bartender, the friend you're sharing this story with, TVs, people in the bar, etc. Imagine acknowledging the bartender when you enter, sitting on the stool, the beer placed in front of you, the action of the game, your relationship with the other people in the room. And how all that makes you feel at home and welcome. Downplay the sell. It's just what it is, everyone knows it. Stay close to the mic for the majority of the recording and turn off mic and shout during the football scoring sections.

Train Central
Radio / 30 seconds

Specs: Deep

SFX: Relaxing music
Ahhh, there's nothing like a leisurely commute.
SFX: Car beep
The freeway traffic.
SFX: Cars speeding by
The friendly motorists.
SFX: "Move over, buddy."
The accidents.
SFX: Car squeal
Five days a week.
SFX: Crash
At the peak of rush hour.
SFX: Multiple car pile-up
Who am I kidding?
SFX: Relaxing music up and under
Starting tomorrow, I'm taking Train Central.

SFX: Train

It'll be good for my blood pressure, not to mention my gas tank.

REVIEW:

Product: Train Central
Key words: Leisurely commute, Train Central
Implied problem: Losing your mellow in commuter traffic
Technique: Allow a second or two between statements for the increasingly noisy sound effects. Start happy then drop pitch and attitude on each line until the solution is introduced and you become happy and mellow again.

Splash-O-Rama
Radio / 30 seconds
Music and SFX: Gentle, nondescript music in the background, which changes to a fun and energetic tune. Waterpark, splashing, laughter, and sounds of kids playing layered in.

Specs: A mom, 30–40. Guys can try reading it, too. Just change "bathing suit" to "Speedo" or "brief." Should sound like you're offering commonsense advice to a friend.

I thought I'd taken the kids to every amusement park ever built. Imagine me, feeding every elephant and riding every roller coaster 'til I turned a nice shade of chartreuse. Yeah, well, you get the picture. Then, last weekend, little Freddie says, "Let's go to Splash-O-Rama waterslides. It's in Jefferson." I said, "Me in a bathing suit? Get real." But you know how five-year-olds can be. So we went. I have one word to describe it. Unbelievable. Slipping and sliding down the giant waterslides. Getting knocked around by big waves in the wave pool. I felt like I was in Hawaii, only cheaper! I didn't care that I hadn't worked out in over five years. No one was watching me. They were all having a great time with their families. Take it from me, the waterslide expert. Next time you need a place to go, make it Splash-O-Rama. You can even get discount coupons on the web. Just log onto Splash-O-Rama.com. Trust me, your family will love you for it.

REVIEW:

Product: Splash-O-Rama waterslides
Key words: Amusement park, Splash-O-Rama waterslides, Jefferson, giant waterslides, wave pool, great time, families, discount coupons, love
Implied problem: Boredom

Technique: Downplay all the information that pertains to you and your family. Reading that information a little faster will help. The story is really about telling your friend about a great experience this place is and how it's the perfect fit for their family.

Oatmeal Bars
Radio / 30 seconds
Music: Calming, professional

Specs: Intelligent, sincere, caring. Should sound like a doctor talking to a patient. Relaxed and confident.

As a doctor, I like to give my patients the best advice. Eat right, get plenty of rest, exercise 20–30 minutes a day, and watch your cholesterol. You want to keep it balanced and healthy. That's why I recommend Oatmeal Bars. They reduces your LDLs, the *bad* cholesterol. And Oatmeal Bars give you six grams of fiber that's needed in your diet. Add a banana with its four grams of fiber and it's a meal. Eat it for breakfast, lunch, or a mid-day snack. Oatmeal Bars is medically proven to help lower your cholesterol. Think of it as a heart-healthy way to a happier, healthier life.

REVIEW:

Product: Oatmeal Bars
Key words: Cholesterol, LDLs, fiber, medically proven, lower, heart-healthy
Implied problem: Poor health and high cholesterol
Technique: Toss off medical information — LDLs, cholesterol, grams of fiber, heart-healthy — as if you offer this advice to all your patients. The last line should sound friendly, as if handing the listener the Oatmeal Bar.

Aunt June's
Radio / 30 seconds
Music: Fun yet subdued

Specs: Male or female. Should sound real, like a situation that happens all the time that is predictable yet disappointing. Introspective.

There he/she was, eating the last piece of pie I'd hidden in the back of the refrigerator. He/she must have known it was there. So I said, "Honey, wasn't that my slice?" "Don't worry. I'll get you another," he/she said. "Right," I thought as I wiped the drool from the side of my mouth. Without even a bit of remorse, he/she picked up the last bite and ate it. Then, he/she got up, went to the freezer, pulled out a triangle box and opened it. Aunt June's Single Slice Pie. He/she heated it for less than a minute in the microwave and handed me a fork. "I think you'll like it," he/she said as it was placed in front of me. I took one bite and all was good again in the world.

REVIEW:

Product: Aunt June's Single Slice Pie
Key words: Pie, freezer, triangle box, Aunt June's Single Slice Pie, microwave, good
Implied problem: Extreme disappointment
Technique: Lower or raise the pitch of the partner's words to separate them from your side of the story. You might add a thoughtful sound (ahh, hmmm, ohhh, etc.,) before you say the client's name because now, it all makes sense. Your partner wasn't callous and unfeeling after all.

Ropaje
Radio / 30 seconds
Music: Retail music with a Spanish flare

Specs: Woman, 40–55. Needs to relate and connect with other women. Confident. Sharing a secret.

I don't know about you, but I've always had a hard time finding clothes that fit. Who said curves are bad? Then I walked into Ropaje. It's a new store that caters to real women. They must have heard us because everything I tried on fit. Pants, dresses, shirts, you name it. And it didn't just fit me, but other women who aren't a size two or don't look like a boy. You should have seen the smiles on the shopper's faces when they checked themselves out. And the styling. Wow! Fashionable, fun, perfect for work or play. Oh, and the best part: affordable. Thank you, Ropaje. You listened.

REVIEW:
Product: Ropaje
Key words: Clothes, Ropaje, real women, styling, fashionable, fun, perfect, affordable

Implied problem: Frustration with finding the right clothes
Technique: Lean into the mic a bit when you get to the body of the copy where she walks into the store.

Redgie Food Processor
Radio / 60 seconds
Music: Romantic Valentine's Day music

Specs: Deep, husky, and masculine. Ironic. Macho and sensitive. Vulnerable and strong.

Guys, that dreaded day of the year is quickly approaching. You know what I'm talking about: Valentine's Day. Seems we never get it right. Chocolates are too fattening, a card isn't enough, and lingerie . . . what can I say. Embarrassing. Thong, boy cut, brief, high-and-low rise . . . confusing. But now I've found the perfect gift. A Redgie Food Processor. No, not for *her* you idiot. For you! You're going to make her a fruit smoothie in the morning, pack her a special sandwich for lunch, and bring it home with an amazing entrée that evening. I know what you're thinking. Me, cook? Get over it. We're men. We can do anything. The Redgie Food Processor comes with a simple cooking guide for guys like us. You knows the ones with six thumbs. Look, I'm just sayin' that if you want to get in good with the lady, give it a try. You'll be thankin' me in the morning. Oh, and the recipes are simple. So, throw some flour on your face so it looks like you worked hard. Now, quit listening to me. Time's a-wastin'. Get the Redgie Food Processor. It's the one in the red box. You'll find that helpful — unless you're colorblind. Then, you're on your own.

REVIEW:

Product: Redgie Food Processor
Key words: Valentine's Day, Redgie Food Processor, simple cooking, red box
Implied problem: Making another mistake on Valentine's Day.
Technique: This is all about personality and relationship with the listener. Your goal is to sound like the last person who would ever cook but now knows how and is proud of it.

Chapter 14

COMMERCIAL CHARACTERS

Now it's time to stretch your abilities a little further. This may be a fun area to pursue or one you prefer not to explore. With a few exceptions, commercial characters are not outrageous. In most cases, they are more like putting on a different hat. Some are big and showy and others are small and demure. How you stand, use your body, contort your facial muscles, and position yourself on the microphone dramatically changes your character. So, if this style of work scares you, keep an open mind. It's not as challenging as you think.

The most important aspect of playing a commercial character is to not be bigger than the product by drawing focus to you. Your character and vocal choices should support the client's information. Here's a checklist of things to consider when using a character voice in a commercial:

- Am I using this voice to show off and have fun or is it an appropriate voice that supports the message?
- Is my job to illustrate the good things about the hero client or the bad things about my client's competition?
- Will people turn up the volume or turn it off when my voice comes on? If unsure, assume that the listener will hear this commercial five times a day for several weeks.
- Define the purpose of your character's job in one word: picky, jealous, unhappy, relieved, excited, etc.

Time to Practice:

Never start with the character voice first. The sound becomes more important than the feelings and blocks the truth and believability required in the story. Instead, start with your own voice and allow the character voice to rise up and out of you naturally. This is a more organic approach. Remember that your job is to support the story and not draw focus to yourself.

Big Refrigerator Co.
"Toaster"
TV / 30 seconds
Visual: Cartoon toaster on a counter talking up to a large silver refrigerator. The toaster bounces around the counter, talking up at the refrigerator. Throughout the ad, people open the refrigerator door, get water and ice from the outside dispenser, and grab food and drinks from different drawers and shelves.

Specs: Cute, young voice. Should show a range of emotions: angry, jealous, sad, pouty, etc.

I know I'm a little toaster but I'm steamed. Just because you're a big refrigerator doesn't mean you can boss me around. Sure, you've got an automatic icemaker and a fancy water dispenser, and everyone opens and closes your door all day long. But they still come to me every morning. I always toast their bread nice and golden brown. You can't do that. So leave me alone and I'll promise not to pop off anymore.

REVIEW:

> **Product:** Big Refrigerator Company
> **Key words:** Refrigerator, automatic icemaker, fancy water dispenser
> **Implied problem:** The toaster is jealous of the attention the refrigerator receives.
> **Technique:** Since the toaster is smaller than the refrigerator, place the microphone a little higher than your mouth and talk up to it.

Sneeze Dust
"Mrs. Clean"
Radio / 15 seconds
Music: Traditional royal British music

Specs: Uppity, conservative British maid.

In Mrs. Clean's house, *dust* is a four-letter word. That's why she always uses Sneeze Dust. After all, whether she entertains friends, family, or the Queen of England she wants everything to be just so. Her rare antiques recapture their original luster every time she uses Sneeze Dust. Put an end to that four-letter word in your home with Sneeze Dust. It always passes the white-glove test.

REVIEW:

Product: Sneeze Dust
Key words: Clean, Dust, Sneeze Dust
Implied problem: Need for perfection
Technique: Since "dust" is a four-letter word, have trouble saying it. There are two ways of playing "the Queen of England": she actually comes to the house or Mrs. Clean's friends think they're royalty even though they're not.

Funride Cruise Line
"Pirate"
Radio / 30 seconds
SFX: Lively music and laughter off in the distance, waves, and boat creaks.

Specs: Open to any type of pirate you can create: original or traditional.

Ahoy, matey! Seems there are some new cruise ships invading me waters! But they don't have the character and history of my vessel. Sure they've got luxury staterooms, round-the-clock entertainment, never-endin' meal service, and three ports o' call. But who needs that when you've got cannons, rum kegs, and gangplanks. Funride Cruise Lines. They give so much for so little. Arrrgh, it'll never last.

REVIEW:

Product: Fundride Cruise Lines
Key words: waters, luxury staterooms, round-the-clock entertainment, never-endin' meal service, three ports o' call, and the slogan: *They give so much for so little.*
Implied problem: Jealous of luxury, food, entertainment and fun.
Technique: Shout as if talking across the ocean to comrades sailing by on another pirate ship. You see and acknowledge them and watch them sail past you after the spot ends. Both ships see and hear the joyous sounds of people aboard the cruise ship. Vulnerability for luxury shows on the slogan line that prompts

the quick dismissal that it'll never last and the return of his rugged, uncaring self.

Sparkle Oh!
"Oven"
TV & Web / 30 seconds
Visual: Close-up of an animated, talking oven

Specs: Anything goes here. Accents, dialects, high voices, low voices, gravelly, a Brooklyn accent, etc. Be creative.

Hello, it's me. Your oven? Phew! It sure gets dirty in here! There's the cheese soufflé that spilled over last week, the meatloaf surprise that splattered grease all over me, and little Sarah's cooking experiment that smells like burned rubber.

Please do us both a favor and get Sparkle Oh! All you do is spray Sparkle Oh! On my inside walls, close my door, turn me to 450, and let me bake. An hour later I'm sparkling clean.

Sparkle Oh! It makes your oven spotless.

REVIEW:

> **Product:** Sparkle Oh!
> **Key words:** Oven, Sparkle Oh, sparkling clean, Slogan: *It makes your oven spotless.*
> **Implied problem:** Stinky, dirty oven
> **Technique:** Sound neglected and sad in the beginning, wishful in the body of the copy, and relieved at the end.

Fieldsit Pillow
"Guru"
Radio / 25 seconds
Music: Sitar

Specs: Peaceful, enlightened Indian guru.

In my business, I do a lot of thinking, a great deal of meditating, and most of all sitting. That is why I use the pillow that nine outta ten gurus recommend, Fieldsit. Fieldsit pillows are made with only natural fibers. And they maintain their firmness even after hours of sitting and meditating. For extended hours of sitting, or sleeping, pick up a Fieldsit Pillow today.

REVIEW:

Product: Fieldsit pillows
Key words: Sitting, pillow, Fieldsit, Fieldsit pillows, natural fibers, maintain firmness, hours, sleeping, today
Implied problem: Sitting, meditating, and sometimes sleeping on the mountaintop is hard on the bum.
Technique: Feel free to change some of the sounds and rhythms. Here's an example: In my bidness, I do a lot of dinkin', a great deal of me-di-ta-ding, and most of all sidding. Dat is why I use da pillow dat nine outta ten gurus recommend, Fieldsit. Fieldsit pellows are made wid only na-tur-al fibers. And dey maintain deir firmness even after hours of sidding and meditating. For extended hours of sidding, or sleeping, picking up a Fieldsit Pe-low too-day.

Warm & Cozy
"Groundhog Day"
TV & Web / 30 seconds
Visual: A groundhog pokes his head out of the ground, looks around at the crowd admiring their clothes, sees his shadow, and crawls back down the hole.

Specs: Scared, cute, quivering voice.

Oh, no! It looks like we're in for a long winter. And I had my spring plans made already. Oh well, back to my cold, underground dwelling. Just listen to those humans complain! They may look funny but at least they know how to stay warm. I wish I could bundle up with a warm coat, a thick sweater, an extra pair of wooly socks and a comfy muffler. Heck, all I have is fur. They're so lucky to have Warm & Cozy. If I weren't so afraid of my shadow, I'd shop there myself.

REVIEW:

Product: Warm & Cozy clothing
Key words: Warm, coat, sweater, socks, muffler, Warm & Cozy
Implied problem: Being cold and not having the right (or any) clothes

Technique: Raise the mic a little higher than your mouth, look up into it and speak, and make your lips protrude so your face is shaped more like a groundhog. Stretch your neck up as you look around at the crowd then compress it again in four short motions to simulate climbing down.

Tingle
"Singer"
Radio / 30 seconds
Music: Opera and theatre/audience sounds

Specs: Pompous, large, confident operatic singer.

When I *sing* it is standing room only. But it wasn't always that way. Before when I sang the front rows were empty by intermission. My manager said, "Either stop eating chili pepper flambé or start gargling with Tingle mouthwash." Well, I wasn't about to give up my chili pepper flambé. So now I *tingle* before every performance. Tingle mouthwash gives me a fresh, clean feeling . . . and a full house.

REVIEW:

Product: Tingle mouthwash
Key words: Gargling, Tingle mouthwash, tingle, fresh, clean
Implied problem: Bad breath and loss of career
Technique: Sing operatically on the italicized words: *sing* and *tingle*. If it's not too distracting, you can imitate your manager's voice. At the end of the commercial, you may want sing a few notes to complete the story.

Sparter
"Talking Teddy"
TV & Web / 30 seconds
Visual: The toy talks directly into camera, showing off all the things he's capable of performing.

Specs: Looking for a cute teddy bear voice for the commercial and the toy. Should appeal to a five-year-old and the parents. The voice must be fun!

Hello boys and girls! I'm new Talking Teddy. Sparter Corporation made me just for you. How about that? Listen to this. I laugh *(giggle)*. I cry *(boo hoo)*. I wear a diaper *(uh oh)*. But most of all I hug people *(I love you)*. I wish you'd take me home with you. Talking Teddy and you can be great friends.

REVIEW:

Product: Sparter Corporation's new toy, Talking Teddy
Key words: New, Talking Teddy, Sparter Corporation, laugh, cry, diaper, hug
Implied problem: The teddy bear will be lonely without a young owner.
Technique: Emphasize "new." Since your character is young, take poetic license and change some of the pronunciations: Talking = talkin', Love = wuv, Great = gweat.

Sundried Plums
"Butler"
Radio / 30 seconds
Music: Classical, stuffy, reserved

Specs: Sophisticated, proper, stuffy. British. Male preferred but could be female.

When I prepare meals for the Uprights, I have to be most careful. Their tastes are quite sophisticated but they do have a bit of a sweet tooth. So when the Uprights right the dinner bell, I always include some dried plums from Sundried. These aren't ordinary plums. They're sweet and juicy and I don't have to fuss with pits. Sundried does it for me. *(SFX: dinner bell)* Ahhh, like clockwork. It's time for their Sundried Pitted Plums.

REVIEW:

Product: Sundried Pitted Plums
Key words: Tastes, sophisticated, dried plums, Sundried, sweet and juicy, pits, Sundried Pitted Plums
Implied problem: Irregularity (of plum brands and digestion) disrupts the employer's schedule and makes the butler's job unpleasant.
Technique: Lift your chin up and look down your nose when you read the copy. Turn your ear to the sound of the bell and say, "Ahhh" after the dinner bell SFX. On the last line, continue the scene by adding a little movement in the direction of the

Upright's room. This lets us know that you are on your way to give them this treat.

Tubster ✦
"Car Race"
TV & Web / 30 seconds
Music: Exciting, upbeat with racing engine sounds in the background

Specs: Should sound like a real track announcer. Stretch out the opening and then speed up and add excitement during the race.

Ladies and gentlemen. Start your engines. The Tubster car races are about to begin. *(SFX: gunshot)* And they're off! Tubster Turbo is on the outside. The Tubster Express is leading the pack on the straightaway. Coming up from behind is Tubster Alley, the newest car from Tubster. They're neck-and-neck going into the loop-de-loop. Tubster Turbo and Tubster Express are falling back. And it's Tubster Alley, the winner! Tubster cars. Fast, safe, fun.

REVIEW:

Product: Tubster cars
Key words: Tubster, car races, Tubster Turbo, Tubster Express, Tubster Alley, and the slogan: *Fast, safe, fun.*
Implied problem: All the cars are good, which one is going to win?
Technique: Since you're selling *fun,* find a unique and fun way to end the spot when you say that word.

News Express
Radio / 30 seconds
Music: This will be selected based on the character, accent and/or dialect performed.

Specs: People with strong accents and dialects, good improv skills, and/or comedic timing.

When I first came to this country my English wasn't very good. I didn't have money to spend on English lessons. Everyday I read the *News Express*. Soon I understand the articles, features, sports, even the comic section. The *News Express* showed me where to get jobs!

My English is much better now. Bet you didn't know I was from ___
_____ [city / country].

REVIEW:

Product: News Express
Key words: New Express, articles, features, sports, comic section, jobs
Implied problem: Having a language and culture barrier that made it difficult to find a job
Technique: The improvised line can either be a surprise twist or an obvious continuation of the story. If using an accent or dialect, feel free to omit or add words or sounds that are appropriate for that area.

Dietfull
"Stomach"
TV / 30 seconds
Visual: Woman sitting at her desk with a salad container she brought from home in front of her. Her stomach talks to her.

Specs: Man or woman's voice. Unique and different. Lots of attitude.

That's right, I'm growling and you're looking at a wimpy salad for lunch when I crave a super burrito with all the fixin's. It's that diet you're on. It's not working. I'm hungry in here! Haven't you heard about Dietfull? It's a delivery service that brings fresh, healthy food to you no matter where you are. At home or at work. You meet with their advisers, they create a plan. You lose weight without starving yourself. It even comes with desserts. Go ahead. Call or email Dietfull today. I can't take this much longer. 1-800-Diet-Ful. You're going to have to talk to the hand, I'm a stomach and can't type.

REVIEW:

Product: Dietfull, dietary food delivery service
Key words: Diet, hungry, Dietfull, delivery service, fresh, healthy food, home or work, lose weight, call, email, today, 1-800-Diet-Ful
Implied problem: Hunger

Technique: The stomach is lower than the head, so look up into microphone. For the phone number say: one eight hundred diet full. No need to spell it out. Add irony on the last line. That's the joke.

Funky Kitty Litter
"Cat"
Radio / 30 seconds
Music: Comedic, whimsical

Specs: Male or female. Comedic. Sarcastic. Confidential.

Pssst! Can we talk? I know I'm finicky but my cat box stinks. Maybe you haven't noticed. Since you're not too regular about cleaning this thing up, why don't you get Funky Kitty Litter. It really hides the smell, especially when you're out of town for a few days. Put it on your shopping list. Funky Kitty Litter. And after you clean out the clumps, sit down. I need to take a nap on your lap.

REVIEW:

Product: Funky Kitty Litter
Key words: cat box, Funky Kitty Litter, hides the smell
Implied problem: Stinky cat box odor
Technique: Cats are lower to the ground than their owners, so look up into the microphone. Since it's confidential, play it close to the mic.

Sammy Cereal
"Sammy Giraffe"
TV / 30 seconds
Visuals: Animated giraffe waves to kids, holds up box of his cereal, pours some in a bowl, and eats it.

Specs: Arrogant and loveable. Should appeal to kids.

Hey kids! It's me, Sammy Giraffe. Handsome, aren't I? That's my tall, spotted mug on the front of my new cereal. Sammy Cereal. Named after yours truly. And it has me on the inside of the box, too. *(SFX: box opening and cereal poured into bowl.)* Giraffe-shaped cereal. Who doesn't like that? Give it a try. It's on the top shelf of the cereal aisle.

And who knows, if you eat it every day you might grow as tall as me. Of course, you'd have to be a giraffe. But it's worth a try.

REVIEW:

Product: Sammy Cereal
Key words: Sammy Giraffe, Sammy Cereal, new cereal, giraffe
Implied problem: Being short and ugly, needing to grow
Technique: There's a nice push and pull in this spot. Internalize and admire your beauty on a few lines and talk to the kids directly on the rest of the copy. Internalized lines are: *Handsome aren't I, Named after yours truly, Who doesn't like that,* and *Of course, you'd have to be a giraffe.*

Elizabethan Faire
"Jester"
Radio / 30 seconds
SFX: Buisine trumpet call. Faire ambiance.

Specs: Deep, commanding, resonant male voice with a flair for the dramatic and an ability to speak in an Elizabethan manner. British accent required.

Huzzah! The Elizabethan Faire is now open. Peasants and royalty arise and enter the gates. Jousters and jugglers. Musicians and magicians. Singers and dancers. There's fun for all. Throw an ax, drench a wench, or soak a bloke. Imbibe in the drink. Partake of the eats. Enjoy the challenges, role-play, and parades. Come one, come all you Renaissance Lords and ladies, peasants, pirates, belly dancers, and knights. Get thee to the Elizabethan Faire now through October 15th. Hip hip huzzah!

REVIEW:

Product: Elizabethan Faire
Key words: Elizabethan Faire, open, now through October 15th
Implied problem: You've waited a year for this event to return, so don't miss it!
Technique: There are so many list items; you'll need to pick and choose which ones you want to stress.

Chapter 15

MULTIPLES

Multiples, paired reads, two-parters, and dialogue spots are just a few of the monikers given to scripts requiring two or more actors to interact with one another. *Listening* and *reacting,* rather than planning and delivering the lines the way you think they should be said, is the key to good dialogue reads. It's about accepting an *action* rather than executing an idea.

In essence, every script is a dialogue because you have to take the listener, to whom you've personalized the message, into account and make sure they understand and are motivated by what you are saying. In dialogue scripts, the actors get to interact with one another and, when working together, don't have to imagine another person on the other side of the microphone.

Guidelines for Multiples

- Listen and react.
- Define whether you're the authority with the copy points or the person who needs help.
- In the beginning, be 180 degrees different from your scene partner (smarter/dumber, worried/relaxed, man/woman, young/old, happy/upset, high voice/low voice, cheerful/sad, relaxed/anxious, etc.).
- Let the story arc naturally until the problem is resolved and you both are on the same page.
- Don't tell your scene partner how to say a line.
- Don't let your mind wander. Stay in the scene so there aren't any dead pauses. The lines should be on the verge of overlapping.
- Highlight your lines and keep your eyes on the script.

- Add realistic emotional sounds and reactions.
- When the written dialogue is incomplete, button it up at the end with a short improvised word, phrase, or sound.

Remember, your character should be different from the other actor, otherwise they would have written the script with only one person in it. Singles are more prevalent in lean times. Conversely, dialogue spots are an indicator of a stable economy because the client has money to pay an additional actor.

Time to Practice:

Dialogue is primarily used in radio commercials and some corporate narration. In either case, assume that an announcer will tie up the loose ends of the story and tell the listener what to do. Your job is to draw focus to a problem and its resolution. The only exception to that rule is when two or more voices are used for variety to interchangeably break up announcer information.

With most auditions and jobs originating from home studios, many dialogue scripts are edited together or performed at different locations and channeled into one studio through real-time audio connections like Source-Connect and ISDN. Auditions are usually restricted to actors reading their lines and responding to a silent scene partner, submitting only their character's lines. When unable to practice with other actors, record one character's lines at a time. Then, edit the two characters' sound files together to see if your responses meld well.

Jam Spread
TV & Web / 30 seconds
Visual: The scene is a kitchen. We just see hand models interacting with each other and the product.

Specs: The man is charming but a bit of a goof-up.
The woman is smarter, is used to his antics, and likes to tease him.

Woman:	What are you doing?
Man:	Making a snack.
Woman:	What's this?
Man:	Hey, put that down.
Woman:	Jam Spread. I've never heard of it.
Man:	Discovered it when I went shopping last week.
Woman:	And now you're hiding it from me.

Man:	I'm not hiding it. See, here it is.
Woman:	Someone's eaten all of it. It's almost empty.
Man:	It must be the Jam Spread pirate.
Woman:	His name wouldn't happen to be John, would it?
Man:	Whatever gave you that idea?
Woman:	You've got Jam Spread on your sleeve.

REVIEW:

Product: Jam Spread

Key words: Jam Spread

Implied problem: Something so good it needs to be kept a secret

Technique: The woman might start with her arms crossed and the guy looking sheepishly upward, having been caught. Give the lines some air between them. Let the picture do the selling.

Illusions
Radio / 60 seconds

Specs: Reporter should be confident interviewer who's upwardly mobile, hoping that this interview will be the big break to move up the news ranks.

Profundo should be flamboyant and a bit arrogant. An accent would be great but not absolutely necessary.

SFX: outdoors with the sounds of people waiting for an exciting event

Reporter:	I'm here with the world famous magician the Amazing Profundo!
Profundo:	Greetings!

SFX: audience cheers wildly

Reporter:	Mr. Profundo, you are known worldwide for your magic.
Profundo:	That is correct.
Reporter:	Your fans are here today to find out about your Illusions.
Profundo:	Ah! Magicians never reveal their secrets.

SFX: audience sounds of disappointment

Reporter:	(whispering) What if I gave you this crisp one-hundred-dollar bill?

SFX: bill pop and crumble as it is grabbed and stuffed in pocket

Profundo:	For my fans I will tell!

SFX: *audience cheers*

Profundo:	My Illusions have the most superb happy hour in all the world.
Reporter:	Your illusions have a happy hour, Mr. Profundo.

Profundo: And my Illusions even provide free hors d'oeuvres.

Reporter: Free hors d'oeuvres? That's amazing.

Profundo: And dancing, too. Nightly until 2am.

Reporter: Profundo, I don't understand.

Reporter: There's no magic to it.

SFX: audience gasps

Profundo: Illusions is the hot new nightclub on Magic Street. The barbeque chicken wings are outstanding. Watch me pull one out of my hat.

SFX: magic poof followed by audience roar of approval

Reporter: Well, the vision is clear. For a little magic in your nightlife, visit Illusions.

Profundo: And tasty, too. Here, try one.

SFX: magic poof

REVIEW:

Product: Illusions nightclub

Key words: Illusions, happy hour, free hor d'oeuvres, dancing, hot new nightclub, magic

Implied problem: Few people are aware that Illusions is open for happy hour and serves free food.

Technique: The reporter is expecting a traditional interview and the magician doesn't deliver it. The magician loves the crowd and knows how to play to it. He throws a curveball to the reporter by talking about the nightclub instead of the magic. At the end, there's room to add a button to complete the story. It could be eating sounds, saying "very good," "can I have another," etc. Use your imagination and think of other endings.

Save-A-Dime

Radio / 60 seconds

Music: Retail store jingle up and under

Specs: Friendly retail announcers. The voices should compliment one another. No specific advice. We'll know what we want when we hear it.

He: It's back-to-school time.

She: And that means time to stock up on savings for the entire family at Save-A-Dime.

He: Right now, Save-A-Dime is featuring boys' jeans, sizes 4 to 14, for only $14.95.

She: And girls' tanks and tops, in this season's favorite colors, from $5.99 to $15.99.

He: We've got jackets in every shape and size starting at only $34.95.

She: And Save-A-Dime has outerwear for every occasion, casual, formal, or sporty.

He: For adults. . .

She: . . . and teens.

He: But that's not all.

She: While you're there, don't forget to check out the latest sweaters, coats, and scarfs.

He: Plus dress pants, and shirts for the guys,

She: And dresses, pants, and sweaters for the women.

He: Save-A-Dime knows how to stretch a budget by outfitting families in style.

She: The latest fashions.

He: At unbelievable prices.

She: When it comes to saving money for the entire family, Save-A-Dime's got the answer.

He: Back-to-school.

She: Or back to work.

He: Start the season right with a stop at Save-A-Dime.

She: It's not just a store.

He: It's a way of living.

REVIEW:

Product: Save-A-Dime discount department store
Key words: Back-to-school, Save-A-Dime, family, latest fashions, unbelievable prices, slogan: *It's not just a store. It's a way of living.*
Implied problem: Economically clothing the family.
Technique: Personality and chemistry between the two actors is what's going to make this spot come alive. Otherwise, it's just item and price information. Work on the relationship between you and your fellow actor and you and the store.

Tempting's Morsels
Radio / 30 seconds

Specs: Looking for two distinct voices to represent and co-brand each company. Should be good storytellers.

VO 1:   Once upon a time there was a cookie company named Tempting.

VO 2:   And a chocolate company named Morsels.

VO 1:   The cookies Tempting made were very, well. . . tempting.

VO 2:   The chocolates Morsels made were irresistible.

VO 1:   Then one day the president of the Tempting Corporation talked to the owner of the Morsels Group.

SFX: *Mumbling*

VO 2:   Together they decided to create a new kind of cookie, a cookie that everyone would love.

VO 1:   That cookie is Tempting's Morsels.

VO 2:   It has the crunchy goodness of Morsels chocolates.

VO 1:   And the chewy goodness of Tempting sugar cookies.

VO 2:   We love 'em.

VO 1:   Try a Tempting's Morsels cookie…

VO 2:   . . . and you'll be hooked, too.

LIVE ANNOUNCER TAG: Tempting's Morsels: available at Shopping Cart, Waysafe, and Food-to-Go.

REVIEW:

Product: Tempting's Morsels chocolate chip sugar cookies

Key words: Cookie, Tempting, chocolate, Morsels, irresistible, Tempting Corporation, Morsels Group, crunchy, chewy, Tempting's Morsels

Implied problem: Desiring a blend of two textures: crunchy and chewy

Technique: The new cookie is targeted to children and to adults' inner child. Therefore, it can be playful, youthful and whimsical. The action in the scene is about two separate items coming together. Find a way to play that action.

Luggage Rack
Radio / 30 seconds

Specs: The couple should be 25–40. Even though they're arguing, it should be upbeat and positive, not angry. It's more about who's going to keep the suitcase rather than the couple breaking up.

Man: Excuse me. What are you doing with my suitcase?

Woman: Your suitcase? I bought this at the Luggage Rack.

Man: You did not.

Woman:	Did, too!
Man:	Remember, you were moving into my apartment and you needed a set of luggage?
Man:	Yeah.
Woman:	Well, I dropped by the Luggage Rack because you told me it was the top discounter of quality luggage.
Woman:	Right, and you bought me this soft leather suitcase with my money. Now I'm using it to move out.
Man:	But what will I do without a suitcase from the Luggage Rack?
Woman:	The same thing you'll do without me.
Man:	What's that?
Woman:	Find a replacement.
SFX:	*Door slam*
Man:	Oh.
Announcer:	Luggage Rack. Great prices. Quality luggage. Too good to leave behind.

REVIEW:

Product: Luggage Rack suitcases

Key words: Suitcase, Luggage Rack, top discounter of quality luggage

Implied problem: Couple breakup and rightful distribution of property

Technique: The dialogue moves pretty quickly. Each person needs to make the point without sounding angry or whiny. At the end, the man has two choices: be sad about the suitcase loss or be happy about his new freedom.

Cameo
Radio / 60 seconds

Specs: Man — He's sleepy sounding until he hears about the car. That turns him on. He gets hopes dashed when she hangs up on him.

Woman — After buying the new car, she's been up all night driving. She calls her boyfriend. They both flirt until he blows it. She is shocked and then angered by his mistake.

Anncr — Casual, cool, confident.

SFX:	*Telephone ring*
Man:	Hello.
Woman:	Hi sweetie. What are you doing?
Man:	*(Yawning)* It's 2:30 in the morning, what do you think I was doing?
Woman:	I couldn't wait 'til tomorrow to call you. I've got to take you for a test drive in my new Cameo.
Man:	Couldn't you have texted? Wait a minute. You got a Cameo?
Woman:	Yep!
Man:	Sporty, sexy, I don't think the world is ready for you.
Woman:	You'll be my first passenger.
Man:	Pick me up at eight?
Woman:	I'll drive you to work.
Man:	See you in the morning, Maggie.
Woman:	Maggie? This is Carolyn.
SFX:	*Telephone click*
Man:	Does this mean I don't get a ride to work in your new Cameo?

ANNCR: The new Miska Cameo coupe. More than just good looks, it's got fully independent race-tuned suspension, four-valve-per-cylinder fuel-injected engine, four-wheel anti-lock brakes, and aerodynamic styling that far surpasses other all sports coupes. Starting at under twentyfive grand. The Cameo. It's a real looker. Dealer pricing may vary.

REVIEW:

Product: Cameo sports car

Key words: New Cameo, sporty, sexy *[The announcer has the bulk of the copy points.]*

Implied problem: Only sexy, cool people own and ride in sexy sports cars.

Technique: Time of day is important in setting the scene. The woman is jazzed and excited but the man is tired and yawning. His tone shifts dramatically when he realizes that she owns the car of his dreams. They get cozy and then he blows it. The story ties neatly into the announcer tag line: *It's a real looker.* Announcer should speed up on the disclaimer: *Dealer pricing may vary.*

Condor Café
Radio / 30 seconds
SFX: City, street ambiance

Specs: Two friends who haven't seen each other in a while run into each other on the street.

Voice One:	Hey! How are you?
Voice Two:	I can't believe it's you! It's been years.
One:	Where are you going?
Two:	I have a lunch meeting at the Condor Café.
One:	The Condor?! I eat breakfast there almost every morning.
Two:	You're kidding. The Condor is open for breakfast?
One:	Yeah. They make great omelets, pancakes, and French toast. I especially like their fresh fruit platter and imported coffee.
Two:	They have all that at the Condor?
One:	Yep. I'm having breakfast there tomorrow. Want to join me?
Two:	Sure. 7:30 okay?
One:	Perfect. Now, you better get to that lunch meeting.
Two:	Right. The Condor Café awaits!

REVIEW:

Product: Condor Café
Key words: Lunch, Condor Café, breakfast
Implied problem: Lack of time to get together and keep friendships active
Technique: Add movement, as if they are walking down the street and run into each other, stop to chat, and then hurry off in different directions. Toss off the laundry list of food items as it everyone knows they serve these things, rather than selling each item. Put thinking and natural response sounds in where necessary to add to the realism. Build out your characters. There's not much information about your characters besides they work and eat. Make strong choices and play their actions.

Flighty Air
Radio / 30 seconds
SFX: "One" is heard through a phone filter. There is ambient noise on the
"Two" side of the phone.

Specs: One is the mother. Two is the daughter. This could also be played as a
father and son. Parent is 55–75. Child is 30–50. This is a typical conversation
between the two of them, except this time the parent agrees to purchase
airline tickets. The two characters should not be whiny or complaining. Stay
positive and upbeat.

One: Sally, when are you and the kids coming home to see me?
Two: Mom, I am home.
One: You know what I mean.
Two: Sorry, Mom. We can't afford to fly back right now.
One: Yes you can.
Two: Brad hasn't sold a house in a month and our credit cards are
near the limit.
One: That's okay. I'll fly all of you home on Flighty Air.
Two: Uhh . . . my phone must have dropped out. I thought I heard
you say you'd pay our way on Flighty Air.
One: All of you . . . except Brad.
Two: You never have liked Brad, have you?
One: His body piercing might set off the metal detectors.

Anncr: This month only, Flighty Air is offering a family fly package.
Purchase three tickets and get the fourth one free. Find out more at
FlightyAir.com.

REVIEW:

Product: Flighty Air
Key words: Fly, Flighty Air, pay our way, family fly package,
three tickets, fourth one free, FlightyAir.com
Implied problem: Financial restraints preventing air travel and
family connections.
Technique: Find places for irony and laugh at the comments,
situation and your very familiar patterned parent/child relationship.

Chapter 16

CORPORATE NARRATION & DOCUMENTARIES

Narration covers a wide spectrum of work. It encompasses long and short form formats; hundreds of pages of copy to scripts that are only a few paragraphs in length. The recording may be used internally by a company or externally with unrestricted public access. It could air on the Internet, Intranet, inside public buildings or transit systems, business meetings, sales calls, museum tours, television, or video. Scripts may contain role-play scenarios, interviews, testimonials, complex business terminology, and lots of sound files that need to be named and delivered a specific way. They may require a casual delivery or a more deliberate, metered reading style. The common thread is that they all inform or educate the listener. Therefore, you must sound knowledgeable and full of pride.

Uses include:

- Software tutorials
- Medical training
- E-learning modules
- School video lessons
- Website information
- Audio tours
- Telephony
- Kiosks
- PowerPoint presentations
- Employee communication
- Marketing and sales materials
- Podcasts

- Recorded announcements aired in public places
- Talking products
- Trade shows
- Travelogues
- Documentaries
- Reality shows

Understanding how the unions define the jobs is helpful to all, even the non-union actors, because it provides a basis for quoting a rate. The general rule is, the more people who see or hear you, the more money you should get paid. Like in commercials, it's not the number of words you say but how many people will hear them.

Union Categories

SAG defines corporate, industrial, or educational narrations as follows:

- **Category I** — Programs shown on a restricted basis that are "designed to train, inform, promote a product, or perform a pubic relations function, and may be exhibited in classrooms, museums, libraries, or other places where no admission is charged. Included are closed circuit television transmissions (such as direct broadcasts by satellites), teleconferences, and sales programs that are designed to promote products or services of the sponsor."

Examples include:

1. A program shown to employees about how to understand their customer base and upsell their product or service.
2. A program about safety on the worksite that does not sell or feature a particular brand or company's product.
3. E-learning training used to update employees on new technologies and policies.
4. A PowerPoint presentation used at a company meeting.

- **Category II** — Programs intended for "unrestricted exhibition to the general public" and "designed primarily to sell specific products or services to the consuming public at (1) locations where the products or services are sold, or (2) places such as coliseums, railroad stations, air/bus terminals, or shopping centers." They "may be supplied free of charge to customers as a premium or inducement to purchase specific goods or services."

Examples include:

1. A program that can be viewed by customers shopping in a computer store about the features of their latest computer product.
2. A program displayed at a trade show about safety on the worksite that sells the benefits of a specific company's product.
3. A DVD given to a customer free of charge or shown on a website that shows how to remodel a kitchen using a company's product or service.
4. A video playing in the salad section of a grocery store about how to make a great salad using their company's salad dressing.

Category II jobs pay more than restricted Category I jobs. For non-union actors who do not benefit from a predetermined minimum pay scale, they should keep the intended medium (radio, TV, Internet, Intranet, DVD, etc.) and target audience under consideration when quoting a job. Finding the current minimum union wage can be attained through the SAG & AFTRA websites.

Non-Union Rates

Many non-union actors use the union base rate to determine their own pay scale, while others come up with their own formulas. Some charge by the hour and number of sound files, others quote a price close to the union rate or set a minimum they are willing to get paid for making the effort to turn on the recording equipment, read the script, edit it, and deliver the finished files. Quote requests for the amount per minute of finished sound files may spur the actor to bid the job at $5 a minute [$300 ÷ 60 minutes = $5]. If sound files need to be broken down into smaller files and named, an additional $1 or $2 per file fee may be added to the quote.

While lowballing jobs is common practice for some beginning voice actors, I do not recommend it. Set a reasonable minimum within the current standards of the business. Giving away your services or selling them below market value in order to get the job is shortsighted and hurts everyone.

Recording Issues

1. **Unfamiliar Terminology.** Medical and technical scripts are filled with acronyms and long, difficult words. Some clients provide a pronunciation list. Others depend on you to do the research. When unsure of a pronunciation, record and deliver an alternative choice.

2. **Getting in The Zone.** Many scripts are the size of a book. It often takes a page or two for an internal metronome to click inside you and hit the appropriate rhythm and tone. When you've completed reading the script, it's a good idea to go back and rerecord the first page or two to match the more comfortable, consistent rhythm of the rest of the script.

3. **Stand or Sit.** Standing is the preferred way to record. When a script is over four pages long, sitting in a chair or stool is the appropriate and expected way to record in order to minimize fatigue. To keep the energy moving forward, lean forward in the chair and keep your back straight. Placing one foot in front of the other helps with this forward movement.

4. **Pacing.** Narrations have more complex sentence structure than commercials. Speaking slower than commercials and breaking sentences into short phrases helps the listener digest the information. Adding an appropriately placed half second to second space for a visual image also allows opportunity for editing adjustments.

5. **Consistency.** Long recordings require that an actor take breaks. Before leaving the booth, take note of your distance and location to the microphone plus the position of your chair, bottom, and legs. If possible, turn sideways to get out of the chair without moving the chair's position.

6. **Mistakes.** When reading long or difficult material, the margin for errors increase. The main thing is to never beat yourself up, apologize, or get frustrated. These negative feelings bleed into your read and delay the recording process. Simply wait a second or two, keep the same positive attitude you had prior to the mistake, and repeat the sentence where the mistake occurred.

7. **Page Turns.** Never turn a page while reading, neither paper nor on a computer, tablet, or mobile device, unless you have expert superhuman abilities to do it noiselessly. The microphone will pick up the paper rustle, tap, or click. Finish

reading the page, stop, adjust the next page into position, and continue reading. It is very easy to edit out these noises when they are in the clear. Many people use an iPad or similar device rather than printed scripts. If that's the case, touch the screen gently so it doesn't make a noise.

8. **Microphone Position.** A common error is for people to lower their heads as the words become lower on the page or shift their heads to the right when a second or third page is placed on the stand. Do not do that! Instead, learn to keep your mouth in the same position from the beginning to the end of the job. You may need to look down your nose or cock your head to the right or left to see the words. If need be, stop and readjust the script.

9. **Naming Conventions.** Most narrations need to be broken into sections. Many companies provide a naming convention, while others depend on you to create your own. Files need a number like 001, 002, 003, etc., at the beginning of the file name to keep the files in order. Otherwise, when delivered to the client, they will be received alphabetically rather than in chronological order. Naming files is a very important part of delivering finished recordings. And be careful: sometimes companies are very cruel and name files with zeros and o's. Ex. 00O30O.

10. **Delivery.** Before recording, confirm how the client wants the files delivered: wav, aiff, a specific mp3 size, etc., if they want it compressed or not, and if they want a certain amount of pre and post recording silence (heads and tails).

Tips For Directing Talent

If you have a visual of where or how the recording will be used, show it to the actor before recording. Hearing a music bed is also helpful for the actor to quickly dial in the appropriate attitude and tempo. Let the actor know the intended audience: doctors, nurses, business owners, middle management, mechanics, engineers, programmers, administrative assistants, shipping clerks, accountants, assembly technicians, iron workers, general public, students, etc. This allows the actor an understanding if they need to play smarter than they are, the same level, or less intelligent. An audience's age also affects the delivery style. Typically, the younger the audience the more casual the read. Conversely, the older the audience, the more direct and formal the style. State if the purpose: information, education, or entertainment. An educational read requires more specific word stress. Knowing the *who, why,* and *where* helps the actor key in on *how* to best deliver the read.

Time to Practice:

Narration is bread-and-butter work for many voice actors. When the recordings are for internal use only, the demands on the actor are fewer. It is not a make or break it situation for the company. Once the information is available to the general public, image is much more important. Your job is to find and reflect the philosophy of the company, sound knowledgeable, and confident. Relate to the listener on a friendly, intelligent, and professional level. Understand whether you are talking to CEOs and other C-class level management, middle management, lower level employees, or consumers. Pride is the predominant emotion.

Point of Purchase

Grocery Store
Use: Video display in the salad section of the grocery store and on the company's website.

Specs: Light, friendly, conversational, and informative. Not pushed or pushy. Real.

Thinking about a salad for dinner? Spice it up with JT's Spray On Dressing. First, start with a bag of mixed lettuce. Rinse it, spin it, and let it dry. Then, put it in a large salad bowl. Toast two cups of chopped nuts and set aside. Almonds, walnuts, and pecans work best. Boil and chop 2–3 eggs. Add carrots, tomatoes, cucumber slices, and shallots. Then toss with JT's Salad Dressing. Sprinkle some cheese on top and the toasted nuts, and you're ready to serve a healthy, delicious salad to your family and friends. Pick up JT's in the salad dressing section of the store.

REVIEW:

Product: JT's Spray On Salad Dressing
Key words: JT's Spray On Dressing, JT's Salad Dressing, JT's
Implied problem: Not knowing what to serve for dinner.
Technique: The first two sentences are the set-up. The body of the copy describes how to make a salad. The final sentence tells

the shopper where to find the product. Point to an imaginary shelf when you say the line to draw the listener's attention there.

E-Learning

Software Training
Use: Online Web class

Specs: Real, friendly, personable, and approachable. Male or female. 30–40.

Hi, I'm Gregg, your virtual trainer. I'm here to help you understand how to use the GQY system more efficiently. This test will only take a few minutes. It is necessary to complete the course before using the product. Let's begin. Press next and follow me.

On the center of the screen is the sketchpad. This is the area where the geometry is created. As you can see, objects are made by choosing a tool from the palette along the left side of the sketchpad. The pointer selects a circle tool and places it near the center of the sketchpad. Notice how easily this simple geometry is modified by adding a line tangent to the circle at a forty-five-degree angle to the horizontal.

Now it's your turn. Follow the instructions. Click next and begin. When you're finished, press "finished." Your score will be calculated. If you need to repeat this exercise, the lesson screen will reappear.

Observe the selection of the line tool. If the line is selected from the modify pull-down menu, it can be attached to the circle by right-clicking on the desired quadrant and dragging the line to the preferred length. Go ahead; try it. Click next when you're ready to move on.

Great, you're almost done. Just a few simple moves and you'll be certified. Select the circle tool. Place it in the center of the sketchpad. Select the line tool. Scroll through the modify menu and select tangent. Now, right-click and hold. A 3-D rectangle will appear. To change shape, simply scroll over one of the shape choices below. You can also select color and movement options. Go ahead; try it.

Congratulations! You now understand the basic operating functions of the GQY system. To learn more, go to Tutorial 202.

REVIEW:

Product: GQY system operating functions
Key words: GQY, center, sketchpad, left side, pointer, line tool, modify pull-down menu, right clicking, dragging, circle tool,

tangent, click and hold, scroll over, basic operating functions, Tutorial 202

Implied problem: Certification needed for understanding and company advancement.

Technique: Using the product should sound simple and easy. You should be loose and relaxed and gesture to locations described in the text.

Talking Product

Car

Specs: Pleasant sounding. Real. Mid-range voice. Male or female. No accents.

Say "drive" to start your engine.

Would you like to hear some music? Say the station or type music you prefer.

Your door is ajar.

Are you sure you want to do that?

Try again.

Hands-free dialing is available. Say the person or number you wish to call.

I'm sorry, I didn't understand you.

Gas tank is low. There's a station in five miles. Would you like me to show you where?

Turn left at the next light.

You have arrived at your destination.

REVIEW:

Product: Intelligent car system

Key words: Drive, music, ajar, hands-free dialing, gas tank low

Implied problem: Keeping focused on the road while driving and performing tasks.

Technique: Each line is a separate sound file. Don't run them together. They are all fairly short. To minimize editing, support each sentence with enough air to sustain it to the end and not have to get noisy breaths in the middle.

Website & Trade Show

Technology

Use: A series of videos and testimonials that introduce and endorse the product.

Specs: Big, dramatic, without being "in-your-face." More suppressed intensity. Knowledgeable and proud with a bit of a tease.

Stop what you're doing! You are about to experience the most amazing product ever — the Elliptical Express. Using Euclidean geometry, Directrix has created a new way to calculate quantum effects. It uses the special case of the hypotrochoid and electromagnetic radion. Genius, right? And it's all right here our new patented device. Let's hear what some of our customers have to say:

Testimonials:

John — *It's amazing. From orientation and position, shape and scale, Directrix has delivered a winning product our company will be using for a long time.*

Fred — *Five degrees of freedom. Why didn't someone think of this before?*

Rhonda — *It all converges on a single point. That makes my job easier.*

So you see, Directrix has taken shape with a whole new product that will change the way you do business. Find out more from one of our sales consultants. They'll put you on the Elliptical Express.

REVIEW:

Product: Directrix's Elliptical Express
Key words: Elliptical Express, Directrix, new patented device
Implied problem: Customers needing an easier or more effect way to work
Technique: Even if you don't know what you're talking about, the audience does. Don't linger on the difficult words. You know them and so does your audience. Say them as if they're part of your everyday conversation.

Museum Guide

Audio Tour

Use: Museum patrons listen on their audio device while they view the exhibit.

Specs: Real, conversational, low-key, and knowledgeable.

You are now standing in front of Paolo Uccello's depiction of *Saint George and the Dragon,* painted in 1470. In no other painting in this collection is his Gothicizing style more apparent. On the right is the armored soldier on a white horse, fighting the dragon. George's fight is an iconic subject of many paintings since the seventh century. William Shakespeare even references the battle in his plays *Richard III* and *King Lear.*

If you look to your left, you will see another version of the same scene painted a few years later, in 1456. Once again the classic image of a damsel in distress is on the left, Saint George is on the right, and the dragon is between them. This painting is called *The Princess and the Dragon.* Note the color and style differences. The green hews of the original painting have turned red. And the sharp angles have become softer to reflect the switch from the warrior's position to the woman's perspective.

REVIEW:

Product: Paolo Uccelo's paintings, along with others in the museum
Key words: Paolo Uccello, *Saint George and the Dragon*, look to your left, *The Princess and the Dragon*
Implied problem: Lack of knowledge about the painter and the paintings
Technique: Your main job is to let people know where to look and move, and casually toss off interesting comments so the listener learns and experiences the exhibit at a deeper level.

Informational Video

Happy Homes Realty
Use: Customer support DVD or link to video on their website.

Specs: Sally and Arnie should be likeable. They represent the listener. The visuals will show the two characters going about their daily business and personal lives. Their lines should sound like internal monologues, figuring out what they should do.

The announcer should be understanding, caring, and self-assured that they have encountered this situation many times and know how to handle it.

Sally:

When John Frank called me into his office, I had no idea he would offer me a management job. My projects have gotten good reviews lately, but I never dreamed I'd be offered a promotion this early in my career. But here it was, a chance to prove myself. I just wish it wasn't in Boise.

What will Arnie think? Will he be willing to give up his job? How about the children? Emily is on the cheerleading squad and Aaron just made varsity. They'll hate leaving their friends. I'll miss my friends and relatives, too. We've lived here all our lives. It will devastate my parents. They're getting older and need me around. But this job is just too good to pass up. There'll be a lot more money, so we can afford to fly back once or twice a year. I've been telling Arnie that we need a larger home. Two more rooms for our offices would be just perfect.

Announcer:

Moving is never easy. It means leaving familiar surroundings and the ones you love. It means packing up your belongings and moving them to another town, another state, sometimes even another country. The relocation experts at Happy Homes Realty understand this concern and are there to ensure that the transition goes smoothly for both you and your family.

It's a well-known fact that the moving process is stressful. Whether your job has a tendency to periodically relocate you or you are moving for the first time, each member of the family has their own set of problems and concerns that needs to be addressed openly and honestly. The key to a successful move is *communication*. That means talking to each member of the family about the move, listening to their thoughts, and respecting their feelings.

Arnie:

When Sally told me about her promotion, I was stunned. On the one hand, I was thrilled for her. I understand how important her job is to her. On the other hand, I'm not sure I'm ready to move. I'm in the middle of designing a new product at work and it wouldn't be fair to the company to leave at this stage of the project. I know I should support her, she certainly was a tremendous help for me when I changed jobs a few years ago, but this is going to have tremendous impact on the family. Will I be able to find a comparable job in the Boise area? What kinds of schools are available for the children? What are the effects of moving while the kids are in high school? How will our lifestyles change?

REVIEW:

Product: Happy Homes Realty relocation services
Key words: Moving, relocation experts, Happy Homes Realty, communication
Implied problem: Moving and making the right decisions.
Technique: Arnie's and Sally's parts are testimonials and should sound very real. There is no selling involved. The announcer is there to put their minds at ease and help the listener know that they'll make the move as smooth and stress-free as possible.

Corporate Event

Pride Corporation
Use: On- or off-site sales meeting or web conference to rally the troops, and build enthusiasm and company pride.

Specs: Real, confidant, assured, and full of pride.

VISUAL	AUDIO
Company Logo	*SFX: Upbeat music* Pride Corporation believes in value, in the day-to-day business needs of the operation, and a system that benefits the bottom line. This is why we have provided TZW for each member of our sales team.
TZW product close-up	It is the personal business solution for product installation, training, service, and support. In short, Pride Corporation understands the value of its investment.
Dissolve to employee photos	And that investment is you.
Videos of sales people & customers	Customer downtime is now a thing of the past. TZW enables you to understand the needs of the customer even before those needs present themselves.

Video clips of product in use	This little device allows you to diagnose the problem, provide the correct solution, supply collateral materials, and schedule a live or virtual meeting.
Close-up of materials	Throughout the coming weeks we strongly urge you to familiarize yourself with the product to provide end-to-end solutions for your customers.
Employee faces morph into Earth and a twirling globe.	It's through your hard work that Pride has emerged as a multi-million-dollar corporation with over 10,000 employees in 17 countries.

REVIEW:

Product: Pride Corporation and its TZW device

Key words: Pride Corporation, value, day-to-day business needs, system that benefits the bottom line, TZW, personal business solution, product installation, training, service, support, investment, you, needs, little device, diagnose the problem, provide the correct solution, supply collateral materials, schedule a meeting, familiarize, end-to-end, multi-million-dollar corporation, 10,000 employees, 17 countries.

Implied problem: Dissatisfied customers and frustrated or overworked employees

Technique: This script is content laden but shouldn't sound heavy. It's about encouragement to be the best, information, and being part of a larger community. Break phrases down so they are easily to comprehend. End each phrase down rather than up. This allows more flexibility to move lines around to fit the images.

On-Site Video Loop

Quality Hospital
Use: Plays in the hospital waiting room to increase awareness, show compassion, and build patient trust.

Specs: Compassionate, understanding, and knowledgeable. Should sound like a doctor, nurse, or hospital administrator.

It wasn't supposed to happen to her. Sue always gave herself a monthly breast exam. She took care of herself, exercised regularly, and didn't smoke. But this time, something felt different. She immediately called her doctor and made an appointment.

At Quality Hospital we know that one out of three women risk developing a breast lump and one in eight women in the U.S. develop breast cancer. Yet, with early detection, treatment is often successful. Our safe, painless, and effective low-dose radiation mammography can detect breast cancer in its early stages, long before a lump is even felt.

We recommend that women fifty to seventy-four have a mammogram every two years. Women forty to forty-nine are encouraged to have screenings based on family history and risk factors.

- You could be at higher risk if:
- You have a family history of breast cancer.
- You are over fifty years old.
- Your first menstrual period was before the age of twelve.
- You've never had children or had your first after age thirty.
- You are overweight or have a diet high in fats.
- You consume an average of two units or more of alcohol per day.

REVIEW:

Product: Quality Hospital

Key words: Quality Hospital, breast lump, breast cancer, early detection, successful, detect, mammogram, screenings, family history, over fifty years old, before twelve, never had children, had your first after thirty, overweight, diet high in fats, two units or more of alcohol per day

Implied problem: Breast cancer and late recognition and treatment

Technique: There are three distinct elements. The first paragraph is the emotional set-up. The second paragraph establishes authority with a little bit of emotion and logic mixed in. The rest of the copy is logical information.

Internal Company Video

Workerbee Company

Visuals: Video montage of people, the campus, and company products. Key words and phrases appear on the screen for approximately 4–5 seconds each.

Use: New Employee training video provides consistent, legal information that contractually protects the company.

Specs: *Strong, trustworthy, and confidant.*

Welcome to Workerbee Company. You have selected an exciting and challenging career in an expanding and competitive industry. Your success is an important factor in the success of the company. We feel confident that you will enjoy working with other talented, motivated people.

As a new employee, it is important that you be aware of our company policies and procedures. You will learn about:

- Performance reviews.
- Benefit packages.
- Training.
- And educational opportunities.

Upon completion of this presentation, you will have a brief opportunity to meet with your supervisor before going to Human Resources.

Let us begin.

SFX: Music and company logo

Performance reviews are conducted on a biannual basis. At those times, your supervisor will schedule a mandatory meeting consisting of an oral and written review. Superior performances are awarded profit sharing at a minimum of 5 percent of your current salary. You will also be eligible for a pay increase dependent on the company's current profit sales margin. Good performances merit a one-time profit sharing payment between 1–3 percent of your current income. Fair to poor reviews receive a warning. Three warnings provide grounds for dismissal from the company.

REVIEW:

Product: Workerbee Company employment rules and opportunities.

Key words: Workerbee Company, new employee, company policies and procedures, performance reviews, benefit packages, training, educational opportunities, performance reviews, biannual, supervisor, mandatory meeting, oral and written review, superior, 5 percent, pay increase, profit sales margin, good performances, one-time, fair to poor, warning, three warnings, dismissal.

Implied problem: If you don't do well we'll fire you and/or you won't receive additional benefits.

Technique: This script style does not lend itself to being the listener's friend. It is purposefully written in a formal style that separates the speaker from the listener. It just wants the new employee to know important, necessary facts.

Telephony: Phone Prompt Systems & Phone Casting
IVR (Interactive Voice Response)
VRU (Voice Response Unit)
Automated Attendant (Virtual Receptionist)

Interactive voice response (IVR) is a telephony technology utilizing voice and touch recognition that all of us have experienced when calling a company or organization. The caller is prompted to touch a number or series of letters on their telephone keypad or respond verbally to audio commands. A voice actor or company employee either records the prompts and uploads them into an IVR platform or dials a number, enters a code, and records the prompts directly into the their telephone system.

Company Voice Mail

Specs: Pleasant, approachable, with good diction and clarity.

Greeting:

You have reached CVM. If you know the extension of the person you are calling, please say or spell the last name now. If you need a listing, say "directory." To place an order, say or press "one." For shipping and receiving, say or press "two." For payment, say or press "three." To speak with a sales consultant, say or press four. To have these options repeated, press or say "repeat."

Connection:

_____(name)_____ at extension number ____(352)____ is unavailable. Say or press "one" to leave a message.

On-Hold Message:

Did you know that CVM has a choice of actors to record your company's voice prompts? To hear a list of our talent, go to CVM. talent.com. We have voices for all types of businesses, from rugged male voices for construction sites to wholesome young women for software companies. Unsure what voice to choose? Simply go online and answer a brief questionnaire. We'll suggest the voice type that is best for you. Or, try our ever-popular guy-and-gal-next-door options. Your listener will think they're listening to a live person. Any choice you make, using CVM will save your company money.

Parsing Numbers:

One	Twenty
Two	Thirty
Three	Forty
Four	Fifty
Five	Sixty
Six	Seventy
Seven	Eighty
Eight	Ninety
Nine	Hundred
Ten	Zero

Parsing Words:

O'clock
AM
PM
Atlantic
Pacific
Eastern
Central
Mountain
Alaskan
Hawaii-Aleutian
Standard Time

REVIEW:

Product: CVN

Key words: CVN, say or spell, order, press or say, one. shipping and receiving, two, payment, three, sales consultant, four, repeated, repeat, and all the parsed words and numbers

Implied problem: Listen carefully, you're not going to get a live receptionist because that would be an additional expense for the company.

Technique: Voice should reflect the heart and soul of the company. Breath support should be even, the voice should have a melodic quality with excellent diction that cuts through the sound limitations of the telephone. The on-hold message is an ad for the company and should be read matter-of-factly. Read the parsed words three ways, with an up, down, and straight-across inflection so they can be programmed into the beginning, middle, and end of a sentence.

Infomercial

Syber Deluxe 3000

Use: TV & Web

Visuals: It opens with unhappy, overweight forty to fifty-year-old person struggling to do a situp. Cuts to product shots. We then see a lean, fit, early-thirties person easily using the equipment, then dressed up and admiring self in mirror before going out on a date.

Music: Pulsing, upbeat, steady electronic beat

Specs: Authoritative, controlled, energetic, proud, confident. Men and women, twenty-five to fifty-five. Should sound like you are the sexiest, most fit, confident person on the planet and it's easy for people to be like you.

The Syber Deluxe 3000 is unlike any other exercise machine you've ever seen. It's compact, lightweight, easy to use, and stores neatly under the bed or in the closet. And, with only fifteen minutes of exercise per day, your body will look leaner, firmer, and healthier.

To begin using the Syber Deluxe 3000, simply step on the easy release bar and snap it into position. Your exercise program is ready to go. It's that simple! The heavy-duty rubber band system adjusts easily to your fitness level. Simply remove the peg from the patented notched-weight system and insert it into the exercise bar. Now, the Syber Deluxe 3000 is ready to tone, firm and strengthen your chest, arms, abs, buns, and legs. And after only fifteen minutes of exercise a day for eight weeks, you'll see unbelievable results.

Shouldn't you get off the treadmill? Order the Syber Deluxe 3000 — guaranteed to give you a sleeker, toned, more beautiful body. And if you order now, Syber Deluxe 3000 will even include a free forty-five-minute exercise video and our muscle-enhancing energy shake.

Don't delay. Call 1-800-S-Y-B-3000 or go to 1800syb3000.tv today to receive your Syber Deluxe 3000 and exercise video at the low introductory cost of only $194.99. It will be billed to your credit card in four easy installments of only $48.75 plus tax, shipping, and handling. But wait! If you order in the next eight minutes, we'll eliminate one of your payments. That's right! You'll only make three payments of $48.75. But don't delay. Order your Syber Deluxe 3000 today. It's the exercise machine that really works.

REVIEW:

Product: Syber Deluxe 3000 exercise machine

Key words: Syber Deluxe 3000, exercise machine, compact, light-weight, easy to use, stores neatly under the bed or in the closet, fifteen minutes of exercise per day, body will look leaner, firmer, and healthier, step on the easy release bar, snap it into position, adjusts easily, simply remove, insert, tone, firm and strengthen your chest, arms, abs, buns, and legs, unbelievable results, order, guaranteed, beautiful body, free forty-five-minute exercise video, muscle enhancing energy shake, call 1-800-S-Y-B-3000, go to 1800SBY3000.tv today, only $194.99, four easy installments, eliminate one of your payments, don't delay, order, today

Implied problem: Loss of confidence and self-esteem

Technique: You are selling youth, ease, confidence, happiness, and simplicity. Shrug, or toss off the assembly information as if it's no big deal. Anyone, even someone mechanically challenged, can put this thing together. Energy and enthusiasm should continue to grow until the very end. Get closer to the mic when you get to the order section.

Documentary

Nature Series
Use: TV & Web

Specs: Quiet, dramatic, behind the scenes. Must be a good storyteller, switching easily from observations to facts.

The deer approaches the opening, unaware of the cougar's presence. Slowly and quietly, Shuka creeps toward his prey. Hearing a twig crack, the deer turns and faces impending danger. There is no time to run before the six-foot-long, 200-pound male cougar pounces on its back and bites its neck. The deer, a favorite food of the cougar, has met its match. He has fallen victim to the balance of nature.

Meanwhile, Carla is at the den watching her kittens. Smaller than males, females have similar reddish brown fur on the upper part of the body and white hair on the underbelly. There are three eight-day-old spotted cubs. Litters range from one to five cubs every other year. In a few months, Carla will teach them how to hunt.

Shuka returns carrying part of his kill. Carla seems pleased with his hunt. As she stands up to eat, the kittens scramble around looking for milk. They mew for their mother, who seems disinterested at the moment.

Off in the distance another cougar howls. It eerily resembles a domestic cat, only much louder. It soon turns into a loud screeching noise. This is the cougar mating call. Cougars do not have specific mating seasons like other animals. They can breed at any time of the year, and cubs reach sexual maturity between the ages of two and three. So, while this family grows and matures, another life cycle begins. We will return three months from now and see if another family's litter has arrived.

REVIEW:

Product: One episode in a weekly nature series program.
Key words: Deer, Cougar, prey, danger, hunt, kill, mating call, return
Implied problem: Survival of the species
Technique: Take your time. Allow for the visuals. Add drama to the last sentence of the first paragraph by breaking it into three sections: He has fallen victim. To the balance. Of nature. The

last couple sentences should hook the audience into watching upcoming episodes.

Medical Training

Med School Course
Use: Online or classroom training.

Specs: Should sound like a doctor talking to another doctor. Intelligent, clear, and direct.

What are the signs of Arteriosclerotic Vascular Disease? The artery wall in ASVD patients thickens as a result of fatty buildup that inflames the walls of the arterial blood vessels. This is primarily due to the accumulation of macrophage white blood cells and low-density lipoproteins that carry cholesterol and triglycerides. Without adequate removal of these fats and cholesterol from the macrophages by functional high-density lipoproteins (HDL), hardening or furring of the arteries occurs, and multiple plaques within the arteries are formed.

Atheromatous plaque has three components:

- Atheroma — in the center of large plaques.
- Cholesterol crystals — in the underlying areas.
- Calcification — at the outer base of older, advanced lesions.

REVIEW:

Product: Vascular disease education and ASVD awareness

Key words: Arteriosclerotic Vascular Disease, artery wall, thickens, fatty buildup, inflames the walls, accumulation of macrophage white blood cells and low-density lipoproteins that carry cholesterol and triglycerides. Without adequate removal of these fats and cholesterol from the macrophages, hardening or furring of the arteries occurs, multiple plaques, formed, atheroma, cholesterol crystals, calcification

Implied problem: If you want to be a doctor, you need to recognize the symptoms before treating the patient.

Technique: The listener is familiar with these medical terms, so you need to be as well. Before recording, confirm pronunciations. Consult online medical dictionaries.

Chapter 17

AUDIOBOOKS

Celebrities and authors voice the greatest number of audiobooks. Undoubtedly, recognizable names help increase sales. However, an actor's or an author's fame doesn't necessarily guarantee that person is the best choice. Many stars are visual talents, not vocal actors. Narrating lengthy text requires exceptional storytelling ability, stamina, and adeptness at immersing listeners in vivid prose. That opens the door for voice actors with unique book-reading skills and a desire to pursue this business.

Readings take on added dimension when the voice talent is able to perform a variety of roles. Using contrasting voices and personality traits give the listener both aural gratification and the ability to rapidly distinguish one character from the next. Your goal is to make each character sound real and true to life. Heavy caricatures and overdramatizations, like making an elderly person sound too creaky and crotchety or a man playing a female role in a high falsetto voice, should be avoided. Instead, make subtle and effective choices. For instance, an enchanted princess may speak softly and wistfully; a strong king may deliver his lines slowly with elongated vowels; an evil villain may punctuate the consonants in a clipped speech pattern. Using the microphone effectively will help, too. One character may be close and centered on the mic, another one may stand a couple inches away and talk at a right angle to the mic, a third character may use the left angle position, a short character may lift the chin and look up to the mic, and a tall character may look down. All these positions should be clearly defined before starting. You may want to make a list of all the characters in the book and their specific physicalities. Then practice them until they are second nature. If you're good at believable dialects, accents, and vocal changes add them in where necessary. Be kind to yourself and don't make it too complicated.

Reading volumes requires vocal stamina and consistency. The fewer mistakes the better. On average, a good and consistent reader can record approximately ten pages an hour. Short books may only take an hour to record and edit. Longer books may require weeks to complete. Ideally, readings should be limited to 4–5 hours a day. Often, schedules do not allow this luxury. An eight-hour day with a one-hour lunch break is not uncommon. When working these long stretches, be sure to take breaks to clear the brain, hydrate, and relax the jaw, mouth, and tongue muscles. Stretch and shake out your whole body. Once refreshed, start again. Short ten-to-fifteen-minute breaks every couple hours will help the process go more smoothly.

There are two types of recording sessions. One is at the recording studio with a director and audio engineer. A fee is set fee based on the estimated recording time or an hourly rate. The less expensive option is to have you record the book in your home studio. In that case, you play actor, director, and audio engineer. A deadline is given to return the completed, edited files. Established audio publishers will fine tune the edits, clean up any unwanted sounds, and add music or sound effects, their company information, and credits before releasing the final product.

Inside the Audiobook Industry

Simon Vance, *AudioFile's* "Golden Voice" and *Booklist's* first "Voice of Choice"

You have narrated hundreds of books in England and the U.S., won numerous Audie and Earphone awards, and were reviewed in the Library Journal as "one of the best narrators in the business." How did you break into the business and what tips would you give someone entering this field?
I began narrating for the Royal National Institute for the Blind in London, in my time off from the BBC, almost thirty years ago when audiobooks were really only available for the blind and partially sighted. I spent eight years learning the ropes (I refer to it as my apprenticeship). I came to California in the early '90s and managed to find a company willing to listen to an audition tape I'd made. They liked me and I've never looked back.

Tips for breaking into the business: Donating time and reading for charity is still a pretty good way to begin — so look around for opportunities in your neighborhood. The thing to bear in mind is that while it's never been easier to set up a home studio and have the potential to record from day one, it's a rare beginner indeed who can produce material of a quality that would interest a commercial publisher. A new narrator needs to find a place to practice his/her craft and to prove they have the ability. These days the Internet offers many chances for practice — one such is www.librivoice.org, which asks for volunteers to read chapters of books that are in the public domain (no copyright fees) and then releases them through the website. This is a way to not only practice, but also to gain valuable feedback from listeners from which you'll be able to get some idea as to whether you're ready to approach commercial publishers.

I should also add that while the equipment and a direction to head in are useful, it's also essential that you work on your "acting" abilities outside of any studio environment. Having a "nice" voice (whatever that means) is a tiny part of the whole. Narrators are "Voice Actors" in the purest sense of the phrase — so think about taking acting classes, improv classes, even work with a voice coach to find the natural "you."

How do you record your books?

I've built up my stock of equipment over several years and I wouldn't expect someone entering the profession to spend the kind of money needed to replicate my set-up when they haven't yet proven they can make a living with narration (or voice work generally). I have a double-walled booth (7" x 6" x 4") in a room in my house in which I recently reinforced the sound proofing on the exterior wall. I have a dedicated DAW (Digital Audio Workstation) for my studio — essentially a PC that is set up optimally for audio recording — and another in my office on which I can edit my finished recordings. Inside my studio I have a computer screen, keyboard, and mouse and, of course, a microphone. I have used an industry standard for many years (Neumann TLM103) but I've recently been playing with a Sennheiser MKH416. These can cost around $1,000 new, so if you're just beginning I would suggest aiming a little lower . . . Harlan Hogan offers a very suitable mic at around $250 but there are even cheaper options around. I recorded my first books on a $50 Shure.

What do you suggest for recording books?

If you are just beginning, look for a reasonably cheap microphone (read the reviews, you'll see which are probably a good bet) and try to find a quiet corner of your house. Use a simple computer and a recording program like Audacity (free) and surround yourself with blankets or some form of acoustically absorbent material (improvise, it can be part of the fun). You'll need at least some technical ability if you're going to be working alone so put some time aside to understand exactly what it means to digitally record your voice using a computer. Then, start working and listening, working and listening — compare your work with that available from somewhere like Audible.com (there are samples available of every book for sale).

Be very aware of the sounds around you — when you are working alone you are responsible for everything that the microphone picks up, so you need to keep one ear on your own work and one ear on the neighbor's dog or lawn mower!

How do you stay consistent over days or weeks of recording?

Pacing is so very important. In a class once a student wondered why her husband (her sample audience) found her voice dull and lifeless at the end of a seven-hour book she had recorded . . . it turned out she had recorded the whole thing in one day! I have *rarely* recorded more than five finished hours in a day and would never dream of trying to remain consistent over a seven-finished-hour day! Audiobook recording requires stamina and endurance. The focus required to be "on" for the entire duration of a day's recording can be mentally (and physically) exhausting.

I generally record an hour and take a break, then another hour and another break and so on. If I feel my voice even beginning to "thin out" then I stop because I know I'll have to match my voice when I begin the next day. This differs slightly from the time spent in a professional studio where there is an engineer and a producer/ director — financial constraints mean you can't have too much "down" time, but then the stress level is reduced because you have two other people listening for mistakes and taking care of all the technical aspects as you record.

Consistency tip: Try to find a natural break in the story to take rests, so that if there is any, even slight, difference in vocal energy it will be less noticeable. By the way, whenever you restart after a break (particularly overnight) always listen to the last few paragraphs recorded to get back into the same rhythm before the break.

What kind of salary can one expect to make?

It's very difficult to say what to expect financially as there is really no "standard." I began at $40 per finished hour (nearly twenty years ago) and I know there are many places where not much more than that is still offered.

AFTRA has started taking a much more active interest in setting a standard "union" rate for this work where once they were willing to have it be calculated on a general "per hour of studio time" basis. This doesn't work for audiobooks where narrators time in the studio for each finished hour can vary enormously depending on the ability of the narrator and, not least, the type of book being read.

Something around $200 per finished hour seems to be the current aim for a professional "union" standard around the country, but don't expect to get that until you've a proven track record. Residuals are rarely, if ever, paid to narrators at this time (if they were I could probably retire on the proceeds from Steig Larsson's Millennium series!) and whether they ever will be remains to be seen.

Time and budget note: Each finished hour requires several hours of behind the scenes preparation in the form of pre-reading, pronunciation and character research, and so on — any week I "finish" 10–15 hours is a good week.

What should go on an audiobook demo?

Begin by thinking about what books you are most suitable for. Check out the publishers you want to send your demo to and where their areas of expertise lie (if they do children's books then include a sample of a children's book).

There are all kinds of opinion as to how many samples and of what duration they should be. My own preference (and it worked for me) is three samples of at least 3–5 minutes' duration each. I chose a classic (Dickens) a contemporary (can't remember what, but a Ludlum or Metzler kind of thriller could work) and a non-fiction narration. In the contemporary (and possibly the classic) include some dialogue that has two people of opposite sexes talking to each other so a potential publisher can hear the way you handle voices of a sex opposite to your own. The non-fiction can be a biography or a history book, for example. The important thing is that your choices reflect contrasting aspects of your talent.

Demo tip: The people hearing your demo may be receiving hundreds of demos every month. They will not respond to every one (if you're lucky you might get a courtesy letter of acknowledgement). But if they hear something they like they could file you away and, when something suitable pops up later, call on you for a full on audition. Don't forget that if you can point to positive reviews for a lengthy reading on librivox.org, for example, that's certainly not going to hurt your chances.

What insights can you give about reading long books?
Make sure you've got a glass of water beside you! Don't spend your evenings out with the lads (or lasses), and it's probably best to avoid those sports events or loud concerts where a lot of shouting is involved. Bare in mind what I said earlier about stamina — make sure you are well rested and healthy.

In the actual recording, if you are using character voices then take notes to remind yourself of what kind of voice each character has – even recording a separate sample to listen to later to remind yourself.

Be gentle in your choices — a gruff voice may sound good for the first page, but hurt horribly by the thirtieth!

Final words of advice: If you've done all the preparation (pre-reading, pronunciation lists, and so on) then you shouldn't have to work too hard, so relax — if you enjoy the story you are sharing, then your listener will too.

Want to become an audiobook narrator? Here's what Audiobook Publisher's Association (audiopub.org) suggests:

1. Apply for the job with a professional demo that showcases your ability to do:

    *   Male/female voices
    *   A range of emotions and settings
    *   Different accents/dialects and languages (when applicable)

2. Set yourself apart from the thousands of others trying to get in. You need more than a "nice" voice.
3. To be considered for narration work:

    *   Research what companies you would like to work for
    *   Find the name of the person who hires narrators
    *   Submit a professional package that includes your demo and a cover letter

4. Network and go to industry events. This is a time to get to know (not solicit) industry professionals. The following is a list of conferences:

    *   Audio Publishers Association Conference
    *   American Library Association conferences

- Publishers Marketing Association conferences
- Book Expo America
- Book London Fair

5. Acting and voice-over experience helps. Take classes at colleges and universities or volunteer for community theatre groups. Consider joining AEA (Actors' Equity Association) or AFTRA (American Federation of Television and Radio Artists) labor unions.

If you have additional questions about breaking into the industry, contact *AudioFile* magazine at guide@audiofilemagazine.com. You may also want to join APA (Audio Publisher's Association) at audiopub.org.

Time to Practice:

I had a lot of fun writing audiobook samples to represent length and style differences for creating demos to submit to audiobook publishers. The three styles are fiction, non-fiction, and children's story. When recording these samples, it's optional whether or not to include a musical intro and outro. Publishers want to hear your vocal range, acting ability, visualization technique, and style. You may find that you are better at one style than another and want to focus your career accordingly. Reading audiobooks takes a lot of time and stamina. Many commercial voice actors are not interested in this part of the business for time and money reasons.

Fiction

This is my humble attempt at a potboiler romance novel. Try reading it with feeling and restrained tension. There should be slight differences in tonal quality between the man, woman and narrator voices. No need to make the voices extreme. You can play around with mic distance when reading the lines that are shouted from other rooms. When it's an internal thought, lean closer to the microphone.

Daze of Love & Money

Dennis slammed the door behind Cheryl and stormed into the kitchen. "I'll kill him!" he fumed as he opened the freezer door and grabbed a handful of ice cubes. One fell to the hardwood floor and shattered, sending ice splinters all over the room. "Just my luck," he mumbled to himself as he threw the remaining ice cubes into a glass and bent down to pick up the icy shards.

"Are you okay?" Cheryl yelled from the living room. Dennis didn't respond. He picked up his favorite single malt and poured it into the ice-filled glass, added water, and took a sip. "It'll be okay," he could hear Cheryl announce with stifled conviction. "Only Alex giving me the fifty grand back will do that," he thought to himself as he gulped down the remaining drink. "Come and join me," came a distant muttering as he fixed himself another Scotch and water. He sighed, took a sip, and walked into the living room.

Cheryl was lying on the sofa, the lower part of her thigh exposed. He was startled by her long, thin legs and temporarily forgot he was angry. "Why didn't you tell me to stop?" "You usually win," she mused. He sat down, smiled and kissed her index finger. A jolt of electricity shot through his body. How was it possible that she could still do this to him? He leaned over and kissed her firmly on the mouth. Her moist, sensuous lips responded, linking their racing hearts together. They fell back on the sofa and were lost in the soft, feathery pillows. For a moment, he forgot about Vegas; and his friend's encouragement to keep bidding when he was down and things kept getting worse. Why didn't he stop when he was twenty grand up? Things would be different now. As she wrapped her legs around his, he temporarily forgot what had happened that evening.

As suddenly as things began, a loud bang, bang, bang at the door startled the couple back into reality. "Who's that?" Cheryl whispered, her heart racing. "I don't know," Dennis confided. The enthusiastic knocking continued as a voice shouted through the door, "Open up!"

"Police?" Cheryl questioned as she stared at Dennis.

"I was stupid but I didn't break the law."

From the distance they heard the voice again, "Dennis, open up. It's me. I need to see you."

"Alex?" Dennis shrugged at Cheryl in disbelief. "He's got a lot of nerve."

Reluctantly Dennis walked to the front door and let Alex inside. His hair was a mess, shirt stained with sweat, and he held something in his hand.

"Couldn't this wait 'til morning?"

"We won!"

"You're drunk."

"We won. I won it back."

"Slow down."

"After you left I felt bad so I thought I'd try my hand at it and I did it. I won back the fifty grand and made a little profit."

"How much profit?"

"You better sit down."

"I'll stand."

"Thirty-five."

"Grand? You're kidding me, right? Is there a camera hidden somewhere?"

"No, for real man. You know me. I've never been lucky. Tonight I was. I could feel it when I told you to keep bidding."

"Where is it?"

"In a safe deposit box."

"Is that the key?"

"You can get the fifty grand back and I figured we could split the rest."

"50–50?"

"I was thinking more 30–70, but why not? 50–50 it is. Let's shake on it."

"Deal. Cheryl, don't go anywhere. I'll be right back."

Cheryl heard the men's voices trail off as they got in the car and drove off to collect their winnings. She opened a bottle of champagne that was sitting in the wine rack. As it popped open and fizzed, she wondered if all the money would be there or if taxes had been taken out. While putting ice in a bucket to chill the remaining champagne, she decided she didn't care. She smiled to herself as she sipped the warm beverage.

Non-Fiction

Often, non-fiction books are more technical in nature and require a more straightforward read. Rather than the primary goal being about entertainment, it's about informing and educating the listener. It's imperative that you sound like an authority on the subject. The information is easy to deliver and it should sound like you personally know the people mentioned and how the device works. Below is a story I wrote about the origin of cameras. The target market is camera enthusiasts, photography students, and history buffs. The intelligence level of the listener is college-level and up.

Photography: A History In Pictures

Joseph Nicéphore Niépce, a French inventor, created the first photograph in 1826. He used a pewter plate covered with the petroleum derivative, bitumen of Judea. He discovered that bitumen hardened when exposed to light and a negative image remained once the unhardened material was washed away and the metal plate was polished. By covering the plate with ink, he was then able to press it onto paper to create a print. Until his death in 1833, Niépce continued to refine his process.

In Paris, Louis Daguerre used Niépce's notes and continued his work, introducing a photographic technique called *daguerreotype* in 1839 that utilized silver on a copper plate. It became popular during the Industrial Revolution, as middle-class citizens wanted their portraits taken. So why are photographs today not called daguerreotypes? Years earlier, in 1832, French-Brazilian painter and inventor Hercules Florence created a similar process and named it *photographie*.

As the photographic race continued, Fox Talbot entered the scene. He read about Daguerre's invention and added an effective fixer. In 1839 he created the first glass negative. A year later, he invented a process called *calotype*. As Talbot spent most of his remaining years defending his patent, George Eastman refined the process of reproducing positive prints and used it as the foundation of his chemical film cameras.

Eastman made many photographic improvements over the next twenty years. In Rochester, New York, in 1884, he developed a process using dry gel on paper. This would later become known as *film*, making photographic plates and toxic chemicals unnecessary. In an effort to make photography easier and more financially viable, Eastman's Kodak camera went on sale the summer of 1888. Its slogan explained it all: "You press the button, we do the rest." The mass-market appeal had started and continued with the introduction of the Kodak Brownie in 1901.

Children's Story

This is a lighthearted children's story I wrote for preschool children. In real life, only a sentence or two would be on each page accompanied by a colorful illustration. Since the audience is small children, feel free to create interesting, fun voices for each of the characters.

Alice The Alien

Garbon and his crew were cleaning out the spaceship as they did every century or so when they ran across a picture with an odd-looking creature in it. He had never seen anyone before who wasn't green.

"Captain!" he yelled. "What is this?"

Captain Zobalt turned the photo sideways, squinted his eyes, and sniffed it.

"Does it smell?" asked Gargon.

"No," said the Captain.

Captain Zobalt took a bite out of a corner of the picture, chewed it for a few moments, and spit it out.

"Does it taste bad?" inquired Garbon.

"Not bad, just bland," the Captain explained.

"Like the dish Chef made us last night?" Garbon said.

"A little better than that," remarked Captain Zobalt.

"What should we do with it?" questioned Garbon.

"We will find its owner and return it!" said the Captain.

"Oh goody," said Garbon, "an adventure!"

Captain Zobalt clicked a few buttons and the spaceship shifted into its fastest time travel mode and sped away.

"Where are we going?" Garbon inquired.

The Captain replied, "To a planet far away called E-Arth."

"E-Arth," sighed Garbon, "I like the sound of that."

Meanwhile back on E-Arth. . . I mean Earth, a little girl named Alice was being driven to school by her mother.

"I hate school! Nothing fun ever happens," complained Alice.

"I packed a green apple in your lunch today. It's your favorite color," said Alice's mother. "You also have on your favorite shirt. 'I Love' on the front and 'Aliens' on the back."

"I do love aliens. I dreamed I was on their spaceship and left a picture of me so they'd remember."

"Oh, Alice," said her mother as she shook her head. "When will you ever grow up and quit believing in such nonsense?"

"It's NOT nonsense," Alice shouted as she got out of the car and slammed the door. She looked up at the sky as she walked inside the school.

Meanwhile, the spaceship was quickly approaching the alien planet. Lights flashed and beeps sounded as Captain Zobalt narrowed down his search for the owner of the photo. "Gladzindo!" the Captain exclaimed as he located the creature in the photo.

On the playground, Alice stood looking up at the sky while the other kids ran around her, played hopscotch, jumped rope, and slid down the slide. The recess bellhad rung, when she saw it! "Aliens!" she shouted as she pointed towards the sky. The other kids looked up for the first time and saw a spaceship. A bright light shown on Alice and two things fell from the sky. Alice caught one in her right hand and one in her left. One was the photo of herself that she had left the aliens in her dream. The other was signed "Zobalt and Garbon." It had two green, scaly creatures in it with yellow eyes and sharp teeth that seemed to smile at her. When she held it up to the sky for the other kids to see, she saw that it had something written beneath their names. It said, "Believe hard enough and dreams will come true." The light went away as quickly as it had shone on her, and a breeze filled the playground as the spaceship sped out of site. Alice smiled up at the sky and waved goodbye to her friends. "Thank you," she said as she carried the pictures to her classroom for Show-and-Tell. Today was going to be a good day.

Chapter 18

ANIMATION, VIDEO GAMES, & TOYS

While each of these areas needs character voices, they all require different techniques and approaches. A cartoon is linear, with one beginning, one middle, and one ending. Video games are non-linear. They have one beginning, numerous middles to accommodate the good, mediocre, and bad player actions, and multiple endings. The character may celebrate a victory, become injured, or die. Playing all these emotional situations requires even more understanding of the character's background and demeanor. Voices in toys are typically very short sound bytes. The target audience is small children who demand excellent entertainment value and fun. Since the sound files are also compressed onto a tiny chip inside the toy, extremely crisp diction and consistent breath support to sustain the sound are essential.

To understand each of these genres, we need to step back for a moment and understand how they evolved. Then, we can embrace and appreciate the styles. Please note that the following historical recounting is from a voice acting perspective and my personal experience rather than a technical vantage point.

• Cartoons

Vaudeville influenced radio and radio influenced the early days of television. Cartoons, when they finally had sound, had the same comedic timing and larger-than-life appeal. Three main actors are attributed to some of the most memorable characters and that we still emulate and replicate today: Mel Blanc, Daws Butler, and Paul Frees. Mel & Paul performed on radio and Daws was a puppeteer.

June Foray, Stan Freberg, and a host of other voice actors of the time contributed to the cartoon styling we still enjoy today.

Mel Blanc, "The Man of a Thousand Voices," worked primarily for Warner Brothers. and later for Hanna-Barbera. His hundreds of memorable creations include Bugs Bunny, Porky Pig, Daffy Duck, Tweety Bird, Sylvester the Cat, Wile E. Coyote, Speedy Gonzales, Pepé Le Pew, Yosemite Sam, and Foghorn Leghorn for Warner Brothers.; Woody Woodpecker for Universal Pictures; and Barney Rubble from *The Flintstones* and Mr. Spacely from *The Jetsons* for Hanna-Barbera.

Daws Butler is most noted for the characters he originated for Hanna-Barbera, which include Yogi Bear, Quick Draw McGraw, Snagglepuss, Fred Flinstone, Cogswell, and Huckleberry Hound; Droopy Dog for MGM; and the commercial character Capt'n Crunch.

The third icon was **Paul Frees**, to whom I had the pleasure of talking many times. (Actually, I did little more than listen. His stories about himself were always fascinating.) He had an amazing four-octave range, from the deep voice of the Haunted Mansion at Disneyland to the little Green Giant vegetable in Jolly Green Giant commercials. He played Ludwig Von Drake for Disney; Boris Badenov for the Rocky & Bullwinkle shows; Inspector Fenwick in *Dudley Do-Right* and Ape in *George of the Jungle* for Jay Ward cartoons; and the Pillsbury Doughboy and Toucan Sam (originally voiced by Mel Blanc) in TV commercials.

In the early 80s, when I was breaking into voice-overs, I worked in the office at Coast Recorders in San Francisco, Paul's studio of choice. He would enter wearing a three-piece white suit with a gold pocket watch. The studio had a special cabinet inside the office where he stored cigarettes and whiskey. Depending on the character he was to play that day, he'd smoke, take a small shot of whiskey, or do both. I asked him how he got into the business. He said that when he started out, he told everyone that he could do a hundred voices. No one believed him. In those days, the recording studios were very close to one another and it was easy to find out what project someone was working on. So, he'd dress up like a cowboy and show up at a studio that was casting a cowboy voice. They'd look at him and hear him talk and immediately hire him. Then, he'd hear about an Italian casting call and dress the part and book the job. Within a week, everyone hiring voices knew he really could do a hundred voices.

Over the years that I got to chat with him, I often sat in on his phone patch sessions. I'll never forget his deep, resonant voice that he called "the cheap Orson Welles" from my favorite commercials. While he was recording one of his trademark characters, the new director on the other side of the phone gave him a line reading. He assured the new hire that he knew what he was doing and that he had originated the character. The woman made another directorial comment. Paul, with much bravado and little restraint, asked to speak to her superior. She put him on the line. He stated his displeasure. The woman was fired on the spot. In those days, voice talent had power!

From the early days of animated silent films, to full-length talking features, to Saturday morning cartoons, to evening adult cartoons, to CG films, 3-D animation, and shows on Adult Swim, cartoons have expanded from childhood audiences to adults of all ages, all influenced by the great voice actors, writers and animators of the past.

• Video Games

In the 1990s, the use and amount of voice in video games took off when floppy discs and cartridges were replaced with CD-ROM. Rather than a few words, grunts, and efforts, whole sentences and complete stories could be told. With the increase in storage capabilities, the demand for good acting also became apparent. In the Bay Area, where many of the big video game companies emerged, the first-place producers went to find actors in Equity theatres. What directors soon discovered was that, while the stage actors were capable of good acting, they liked playing to the back wall. Volume issues on the mic coupled with down sampling and compression to conserve space on the disc made it necessary to train actors in a new style of acting.

Since I was a voice actor and instructor, and I owned my own voice acting school, I was approached to direct and teach actors how to perform more effectively. I cast and directed dozens of games for Sega, Sony, and other large game companies (many of which were acquired, merged, or became defunct a decade later) and taught the actors how to *implode* rather than *explode* on the mic. At one point while directing *Dark Wizard,* I had to go inside the studio and pull my student J. S. Gilbert's arms and have him resist me so I could get the proper intensity for the scene. A new voice came out of him that he said he'd never be able to replicate. Since then, he's used it in numerous other games. Over the years I went on to cast, direct, and train actors in other games like *Spawn, Aliens, Star Wars Chess, Mario's Time Machine,* one version of *Mavis Beacon Teaches Typing, D2, Skies of Arcadia, Mother Goose's Farm,* and numerous others. Since then, imploding with proper intensity on the mic has become the norm.

DVDs with ten times the storage as CD-ROMs brought forth another growth opportunity for voice actors. 3-D, motion capture, high-definition video, cloud computing services, and motion-sensor games have resulted in greater realism visually and technically and therefore even more truthful voice acting to match the picture.

Of course, during all this time in the U.S., other countries were inventing video games as well. Which each new game that enters a market, it needs to be localized to that area's language or dialect. Actors with the ability to look at a short scene, time out the lip flap, and deliver an emotionally charged performance that matches the facial and body movements in one or two takes are actors who work a lot and are in high demand.

Currently, there are many large video game companies producing base games with 10–50 hours of game play. That means multiple recording sessions for voice actors and repeat business a year or so later when they release the expansion packs. Styles include MMOG (Massively Multiplayer Online Games that handle hundreds or thousands of players), MMORPG (Role-Play inside the MMOG where players interact inside a virtual world), Strategy (requires the player to think and plan), RTS (Real-Time Strategy, which adds positioning and maneuvering capabilities), FPS (First-Person Shooter — weapon-based combat gun and projectile weapon shooting from the player's perspective), Action, Sci-Fi, Horror, Racing, Sports, Military, Realism, Fantasy, Hop and Bop, Puzzle, Exercise, and an assortment of games for kids of all ages.

· Anime

Merriam-Webster Dictionary defines anime as "a style of animation originating in Japan that is characterized by stark colorful graphics depicting vibrant characters in action-filled plots often with fantastic or futuristic themes." The drawings are detailed and typically have fewer frames per minute than the American cartoons mentioned earlier. Many stories originate from Manga, the Japanese form of comic book that is popular among children and adults. In the 1980s, anime started gaining favor in other countries. While still a niche market, its global popularity continues to increase in films, television shows, DVDs, and on the web.

The Japanese voice actors who originated the parts are very serious about their profession and are stars in their own right. With each new release, they are interviewed by the press and discuss the complexities of their character in great detail. The majority of anime work outside of Japan requires ADR (automated dialogue replacement). While other North American cities localize anime, Los Angeles and Canada perform the majority of it because they are equipped with the talent and studios necessary to record each file quickly and stay on budget.

My anime experience in San Francisco is with two titles: *JoJo's Bizarre Adventure* and *Saikano*. I casted and directed both of them. It took three months in the studio to complete the first twelve episodes. Over time, top talent was able to record 45–60 files an hour while other actors never recorded over 15–20 files an hour. Of course, some of the files may have only been a breath or a grunt. In contrast, 10–15 files per hour are common in high-budget cartoons but it is expensive on shows with small, targeted audiences and dozens if not hundreds of episodes. From a voice acting perspective, it is easy to evaluate the speed at which an anime episode has been dubbed by the quality of the performance and the exactness in matching the lip flap. That's why many hardcore fans prefer the original subtitled versions to the ones that are localized. As a voice performer interested in this type work you must work hard to quickly match the flap without jeopardizing the authenticity of your performance.

• Toys

If you walk into a toy store, it appears that almost every toy talks. As a kid in the 1960s, I had a Chatty Cathy doll. You'd pull the string and a little record player inside the plastic chest would play her voice. After time, the record must have slipped from its position. So when I pulled the string, rather than giving a short, happy greeting, Chatty Cathy let out a slow, demonic, incomprehensible message. I LOVED it!

Skip ahead to the mid-'80s. Cassettes inside the toys played messages recorded by voice talent like in the extraordinarily popular animatronic bear, Teddy Ruxpin. A decade later, electronic learning toys became the craze. Leap Frog rode this wave and quickly became the fourth largest toy company in the U.S. behind Mattel, Hasbro, and Lego. This time they put the voice on a chip. Finding a voice that everyone liked and had cut through value when down sampled to 8 bit. Clarity, diction, articulation, vocal placement, and range were major factors, in addition to acting ability, in who could voice a product. I cast many of my students in their early talking books and interactive toys. The actress who went on to play their main character, Leap, was attending my characters class. In addition to the traditional casting session, I had everyone in the class audition for the role. For over ten years, she recorded voices for the company on a regular basis.

While toy technology and moveable parts became more prevalent, the need for unique, fun, and engaging toy voices increased as well. Over the past twenty years I've voiced, casted, directed, or recorded dozens if not hundreds of toy voices. In a talk with one of the founders of Worlds of Wonder, who went on to form his own toy ideation company, he told me that some years ago a toy with very simple technology outsold all the other toys that Christmas because the voice was so funny. People walked by the store display, heard the voice, and had to have it. This was a wake-up call to the toy industry that the voice, in addition to the latest technological breakthrough, couldn't just be good, it had to be amazing!

Now, the chip inside the toy has improved but is still not perfect. Certain sounds have to be over articulated or even changed to a different letter ("d" instead of a "th") depending on the unique properties and manufacturer of the chip. The toy may be plugged into the computer for additional information or personalization. This provides a steady income for the talent. Several of my students have spent months and even a full year recording names and phrases for one toy. Technique for voicing dolls often involves concatenation (individual sentences or phrases that will be linked together through computer coding to sound as if they were recorded at one time) and parsing (individual words, phonemes, and phrases that will be inserted into a concatenated sentence). This requires precision on the actor's part and the ability to provide multiple inflection endings — up, down, and straight across — so the parsed word can be at placed appropriately in a sentence. A voice actor who understands the pattern and can deliver it each time in a fresh, fun, exciting, and new way is a voice actor who can work in this area.

- ## Mobile Games, Animated Greeting Cards, & Casual Gaming

Another use of character voices is in mobile and smart phones, PDAs, portable media players, tablets, and other small or lightweight handheld computing devices. There are a multitude of game apps with limited amounts of voice, sound effects, and music that require short, cute, funny, or dramatic emotive sounds, simple words, or short phrases. Others take a more cinematic approach and have characters set up the scene. I work with a company that provides mobile greeting cards to a few of the major mobile service providers. Every month we record a batch of seasonal greetings. Each recording must be humorous and clean. No breathing sounds, no laughs, no sighs. It must have crisp, clear diction and no slurred words. The delivery can't be too fast, either. If the line is programmed into the avatar with these errors, its animated mouth spasms, wiggling back and forth uncontrollably. This is not very romantic when sending out a Valentine's Day greeting. Personality, vocal punch through, and consistency of the recurring characters at each session are essential.

INSIDE THE ANIMATION WORLD

Bob Bergen, voice actor in hundreds of commercials, imaging branding for radio stations, animated features including *Tangled,* *TinkerBell, Spirited Away, A Bug's Life, Iron Giant, Cars, The* *Emperor's New Groove, Up,* **and** *Wall-E,* **plus numerous interactive games. An Annie Award nominee, he stars as Porky Pig in Cartoon Network's** *The Looney Tunes Show.*

When creating a character, what's the most important thing to remember?
All characters have a voice. But not all voices have character. Animation voice-over is all about the acting: giving life to the words on the page. The script is a skeleton. Your job as the actor is to give it a body. Most importantly, commit to your choices. Commit to your character. Don't concern yourself with the sound as much as the personality and heart of the character.

Can you offer a tip to those interested in breaking into the animation business?
Study acting and improv before studying animation voice-over. Without solid acting skills you will be spinning your wheels in an animation voice-over class.

What comprises a good animation demo?
When it comes to a demo, originality in character is key. No one needs another kid's voice, or witch, or superhero. They need original kids, witches, and superheroes.

Check out the demos of your L.A. competition on Voicebank. Dee Bradley Baker, Daran Norris, Grey DeLisle. You need to be better than those already represented and working. And if you aren't, don't make a demo until you are. You'll get one shot per listener.

You want your characters "doing," not just "saying." They need to have some kind of action or interaction going on, rather than just commenting on a situation. This will show off your acting skills as well as your vocal skills. Each character isn't just saying wild lines. These are scenes, with an unheard scene partner. Who is this scene partner? What is the relationship between the characters? Where are they? Having all of this figured into the small clip or scene will add perspective and interest. Even a 5–10-second clip will be enriched in character with these layers figured in.

You also want contrasting characters and intent next to each other. No intro or exit music between characters. No technical fading out or drop of acting energy at the end of each byte. You want voice, attached to voice, attached to voice. Often a demo producer will have establishing music or sound effects at the top of each byte to let the listener know the demo has moved on to the next character. This shows off the work of the producer, not the actor. Better to allow the contrasting character, contrasting energy, or intent let on that you've moved on to another character.

Never tell a story. The demo should sound like a montage of clips from actual cartoons presented in a minute to a minute and a half. Never repeat a character. No back and forth conversation between two characters. Start the demo off with a character using your own voice. And every character should be *you*. No partner reads.

Never use copy from workshops or classes. Class scripts are usually actual auditions, and the agents and casting directors have heard them a million times. Comic books are great resources for animation demos. And make sure you use a producer who knows what the agents and animation casting directors are looking for in today's market.

Finally, never produce your own demo unless you are a seasoned demo producer with a successful track record. The demo needs to move fast enough so the listener doesn't get bored, or have the urge to fast forward to the next spot. And the demo should leave the listener asking for more. More means a meeting for representation, audition, or job.

Ned Lott is a freelance producer, voice director, and casting director. He has worked on feature-related projects for Walt Disney Company, Pixar, Nickelodeon, Warner Brothers, and Universal, including *Cars, Finding Nemo, Lord of the Rings, Coraline, Pirates of the Caribbean: Dead Man's Chest, At World's End*, three animated features out of South Africa and France, and seven Studio Ghibli titles, including Hayao Miyazaki's Oscar™-nominated theatrical release *Howl's Moving Castle*.

You started out in the '90s directing video games for The Learning Company using primarily non-union talent, you then became the senior manager at Disney Character Voice, Inc., and hired union talent in films and video games, and now you're a freelance director. What's the difference between directing union actors and non-union talent?

With non-union talent there are so many levels of talent that the strongest actors have an opportunity to rise to the top with solid acting and character voice skills. In directing non-union, you often don't know what level you are dealing with, so it can be a challenge to find top-level talent in a short timeframe. Overall, union actors tend to be more consistent in their skills. Since they've had to prove themselves to get into a union, they are automatically on a stronger level, and therefore the expectation is to find even higher-level talent in that same short timeframe. With that said, I've found equally talented actors on both sides and continue to strive to find new surprises.

Can you name some of the union actors you've directed?
I've worked with many of the industry's top talent, including Christian Bale, Lauren Bacall, Shia LaBeouf, Billy Crystal, Whoopi Goldberg, Dakota Fanning, Anne Hathaway, Angela Lansbury, Geoffrey Rush, and Uma Thurman. I also cast Liam Neeson as the voice of Aslan for *The Chronicles of Narnia: The Lion, The Witch And The Wardrobe, Prince Caspian,* and *Voyage of the Dawn Treader.*

When selecting talent, what do you listen for in a demo?
If it's a demo to showcase an actor's talent, I'm listening for strong characters, acting, and reading skills every time, and it helps where the demo is good quality. I like to hear something that is unique and memorable, that helps that actor stand out. In regards to a specific demo for a part, I'm always listening for a perfect fit…the voice that I hear when I look at the image of the character and know that it would come out of the mouth of the character.

Is there a difference between demos targeted to video games versus cartoons?
Seems like the acting for video games and animation projects for TV and features are becoming similar…as technology increases, many more video games are having stronger acting segments and solid dialogue. So my feeling is that both demos can be the same, as I want to hear strong acting and great characters for both.

Besides good acting, what do you listen for when selecting a voice?
Strong believable characters, good reading skills, a nice fit with the other voices in the cast, a voice I'd want to listen to for hours and hours.
Can you offer insights into the use of voices in social games, like the ones you see on Facebook?
With social gaming, there are going to be quite a few new opportunities, and I encourage actors to research which companies are producing

them to try to get in the door for voice parts. There will be many types of roles, both non-union and union, and the actor should be willing to go for the small parts starting out. I recently directed my first social game voice session and it reminds me of the early interactive days before CD-ROM. Small parts and quick sessions, with lots of potential around the corner for larger parts and solid work.

Mark Evanier is the writer-producer of the *The Garfield Show* that is syndicated around the world and *Garfield and Friends*, seen on CBS for seven years. He has written and/or voice-directed *Scooby Doo, Mother Goose & Grimm, Dennis the Menace, Felix the Cat, Dungeons & Dragons, Richie Rich, CBS Storybreak, ABC Weekend Special*, and many more.

What's your main criterion for casting a character?
The main thing I look for in casting is acting ability. The actor who says "I can do 200 voices" is (a) deluded as to his own versatility and (b) selling quantity over quality. That's really a sign of amateurism and besides, I don't need someone who can do 200 voices. I need to find the person who can do the one voice I need and maybe double or triple. The original voice of Garfield, Lorenzo Music, had a long, lucrative career in cartoons and commercials doing his one voice. He had a unique sound and when you gave him a script, he found every joke on the page and delivered it to perfection.

Do you have any other casting tips?
The other thing I don't need is mimicry. The fact that you do a great Homer Simpson is nice, but I'm not likely to be casting that role. Save that for if and when you have a chance to submit for a specific voice match assignment.

What do you listen for in demos?
I listen to demos and ask myself the question, "What can this person give me that I can't get from the actors I know and have worked with in the past?" Once when I had to cast a witch, I waded through the demos of about sixty actresses, all of whom were pretty much replicating June Foray's witch voice. I didn't need any of them because if I'd decided that's what I wanted, I could have hired June Foray...which I did. A witch voice that didn't sound like June's might have caught my ear, but there wasn't one.

How did you become a voice director?

I became a voice director in self-defense. In fact, I think of myself as a writer who extends that job to casting and direction. My first voice directing job was on a prime-time animated special I wrote for NBC. When it came time to hire a voice director, all the good ones were unavailable. I looked over a list of who was available and told the network folks, "I can't do a worse job than any of these guys." They agreed and so let me cast and direct. I hired a voice cast so good that a rhesus monkey could have directed the thing and the show came out fine. Since then, I feel the main part of my job is casting. And my second most important role is to set the right atmosphere where everybody has fun and no one feels defensive if they screw up and have to do multiple takes.

Can you describe your directing process?

I cast the roles when I write or before the session, but I never tell the actors up front what I'm hearing in my head. Instead, I'll say, "What would you like to do as this character?" I'd rather hear what they'll come up with and sometimes it's much, much better than what I have in mind. It's the same with simple direction. I may have in mind the way I imagine a line being read but rather than impose that on the actor, let's hear what the material suggests to them. I can always give the actor more direction later, but I can't take away what I've told him.

During the job, do you bring each actor in individually or as an ensemble?

I don't like to work in splits. I vastly prefer "ensemble style" where the entire cast is in the room, playing off one another. I pass out scripts, assign roles, and then give them a brief description of the action. Their script just has the dialogue but mine has the dialogue (with matching numbers) and all the stage descriptions, character descriptions, etc. I try to make the process quick so we don't rehearse. We start recording and if necessary, dump the first takes. Ideally, we do twenty or thirty lines in one take — until we get to a good stopping point — and then I will offer criticism in as non-threatening a manner as possible, and we'll do pickups on the lines that bother me.

Do you ever cast new talent or do you stick with actors you've used in the past?

The people I hire are the people I hire. I tend to favor those who've performed well for me in the past but there are always new people.

Ultimately, it comes down to a hunch. Actor A seemed more like the character I had in mind.

Is there a difference between the director and actor scripts?
Absolutely. Here's an example from the first six scenes of a *Garfield* script I wrote titled "The Perfect Pizza."

Full Script:

```
                        "MOTHER GARFIELD"

FADE IN:

EXT. ARBUCKLE HOME - AFTERNOON

It's a very nice day as we PUSH IN on the scene and go to --

EXT. SIDE OF THE HOUSE - CONTINUOUS

Jon's metal trash cans are lined up along one section under a
window.  A stray cat named HARRY (rather scrawny and tough-looking)
wanders up and begins opening trash cans, rooting around inside,
slamming down the lids, etc.  Making a lot of noise.
                        HARRY                           <1>
            [HUMMING]

INT. ARBUCKLE HOME - CONTINUOUS

Garfield's trying to sleep but the noise of the CANS and HUMMING
wakes him up.  He gives an annoyed look to CAMERA.
                        GARFIELD                        <2>
            Waking me up is a crime punishable by
            no less than fifteen years in a maximum
            security prison.

Garfield settles back down and tries to resume sleeping.  But
after a few more seconds of the CANS and the HUMMING, he's awake
and he gives us another look.
                        GARFIELD (CONT.)                <3>
            Or at least, it should be.

Garfield gets up and heads for the source of the noise.
                        GARFIELD (CONT.)                <4>
            All right, I'm up.  Let's see who's
            too stupid to not be sleeping at this
            hour.

EXT. SIDE OF THE HOUSE - CONTINUOUS

As Harry continues going through the cans, Garfield appears in
the window.
                        GARFIELD                        <5>
            Oh, it's you, Harry.  What are you
            looking for?

                        HARRY                           <6>
            Leftovers.
```

Voice Script:

<1>   HARRY
            [HUMMING]

<2>   GARFIELD
            Waking me up is a crime punishable by
            no less than fifteen years in a maximum
            security prison.

<3>   GARFIELD
            Or at least, it should be.

<4>   GARFIELD
            All right, I'm up. Let's see who's
            too stupid to not be sleeping at this
            hour.

<5>   GARFIELD
            Oh, it's you, Harry. What are you
            looking for?

<6>   HARRY
            Leftovers.

<7>   GARFIELD
            In this house, nothing is left over.

<8>   HARRY
            So I see.

<9>   HARRY
            What I really had my appetite set on
            was that nice, plump, juicy bluebird.

<10>   HARRY
            Mmmm. Does that look like good eating?

<11>   HARRY
            But I'll bet you've had your eye on
            that one for a while, right?

<12>   GARFIELD
            Not right. I never chase any bird
            smaller than a roast turkey with
            stuffing, mashed potatoes, cranberry
            sauce and that creamed corn that Jon's
            mother makes.

<13>   HARRY
            What? No bird chasing?

<14>   GARFIELD
            I gave it up. Too much work, too
            many feathers, not enough drumsticks.

<15>   HARRY
            Come on. A cat never gives up bird
            chasing.

Time to Practice: Age Range

Age range is important when building your stable of characters. You need to think like them, move like them, feel like them, and speak like them. Study people in each of these age ranges. Select and write down their most unique qualities. Record *their* voice and practice. Record *your* voice and see how well it matches. Take your time. Write down everything your character likes and dislikes. This will give your character strong opinions.

Baby

Whaa! I wanna go back in the dark again where it's warm. Let me back in! Whaaaaaaaa! It sure is bright out here. Who are you? Put me down! Upside down, cool. Whaaa! That smarts. You hit me! Hmmmm. You people look nice. Do I belong to you? Hey, what are you doing? I can't move my arms. Ah, nice and warm. Whaaaah! I'm hungry. Whaaah! Give me something to eat! Where's my thumb?

Five-Year-Old

Being five is not easy. I keep stubbing my big toe on the bottom of the swimming pool. I wanna go swimming in the big pool! Mommy says if swim right and don't doggie paddle, things like this won't happen. I don't get it. My toe hurts when I swim, not when I stand.

Ten-Year-Old

What's happening to my body? I hate it! It's so embarrassing. I wish my bother/sister would move to Australia. That's on the other side of the world, where he/she belongs. He/She likes to turn out the lights in the bathroom when I'm taking a shower. He/She is such a jerk.

Fifteen-Year-Old

Do you think that girl/boy who sits next to me in math is cute? Yesterday she/he asked to borrow a pencil. It's got teeth marks on it. That's cool. She/He probably thinks I'm a dork with these stupid braces.

Twenty-Year-Old

College is sweet. You get to live away from home and stuff like that. Lots of hotties, know what I mean? Costs some bank. The 'rents nag that money doesn't grow on trees. What do they think credit cards are for? Duh. Get a life.

Thirty-Year-Old

What are you doing this weekend? Cool. See you at noon at the coffee shop. Need a double skinny mocha latte after last night! We'll chill there for a while and then go for a ride. Gotta pick up the jacket I left at the club.

Forty-Year-Old

Honey, will you pick up the dry cleaning on your way home? I'm taking Johnnie and Sally to soccer practice after work. Oh, the car is making a weird noise. Can you take it to the shop? Have a big meeting on Thursday. Hey, what should I pick up for dinner?

Fifty-to Sixty-Year-Old

Can't believe it. Our daughter, married. Guy is nice enough. Been living together for years. He's in management. That helps. Why do weddings have to cost so much? Should have let them elope.

Seventy-Year-Old

Oh, look, honey. Our social "insecurity" check arrived. We can take that cruise. Always wanted to see Alaska. Hear it's beautiful. Humpbacks and orcas, sea lions, and fresh salmon. Sit back, relax, and enjoy the scenery. Should we ask Fred and Martha to join us?

Eighty-Five-Year-Old

Do you want to see pictures of my great-grandchildren? I've got ten. That's Bobby. Or is it Ted? The old memory's not what it used to be. Darn cute kids. Play too many video games. Should go outside. In my day, I used to shovel snow for entertainment.

Time to Practice:

The following scripts are an assortment of applications and performance styles to practice your character voices. You should build a stable of ten go-to characters that you know completely, inside and out. From there, you can layer on accents, ages, and different physical attributes quickly when auditions or jobs come up. It's too late to create an in-depth character on the spot. It needs to have a foundation. Don't stand like yourself unless you're using your own voice as a character. You'll have a tendency to drift back into your natural voice. Stand a unique way for each character, use a different set of muscles, and position your mouth, tongue, and teeth in a unique and different way. For your speech to be clear and understandable with these added impediments, a new rhythm, vocal placement, and attitude will result. It will feel odd at first. Later, your body rather than your mind will know how to play that character's actions. Don't forget that it's all about action; after all, the characters are "animated."

Good Versus Evil
Video Game
Style: Fantasy Realistic Cinematic

Specs: These two characters are polar opposites competing for control of the Great Island World. The Evil Sorcerer requires a low male voice that is slow, steady, and commanding. The Good Queen needs a mid to low female voice that's strong, authoritative, and has a lot of heart.

Evil Sorcerer: I am the great lord of wizardry and ruler of Geldon Island. That is, until it was taken away from me 2,000 years ago during the Battle of Darkness and Light. It was then that a spell was placed upon me by Queen Lordat. She exiled me to a cave beyond the Seas of Zarti. There, I was destined to live eternally as a granite statue. I need you to open the Jar of Turbulence. Only then will the spell be broken. Help me to regain my land and return it to darkness. The people's joyous laughter must be silenced so darkness and terror can reign forever.

Good Queen: For 2,000 years, Geldon Island has prospered. I, and the kings and queens before me, have fulfilled Queen Lordat's wishes and kept the Jar of Turbulence sealed and the Evil Sorcerer frozen in a granite statue. Now, Prince Reuben has mistakenly opened the Jar. The spell has been broken and the Evil Sorcerer is free once more to wreak havoc on our people. Our rich, golden lands are threatened with darkness and destruction. We must gather our allies together and fight. We need your help. Goodness and light must prevail.

Math Fun
Video Game
Style: Edutainment for children in grades 1–2

Specs: The main character is a cute bear teacher. Voice should appeal to young children and have a nurturing, instructional quality. Talent must be able to concatenate and parse. Do not read the lines as one continuous thought. Each parsed word should be read three ways: with an uplifted inflection (for the beginning of a sentence), straight across (for use in the middle of a sentence), and with a downward inflection (to end a sentence). Each line is a separate sound file that will be used in different places in the game.

Okay, class. Settle down.
Welcome to Math Fun!
Today's lesson is counting with coins and dollars.
Let's begin!
If Jimmy has _____ quarters and Alison has _____ dimes, how much money do they have?
That is correct. The answer is _____.
_____ dollars and _____ cents can buy Alison and Jimmy an ice cream sundae.
Good job.
Try again.
Congratulations!
Record each of these numbers three times with different inflections:
One   Two   Three   Four   Five   Six   Seven   Eight   Nine   Ten

Military Action
Video Game
Style: Action Military

Specs: A soldier in a combat zone. The scenes are tense. Must sound real and believable. Use these lines to show a range of intensity and emotions.

Target in sight at 3200 Northwest of my position. I'm going in.
Copy that. Take him down and stay clear of civilians.
It's going to blow. Go, go, go!
Meet back at the rally point.
Watch your lines of fire.

Be careful out there. These are your enemies. Shoot at them, they will shoot at you. Assess the situation before making a move.

Western Round-Up
Video Game
Style: Children's Game

Specs: This can be a little kitschy to appeal to a young audience. Over-the-top cartoon characters okay. Must be fun! Add additional vocal sounds and gestures to fill out the lines and show attitude.

Look out! You're going to fall into the ravine!
That was a close call.
Don't move. There's a rattlesnake.
Oh no. STAMPEDE!
I don't know if I can make it.
You'll have to lead the herd.
Better luck next time, partner.

Space Attack
Style: Sci-Fi Horror game

Specs: The music bed is steady and suspenseful. Actors need to show suppressed fear and be prepared to scream.

Well, today is going to be a piece of cake.
Whadda ya say I beat you in chess one more time.
I heard something but can't see it.
Computer. Coordinates. Where did you last see the alien?
Ahhhrrrrggggghhh!!!!
(gasp) If you ever get off this planet, give *(cough)* this to my mother. *(death rattle)*
You're not going to beat me you slimy piece of dung.

Duck!
Style: Casual Gaming

Specs: Need cute voices to play birds, ducks, squirrels, fish, and dogs in this comedic shooting game. The ducks fly, get shot, dive in the water, etc. Sometimes the other characters get shot or comment on the action. Each sound file is 2–5 seconds long.

Record a spectrum of emotions for one or all of the characters: happy, scared, flustered, running or flying, bored, wounded, dying, etc.

Sam The Fighter
Style: MMO Video Game

Specs: Looking for a series of grunts and efforts while running, jumping, and sword fighting.

A series of breaths to use while the character runs.
Grunts for jumping over obstacles of different sizes.
Hi, ya!
Ugggghh.
You're mine.
Take this, loser!
Ahhhh.
Hmmmm.
Gotcha.
Ha, ha, ha.
I'm not violent, you just make me that way.

Clown Fighter
Style: Cinematic Casual Game

Specs: This adult game app for the phone is targeted to adults. Not your typical fun-loving clown, it should have a sinister and strange sound. Low, gravelly voices are good. Looking for a unique sound.

So, you had the courage to find me. Not running like mice from the apocalypse going on around us. That's my kind of hero, someone not afraid of the unknown. *(laugh)* Alrighty then, let's get a move on. Choose a door, any of them. You'll find the answer inside. Time's a wastin'. We got some killin' to do. And let's hope that's not you.

Cutie Doll
Style: Animatronic Doll

Specs: Should sound like a realistic baby. The crying should not be piercing and annoying but have a cute quality. We'll record phonemes and assorted baby sounds.

Da	Dada
Ma	Mama
Gurgling sounds	
Laughs	Cries
Pway (play)	
Mine	Dat's mine
Gimme	
No	Uh, huh

Fantasy Life
Style: Fantasy World fighting game

Specs: The setting is medieval England. Mordak is a warrior. Glendalin is the beautiful queen, forced to protect her territory. Both have slight British accents.

MORDAK:

Confident:	Men, stand ready. We will not let them defeat us. We must rally together and do everything in our power to slay our enemies.
Shouting to his army:	Hold strong, men. Defend the castle.
Encouraging:	Keep fighting. Don't give up.
Under his breath:	They defeated us. Next time, they will not be so lucky.
Commanding:	Stay behind and take cover. Archers! Man your posts. We will not leave until this castle is in ruins.

GLENDALIN:

Decisively:	We must defend the castle and our territory no matter what. It is my duty as the queen to my family and to my people.
Preparing for battle:	Hold fast and fetch me my armor.
Orating to the crowd:	Be not afraid my people of Xethera. Our army is strong and powerful. You must clear the area for battle.
Satisfied:	Well played. Our enemy has retreated.
Regally:	Bow down, Ogalith. I anoint you Knight of Xethera, keeper of the peace and ruler of my heart.

Power Up
Anime

Specs: The characters are drawn in the typical wide-eyed, spike-haired fashion. They seem ordinary until they are challenged to battle and must summon their powers. They stare coldly at each other before fighting. The fighting scenes are at all different speeds: slow motion, normal, quick cuts, and fast.

SKADE

We meet again, Hojo. It is not my custom to fight a woman but this time I will make an exception.
He summons his powers.

HOJO
Raising her arms above her head.
For you, I will, too.
Shouting.
Stars and Moon unite. Restore my might!
She puts her wrists together for her power up. A beam of light shoots out of her hands, up into the heavens.

BOTH
Ahhhhhhkeeeee!
They fly through the air and attack each other.
Argh! Zoi. Kahhh.
Grunts and fighting sounds as they punch, kick, spin, and fly through the air.

SKADE
This time, you will not win.
He releases a magic snake from his power belt that wraps around Hojo's body.

HOJO
What the…?
Struggling to understand and find freedom.

SKADE
I told you I was more powerful
He laughs.

HOJO
Two can play at this game, Skade.

A piece of her clothing rips off, flies through the air like a projectile missile, and pokes him in the eye, releasing the snake's grasp.

SKADE

He grabs his eye and shouts in agony.

Ahhgghhh!.

HOJO

Now we see eye to eye.

She leaps up into the sky and flies away.

Montabulous Creatures
Cartoon

Specs: The scene takes places in a very colorful office. Outside the window is construction and tall silver buildings. The characters are green and octopus-like.

    Gloria is a bored secretary who delivers her lines in a flat, monotone manner. She might have a New Jersey accent.

    Montabulous is the leader of the alien planet. His wife and secretary henpeck him. To show his power, he's always devising wild plans to change and improve the planet. Any chance he gets, he uses the planetwide public address system to talk to the inhabitants.

MONTABULOUS

Greetings, space creatures. This is your trusty leader, Mr. Montabulous. Now, I know you have been wondering what all this construction is about here on Yelbot. Well, I've come up with a fabulous plan to capture earthlings and have them be our servants. I just love a good mani-pedi in the morning. With 120 finger-and toenails, it takes some time. Now, through our telekinetic abilities, you'll see how it works.

Intercom buzzes.

One second.

Clicks button on phone-like object.

GLORIA

Over speakerphone.

Mr. M, you've got a call on line five.

MONTABULOUS
Hang on while I take this call.
He talks under his breath so the listeners won't hear.
Yes honey, I'll pick the cream puffs up on my way
home from work. Right, I'll get the green, not the
red, space juice, too. Look honey, I'm doing my
State of the Alien report right now. Can I call you
back later? Okay. Right. I'll remember. Tentacle
kisses back at ya. No, I can't do that right now. Oh,
all right. Muah!
He throws a big kiss at her and clears his throat.
Now, where was I?

GLORIA
Over speakerphone.
You were about to tell us about your plan.

MONTABULOUS
Right. Can you cue the music for me, toots?

GLORIA
Over speakerphone.
Cue it yourself, sir. I'm busy.

III. GETTING THE WORK

Chapter 19

THE DEMO

The demo is a voice actor's audio résumé. It is used to obtain a talent agent. Producers listen to audio demos to ascertain if a voice or style matches the job or audition specs. In addition to vocal quality, it should showcase acting range and ability, versatility, believability, timing, diction, and emotional depth. Commercial demos are targeted to advertising agencies and production companies. Industrials are geared to businesses and production companies. Character voice demos are directed to animation, toy, and videogame companies. Audiobook demos are sent to audiobook publishers for book narration consideration.

TYPES OF DEMOS

Commercial, narration, and animation demos are the standard. Each of these categories has subcategories that target very specific areas of the business. Here's the breakdown of demos one could potentially produce:

Commercial

- TV & Radio
- Promo
- Political
- Foreign Languages & Accents
- Trailer
- TV Affiliates
- Radio Imaging

Narration

- Documentary
- Corporate Industrial
- Medical
- Audiobook

Animation

- Cartoon
- Interactive Games & Toys
- Animal Sounds
- Sound-Alikes

WHAT DO YOU PUT ON A DEMO?

Demos are approximately one minute in length. They are comprised of short sound bytes rather than full scenes. Ideally, they are real jobs that you have voiced that are mixed with music and sound effects. For some, the demo may be a mixture of real jobs and ones created to fill in gaps or expand into new areas of the business. Someone just entering the business will need to record every element from scratch.

Commercial

When coming up with scripts for a commercial demo, do not use existing copy from websites that provide audition and job scripts intended for practice purposes only, this book, or ads you've seen or heard. Be original. Newspaper, magazine, junk mail, and web print ads are great resources. Using copy points from the print ads, create new scripts that are style-specific, i.e., real person, announcer, spokes, etc. In the edit, juxtapose styles. A soft, slow, intimate spot may segue into a more high-energy read.

Narration

Website tutorials, technical materials, medical information, travelogues, history books, science data, how-to guides, encyclopedias and other long form reference materials are fodder for a narration demo. Use the most interesting 8–15 seconds from each that showcase a specific strength. Depending on the market you wish to pursue, it may be more technical or more documentary in style. Intelligence, storytelling ability, and authoritative pride are strong assets to showcase in an industrial narration demo. Audiobook segments should be reserved for a separate audiobook demo.

Animation

Compile a list of your most solid characters and write a line or two of dialogue. A high-concept demo, where the characters talk to each other or interact in some way, is very hard to pull off successfully. Instead, record short snippets of dialogue from each of your characters and edit them together. The characters must be well developed and show strong acting ability, action, consistency, and a wide variety of emotions.

SHOULD YOU PRODUCE IT YOURSELF?

No matter how talented you are, it's hard to step away and look at yourself as a product. Having all the right recording equipment doesn't mean you can make a demo for yourself, either. You need another ear to direct and coach you through the process. Do the research to find people in your area who have the best reputations. Listen to the demos they have produced. If you think the person or company is a good fit, then set up a meeting. If you want a particular sound that no one in your area is producing, you may need to go to a different city or larger market to record your demo.

If you have not studied voice acting prior to making a demo or have only taken a one-or two-day workshop, do *not* cut a demo! That is not enough time to fully understand the nuances and requirements of the voice-over business. If you have practiced all the scripts in this book but never received an evaluation from a voice-over coach, you should study with a coach or take voice-over classes before producing the demo to make sure the delivery is on target and not locked in your head. You only have one time to make a first impression, make sure it's your best.

BRANDING YOURSELF: FINDING YOUR NICHE

The first cut on each demo is the most important. Lead with your "money voice." It should showcase your personality and signature way of interpreting copy. The last spot should be a callback, a reminder of who you are and what niche you fill. No matter how outrageous or diversified the spots are in the middle of the demo, the listener should never lose focus of who you are and what you have to offer.

Here are a few niches. Note that these attributes are often listed in the copy specs. Sometimes the talent descriptions are a perfect fit for your style, sometimes not. Versatile actors may fit many of these categories, which makes it harder to brand the actor but easier for the actor to find work.

- Young and cool
- Warm and sincere
- Offbeat and sarcastic
- Confused "other guy"
- Wry and dry
- Deadpan
- Bold and "in-your-face"
- Snarky and ironic
- Imaginative storyteller
- Clean and straightforward

WHAT DO YOU DO WITH A DEMO?

The main purposes of a voiceover demo is to:

- Submit to talent agents for representation.
- Post on talent databases.
- Email to clients.
- Showcase on your personal website.
- Include in pay-to-play sites for job opportunities.

When posting or sending a demo, it is best to describe your niche or niches, rather than the ads you've voiced. On pay-to-play sites, rather than or in addition to posting your entire demo, you may want to cut them up and label each clip to get more visibility on the sites. The company's title does not lend as much hiring information as a description of the actor's voice and personality.

When you have voiced an ad for a company and wish to post that company's logo on your website, you may not necessarily have permission to do so. Many companies have very stringent rules about where their logos can appear and who can use them. Just because it is easy to grab and drag a company logo off a website does not mean you can. Check the *use* guidelines on their websites.

UPDATING DEMOS

The lifespan of a demo should only be as long as you feel comfortable sending it out and having people hear it. For some, this may be six months. For others, six years. Does it accurately depict your current abilities? Have technology, styles, and attitudes changed so that it sounds dated? Did you just voice a new job that you know would be a fantastic addition? Do other people's demos sound better than yours? Stay on top of your career and change your demo as often as you need to stay competitive.

Chapter 20

GETTING AN AGENT LOCALLY & BEYOND

Having one or more talent agents isn't absolutely necessary to work in this industry but it sure as heck helps! Talent agents have connections to higher paying jobs. They work with you to earn income together. They negotiate the best financial rates possible. They act as liaisons between the talent and producers, directors, writers and casting directors. An agent is someone you should trust, respect, and talk to for career guidance. Reputable agents never require a registration fee. They work on a commission basis. If you don't work, they don't get their percentage pay. Should an "agent" ask you to pay a fee up front, keep your wallet in your pocket and walk away.

WHERE ARE THEY?

Major and secondary markets have numerous voiceover agents. Smaller markets may or may not have voiceover agents, or for that matter, talent agents of any kind. To find a comprehensive list of talent agencies around the country, go to the SAG.org website. There you will find a listing of SAG franchised and ATA/NATR agencies [Association of Talent Agencies and National Association of Talent Representatives]. From that list, you will need to do additional research. Go to each talent agent's website and see if they have a voiceover department. Unless you are interested in pursuing an on-camera career, remove the agencies that do not have a VO department. Next, locate the appropriate person to send your demo. Do NOT send the demo to the president or vice president of the agency. They will not have time to listen. If it is unclear who should receive the demo, call the agency for clarification or ask fellow actors in that market.

REQUESTING REPRESENTATION

When seeking talent agency representation, you should not take a blanket approach. "To whom it may concern" headings will get you nowhere. Every agency has a procedure for submitting that should be adhered to and respected. Most accept emailed demos and notes, others require hardcopies [formal cover letter and demo on CD or USB flashdrive]. Do your research before submitting. Having someone "walk in" your demo is best if you know someone who has a good rapport with that agent and can put in a good word for you. In whatever manner you submit your materials, your note should be brief and informative. The agent should get a clear idea of who you are and whether you're a good personality and performance fit.

Lots of people submit demos to agents every week. Listening to the demos, while necessary in finding the next big money maker for the agency, is not on the top of their priority list. It will take weeks, even months, to receive a response. If they want to represent you, you'll get a call or email to come in for an interview. If they're not interested in you, you'll either get a note that says they're not interested at this time or you will hear nothing at all.

What you say in your submission information may prompt a quicker response. Here is a list of some information to include, in addition to your basic contact information:

- Personality information: what makes you special
- Acting ability/background
- If you have ISDN
- Areas where you excel; your versatility

Be creative in how you word this information so it shows your personality and business sense. Don't be too cute or too dull and dry. Find a way to say the most in the least amount of words.

SIGNING WITH AN AGENT

There's a lot of anticipation and excitement leading up to getting an agent and very little pomp and circumstance during the actual "signing" process. You may or may not have to sign a General Service Contract (GSA). A handshake or verbal agreement may be satisfactory. Some actors may be brought into the agency on a trial basis before the agency makes the official decision to create a long term relationship with that actor.

Most agents want exclusive representation in their market. The actor can seek additional talent agency representation in other areas, but not in their city or market. Having multiple agents is good for increased booking opportunities but tricky when multiple agents request you for the same audition or job. Establish your primary agent and defer to that agency when in doubt.

Only acquire the number of talent agents that you can service easily. Be aware of time differences and how they will impact your schedule. Find a balance between personal and work life that works for you. After an audition is submitted you will either hear nothing, get a "check avail" to see if you're available to record the job on or by a particular time, or receive a booking.

While an actor/agent relationship is intended to last a lifetime, there are times that an actor and talent agent are no longer a good fit. Changing agents is never pleasant. If you feel this is a necessary move for your career, arrange a meeting with the current agent to discuss your decision. If that is not possible, write a sincere and thoughtful note. Keep the information positive and professional. You want to leave that bridge intact should you need to cross over it again in the future.

AUDITIONS

The majority of auditions are recorded in your home studio. A script is emailed to the talent and an mp3 is emailed back. Those without recording equipment or who desire personal direction can go into the agency during a designated time slot. The audition starts with a name slate [First name, last name] followed by an edited, professional performance of the scripted material. Each agency has its own naming conventions. You must follow them or you run the risk of not being included in the audition. Dashes, underscores, spaces, and upper-and lowercase conventions should all be followed. Actors with multiple agents need to pay particular attention to these subtle differences. Submit your auditions on or before the deadline date and time.

UNDERSTANDING AGENTS

Talent agents have their own unique way of evaluating talent. The following interviews are provided to give you insights from their side of the business.

Robyn Stecher, executive vice-president, commercial department head at Don Buchwald & Associates, Inc., in New York

As a talent agent, what insights do you have about actors?
I've been an agent for over twenty years. I believe that acting is a calling. I don't think an actor *chooses* this career, it calls to them. They *have* to pursue it. Otherwise no one would naturally pursue this way of life. It's too difficult.

Do you represent a lot of actors?
We have a relatively large roster. It's sized according to what the market needs. We're an exclusive agency. We don't freelance and therefore our clients do not have representation with multiple commercial talent agencies. We represent actors based on the needs of the market place and based on the number of agents we have servicing the clients.

What type of work does the Commercial Department primarily get?
We have eight agents working in all the areas of commercial work. That covers TV voice-over, radio commercials, animation, promos, documentary narration, industrial narration, politicals, audiobooks, trailers, on-camera commercials, hosting, and celebrity endorsements.

What's the most popular voice actor or style?
The biological voice is less important than the ability the talent has to interpret copy.

How many new actors do you take on each year?
That's really dependent on what the market is asking for. We are highly selective and bring on very few each year because we want to properly service our signed clients. For example, we don't want to overburden our list in a specific age or age range. We represent an actor for most of that person's lifetime. When we take on someone new it's because we believe they are unique and they'll develop become someone special in the business.

Have pay-to-play voice-over sites and an increase in non-union jobs affected your agency?
There's a big difference between union and non-union talent. The non-union market definitely undermines the established standards. The more non-union work, the more erosion in the marketplace. The

major ad agencies have been doing some non-union work, however, I believe they are still hiring primarily *union* talent.

One observation I have made is that while we haven't lost agents, we haven't gone out of business, and we are not smaller than we used to be because of it. On an individual basis, our clients are being hurt by this.

Is there a percentage of union work going away?

Yes, the commercial strike of 2000 was the beginning of this downward trend toward non-union talent, however it is only in the last few years that we are starting to really see the damage and harm to our industry with these pay-to-play sites. A realistic vision of this trend, along with simple math and common sense, points to the very real possibility of a continuation of huge income loss for union talent and eventually monetary losses for the agencies who represent them.

How do you receive demo submissions?

Electronically, by mp3 for the most part. Most of the websites will tell you to whom you should send the demo. Use your judgment. The higher-up executives will not likely be the best candidates to hear developmental talent.

Who do you like representing?

The more valuable performers are more versatile. We're really excited about a client who gives a great commercial read and can read promos, and voice commercials and perform documentaries. Someone who's limited to commercials, it's going to be tougher for them. They're still going to make it and have business but they're relying on a particular sector. And that's where you see the big falloff in job opportunities and income.

Do you represent more men then women?

Both men and women are fairly equally represented.

What suggestion can you offer actors?

Find yourself on television. Find who *are* you? Can you voice commercials and record documentaries? Are you good at characters? Can you voice video games or animated films? Chances are you're going to get an agent and do very well. If you're the performer who has a very character-y voice only, your income potential will be very limited.

Can you offer any other advice?

Work on your acting, your improvisational skills, and your interpretation. Take classes. That's what makes you a better voice performer, especially if you're coming up in this business. If you're well seasoned, keep working on yourself.

Do you help actors transition into different types of work?

I think the next question is better and speaks more broadly to the topic.

This is a fickle business. An actor can be hot one year and cold the next. How do you help an actor when that happens?

If someone's bookings flatten out, we talk with them and ask for their feedback as well. We'll say something like, "We've noticed a shift in how your auditions are going." Then we offer some advice. If they're well-established actors, we can't say, "Go take a workshop." We have to help them make a shift to a different style read. We work very closely with our performers at all stages of their career to ensure that together we are creating the possibility for the most income.

Since most actors have home studios, do you represent people around the world?

We have a lot more people from out of town on our roster now than in years past.

Do you still audition people in your office?

We have one or two booths running auditions every day. Each of our agents is very conscientious. We each have our own production company and advertising agency clients. I work on my accounts, the other agents work on theirs. As the jobs come in, we each set them up and decide whom to call in. We rely on our booth director to make sure the reads are the best they can be.

Any parting words of advice you can offer voice actors?

If you are starting out, get into some good classes. Get a good coach. Take this profession seriously. You need to know something about the industry. It's not a hobby. I think people think that because "Everyone says I have a great voice," that they can make money. It doesn't work that way. This is a full-time commitment. It's also a job, so you have to be available Monday–Friday from 9am–6pm, sometimes later. Having your own recording studio is an absolute plus. Be realistic about how long it's going to take to get an agent —

how long it's going to take to get a job. Look for the best work, aspire to be a professional, and it could take a while.

Vanessa Gilbert, president of TGMD Talent Agency in Los Angeles

When Steve Tisherman retired, you, Kevin Motley, and Ilko Drozdoski bought The Tisherman Agency and changed it to TGMD. You continue to focus on the quality of the performer rather than the quantity of talent in your roster. One of your famous actors was the iconic trailer voice actor Don La Fontaine. Can you share a "Don" story so we can get an idea of what kind of person he was?
He came into the agency on a Jewish holiday. My son Ben, who must have been six or seven at the time, and I were the only ones there. He asked Ben if he'd like to go keep Don company and ride in his limo to all his recording sessions that day. So, Don took Ben to his twenty or so work calls that day: Buzzy's, Bell Sound, Woodholly, CBS, NBC, etc. Ben came back with all of Don's scripts with his doodles on them. Don and Ben did that one more time after that.

What can trailer announcers expect to make?
Scale plus 10 percent is a bit less than a $1000 per trailer. Actors do make more because they often record several a week. I wish it were under a union commercial contract because it's selling a film and *not* on a day player's contract. Trailers play in the theatre. TV spots play on the web, airplanes, and in hotels, and lord knows where else — Blockbuster, for one rate. Trailers pay no residuals. If so, it would be a good payday.

When you take on new actors, what is the most important thing you listen for in their demo?
I listen for believability, sincerity, and if they understand the art of voiceover. After that, I listen for a voice quality.

Do you submit every audition?
I listen to the best guys first because they set the bar. After that, everyone has to get at least close to them to make it to the client. If someone isn't believable, no, I don't submit that person. That's to protect integrity.

If a talent continues to not make the cut, what do you do?If I don't think they are "getting it," I suggest that actor get in a workshop. If they don't take voice-over seriously, I have to cut him loose.

Since most people are submitting mp3s these days, you must get a lot of demos.
I don't have time to listen to them. My booth director listens to them all and brings to my attention anyone who would be a good fit for the agency. Unlike some agencies, we do send a response to everyone, even if it's a "no, thanks."

How much money can a voice-over actor make for an ad on the web?
A minimum of triple scale is what the union has decided as base pay.

On your website, you have a fantastic quote about the VO business.
It says, *"Voiceovers move quickly, it's the purest form of art, the purest form of acting. You have to harness your heart and your brain and channel it through your voice, reducing big concepts down to their emotional essence. I love the process."*

How many new actors sign with your agency every year?
We lose about five actors or so a year due to death or leaving, so I have to replace them. We represent actors for commercials that also do voiceovers and others who just do voiceovers.

Is your agency divided into departments: promo, animation, commercial, trailer, etc.?
Our agency isn't. All the agents work in all the different mediums. We love it when an actor has an understanding of every single medium and can shine. It's sad that talent have to be studio engineers in addition to being voice-over actors. It is rare when a talent can cross over with ease.

Do your actors have to live in LA to get work through your agency?
We represent talent from all over the world. They can record from home. The only place it gets tricky is with commercials where the producers want the talent to come into the studio and look at the picture so they can match their read to the visuals. With a lot of talent having capabilities to do that at home, it's becoming less and less of an issue.

Over the years you've seen a lot of changes in the industry. What's your biggest challenge now?
Sites like Voices.com and Voice123.com are making it much more accessible for non-SAG, non-AFTRA, non-quality work. The impact is huge. The pie is bigger and the pieces are smaller. A lot of the agencies aren't SAG anymore, they're ATA. We're a union agency.

Every one of my actors is proud to be a member of the union. We do everything to provide union opportunities and we'll keep heading in that direction.

Do you have any pet peeves about actors when you want to book them, check their availability, or bring them in for an audition?
"Pick up the phone!" That's my main one.

How hard is it to deal with actors who live in a different area of the country?
With ISDN and home recording studios, everyone has to be an audio engineer. We do pay a booth director to come in every day from 10am–2pm to record actors.

How long do you like your demos?
A minute. People can shut it down when they want to, so it doesn't matter that much if it goes over.

I'm sure you use Voicebank.net to receive and post auditions. What do you like about the site?
Keeps most of the casting process "simple." I'm really excited about their specialty voice feature where we can post talent in categories like yodeling, screaming, laughing, crying like a baby, or foreign languages. It makes the search easier. I do miss the one-on-one communication of days past.

Any words of advice you can give an actor?
Approach everything with sincerity. Don't try too hard. Be who you are. Take classes. Know what you're doing. And *answer the phone!*

Joan Spangler, Look Talent Agency in San Francisco

What's the most important element that you want to hear in a demo?
The actor has to have an ability to act. It should have heart and truth. I want to buy into whatever is going on. I want to be unaware that I'm hearing a commercial.

Let's say that you listen to several submissions. All have wonderful, truthful reads but sound alike. How do you select which talent to represent?

If they all sound alike and have a "selling" quality, I might be interested in meeting with them all. From there I can make a decision. Otherwise, I'm looking for a voice quality.

On demos, do you prefer commercial spots to be ordered in a particular way?

No, the only thing that really matters is that I like to have the first spot be just a real person talking about something personal. After that, I really don't care which order the spots are in. I find that most people don't know what their real sound is and hide it fourth or fifth. I suggest that the actor open the demo with that "real" spot. This way, the listener immediately has a strong image of that person.

How important is it in a secondary market (not L.A., NY, or Chicago) to have separate demos for commercials, narration, animation, etc.?

Unless a client has incredible strength in many different areas, I don't think it's a good idea to do it. For actors with a lot of versatility, having multiple demos is useful, especially if it helps avoid confusing people.

As a voice-over agent, what do you consider your hardest job?

The toughest thing that I do is say "no" to someone who's never going to be able to do it. The next hardest thing to do is find the right niche for people who are good but not multiple-voiced.

Is there a drop-off of voice actors losing interest or moving out of a market?

I'd have to say no, not necessarily in the voice business. Theatrical and on-camera talent tend to move on to Los Angeles or New York to do film or Broadway. Voice people seem to stay in the Bay Area. Voice-overs are something they can do locally without having to move around the country. Of course, some people eventually get bored with doing it and stop. For people who thought they were going to be wonderful but for some reason it just doesn't happen, they move on and go back to medical school or explore other career avenues.

Do you have any pet peeves about actors during the interview process?

Many times it is a matter of good and bad manners. Unfortunately, I think that many people just didn't have good manners taught to them when they were growing up. They don't know how to be businesslike in a meeting.

What percentage of talent versus business do you think an actor should have?

I would rather represent someone who has 70 percent business and 30 percent talent than the other way around. People who understand that it is a business are on time, they promote themselves, and they're always creating new material. It's just a lot easier for me, on the business end, to represent them. Someone with a lot of talent who doesn't return calls or emails and doesn't understand how important it is to write thank you letters to producers after the first job isn't going to get the next job.

The actor and the agency need to work together. Obviously, it's always going to be that the actor does the majority of the work because the actor has more time to do it than the agent. The agent should be the touchstone for what it is you're doing. And if you plan to do a promotion, you might want to run it past the agent first. Certainly with any new demo you want the agent to listen first, make sure that it's in the correct order, and that you're covering what's important in that particular market. You then have to do the work to fix it.

Do you have any tips to offer voice actors?

I've always felt that improvisation is the common denominator in actors who work the most. These people can go into a studio and fill in a word here or there, or an attitude, or anything that creates something new off the page. It makes the writer look good and it makes the producer and director look great! They'll remember that and bring the actor back for more jobs.

Chapter 21

MARKETING YOUR TALENT

Self-promotion and marketing are essential for freelancers. It is critical to building name recognition, getting auditions, and booking jobs. Even if you have a talent agent, or several talent agents around the country, you cannot expect to get all your work through your agency connections. Agents represent many actors and cannot concentrate their attention on just one person. Pay-to-play sites have thousands of voice listings. You, on the other hand, only have one person to focus on: yourself. Therefore, *you* must take control of your marketing.

To begin your marketing campaign, think of yourself as a product. What voice qualities do you possess that are unique, different, or interesting? Is it your voice quality? Style of delivery? Versatility? Humor? Years of experience? Is there something special about your name? When voice actor Joe Paulino started his career many years ago he used the slogan, "Not just another rubber voice." It was a clever and successful way to alert clients of his versatility and humor. When I began my career, I used to hand out Clark candy bars. It was my way of elevating a common name, Clark, to a more memorable status. Candy, I found, not only remained on the hips . . . but also on the lips of producers, casting directors, and agents.

In this section, I've broken marketing elements into five sections: Social Networks, Branding, Awareness Campaigns, Websites, and Building a Client List.

Social Networks

LinkedIn, Facebook, Twitter, MySpace, BranchOut, and other networking sites can all suck up an actor's time. The majority of it is typically used to network with fellow actors. On occasion, a real job comes through. Take time to define your services and be strategic about who to "friend." For business purposes, you may need to separate your postings into two sites: one for friends and family and one for the business. The boundaries can get pretty muddy. Mixing the two may be right for you, too. Make a decision about how you want to use these Internet connections and work towards your goal for building a support system, client base, and jobs.

Branding

Branding a cow is painful; branding an actor is not. It's about taking the time for self-reflection and exploration to come up with the proper approach that is unique to you. Every day we see logos, and hear music, sound effects, and tag lines that immediately identify a company. You need just as recognizable a brand in order to stand out from the pack. How you feel about yourself and the service you provide helps you establish your rate card. You need to consider:

1. Name recognition
2. Value
3. Quality
4. Trust

The higher your rankings in these four areas, the more you can charge. If a talent gives away their services or undermines industry standard rates, they are sending a message that their services have little or no value. It may bring in jobs initially, but those buyers, once they have a budget, will go elsewhere for a higher-level performer.

Someone with a résumé of high-profile jobs garners more trust than someone without a track record. Saying you voiced a national product when, in actuality, you recorded something for the local office or dealership down the street does not build trust. Be honest. Call it what it actually is.

The process of name recognition has four steps: Who is this person? I've heard of that person. Give me that person. Get me someone who sounds like that person. At first they don't know you. Then your name sort of rings a bell, but they're not sure. Next, you are in demand and working all the time. Finally, you are so popular your rates go up and certain people can't afford you anymore. They still like you but want someone who sounds like you, only cheaper. By the very nature of obscurity, the actor spends a lot of time at "cattle-call" type auditions where the chances of getting the job decrease proportionately with the amount of people auditioning. You want people to remember you and request your services.

Being a seasoned actor, and having a great microphone, well-equipped recording studio, and ability to engineer the job provides a higher quality product than someone talking into an inexpensive microphone placed on the desk right next to his or her computer. You're only as good as your weakest link, and non-union actors need to charge accordingly.

I spoke with a voice actor who is also a partner in a graphic design firm. This is what he had to say about branding:

Ian Price is an experienced graphic designer with practices in London and San Francisco. He co-founded Price Watkins Design in England and set up the U.S. satellite branch, Price Watkins Media, Inc. He is also a voice-over and on-camera actor in both countries.

What exactly is a brand?

A brand is the *promise* of something. That something is intangible; it could be a guarantee of quality, a sense of prestige, or of reliability. Brands offer a differentiating factor that makes it easier for customers or clients to choose between the many competing product variants.

Why do voice actors need to brand themselves?

To give a supermarket analogy: faced with a dozen types of coffee on a shelf, how do you make a choice? You may be a connoisseur, in which case you can make a rational, reasoned choice. But if you're very busy and you just need to get the shopping done quickly you'll probably go for a recognizable brand.

This is the feeling you need to evoke with your own branding — to create something that feels familiar and reassuring and will instantly remind the client of your own particular qualities in a positive way. Therefore, the look and feel of your website and mailings should have the best possible shelf-appeal.

How hard is it to brand one's self?

Thinking of yourself as a brand involves a bit of a mental jump because it's not about you as a person. The process can be somewhat disconcerting because it is partly about how others perceive you as opposed to how you'd like to be seen. It's primarily about what image and values you project.

To explain this in more detail we'll need to think about what sort of *image* you and your voice portray — this can sometimes be quite different from the image you have of yourself. For example, is your voice more suited to cartoons but you look like an urban sophisticate? Do you sound like Minnie Mouse but look like Jessica Rabbit? Or do you resemble Elmer Fudd but have the dark brown velvety tones of a jazz singer?

What constitutes strong branding?

It must be a clear impression of what you bring to the party. For example, your business card must be a strong reflection of you as an actor — not necessarily you as a person. Although in some lucky cases these two do coincide. You clearly need something that's strong, professional, and memorable. But it's key that the memory left behind is of you.

How can it be memorable?

Brand *tone* is a bit like first impressions; you make assumptions about a person based on things like the way they look, who they associate with, or maybe their accent. Similarly you might judge the tone of a brand by its design. A brand talks to us in a way that reflects its persona: it might be modern and friendly like Apple, exclusive and luxurious like Dior, energetic and on-the-go like Coke, or adventurous and wholesome like Patagonia. The tone must be a true reflection of the brand values; otherwise you might be speaking to the wrong audience or misrepresenting yourself.

What process should an actor go through to create his or her own branding?

You should go through the same thought processes that big companies use so it will be just as memorable.

What items should we consider when building our brand?

When creating a brand for a voice actor, I consider the following:

1. Think about the qualities of your voice. Is it bright and breezy, authoritative, laid-back, or quirky? Seek advice on this from fellow actors, classmates, tutors, agents who represent you, and people who have hired you. Be prepared for the answer. The natural voice quality you think you have might be quite different from what others hear!

2. What kind of energy do you typically bring to a read? Are you a spokesperson, a trusted neighbor, or are you high energy and bouncing off the walls?
3. What sort of clients would be drawn to your particular style of voice? Would it be luxury goods stores, carmakers, grocery stores, or documentary filmmakers? Think about which categories of work your voice is likely to be useful for, and write them down.
4. Pick out colors, textures, and images that appeal to you — for whatever reason. It can be useful to create a mood board for yourself or a graphic designer. Tear out pages from magazines showing elements that you like, or assemble a collection of favorite objects.
5. Repeat this exercise with items that you find unappealing.

All of this will create a background to inform the look of your brand.

How will actors use their brand?
Outputs for a brand may include business cards and other stationery, websites, and marketing or promotional materials. In terms of how much control you have over your brand, you should end up with something that you feel is a true reflection of you as an actor, leaves a good and accurate impression of you, and is a useful reminder of your talents.

How do you know when it's right?
When working through visuals towards a final design, I always tell my clients that if it looks or feels wrong in any way, then it *is* wrong. Don't be bamboozled by design-speak or feel that the person who's creating your look is an expert and must therefore know best. Never forget that it's *your* brand and you must feel confident in how it works for you and be proud of how it looks.

What's good and what's bad branding?
It's a useful exercise when we're developing our own brands as voice-over artists to think about what sort of imagery and icons the most well-known brands have adopted. Generally the most successful will not have taken the most obvious route and there is an element of surprise or fun in their approach. It's a good idea to avoid well-known visual clichés. While there's no particular reason not to use a microphone or a clapperboard, do keep in mind that these are often the first things that everyone thinks of when creating a brand in this

business. They can be made to work, but why limit yourself by using images that nearly everyone else in the business has already thought of? The idea is for your marketing to stand out, so why not surprise them with your brand?

What process is involved in creating a brand?

To start on the creative journey, here are some initial questions to ask yourself when thinking of your voice as a brand:

- How would you describe your sort of voice-over to others?
- If your brand was a color, what would it be and why?
- If your brand of voice-over was a person, describe him or her (note that this person is probably not *you*!).

When you're working on your brand keep the following points in mind:

- Avoid obvious visual clichés
- Consider what imagery might set you apart
- Don't use visuals inappropriate to your brand, e.g., don't be a sports car if you've got a jalopy kind of voice
- Think carefully about the impression you want to create
- What do you imagine the reaction of a recipient would be to your branding? Will they be impressed, surprised, shocked, delighted? Is this the reaction you want?

Can you share some generic layouts so actors can get a better understanding of brand and style?

Here are some examples of branding I created for fictitious people to help get one in a creative frame of mind. Below each design, I describe why the branding works for that individual.

Barbara has both a distinctive voice and a distinctive look. Her voice is quirkily modern and she has a mass of red curls; the idea of this card was to bring them together to make a memorable image so that anyone who sees the card in the future will easily bring Barbara to mind.

Oliver is lucky enough to have the memorable initials OH, so this is a great opportunity to use a speech bubble in a non-clichéd way as a reminder of Oliver, and just to drive the point home, the bubble points directly at this name. It's a surprise because his voice is suited for business and industrial work — which is reflected in the business blue palette of colors used for the card, as well as the steely glint across the back. So there's an element of seriousness but Oliver still looks like a fun guy to work with.

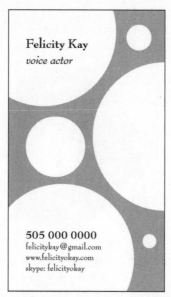

Felicity Kay's bubbly voice personality is indicated by the graphic take on bubbles on her card. Her voice is suited for a young, contemporary audience and there's a fashionista feel to the colors chosen for the card. In fact, Felicity couldn't decide on one color so she had a range printed and will choose the shade depending on her mood and who she's giving the card to!

Tony has a big, bold, newsworthy voice — he would be your headline reader of choice. A punchy take on a business card was a good solution for him. No-nonsense, bold typography combined with a version of a typewriter font to give that newsroom feel.

Millie has a very versatile voice — she can be a spokesperson, a fun girlfriend, and does a great range of kids voices. This range was captured in a childlike cartoon drawing of Millie making an important announcement with a megaphone. The overall result is a charming combination of her talents in visual form.

Keep it consistent — some key design points to remember

When you're putting together your own ideas for websites, emails, postcards, and business cards, there are some key points to remember.

- Make everything suitable for a general audience, so no inside jokes or obscure references. Remember that it's not just going to your friends, it will be seen by people who've never met you and don't know you. This is your chance to show yourself in a good (and memorable) light.
- Don't forget to include all of your essential information. It may seem obvious, but it's surprising how many people forget to add their name, phone number, and email address as a bare minimum. These can be on the front or back of your postcard or business card — but they must be there and easy to find.
- Don't use wacky typefaces that are hard to read. This is not an eyesight test, it's about getting you out there — this

information must be easy to find and easily legible or you've wasted lots of time and effort.

- There are some ideas for business cards shown above — use both sides of the card for more impact and make sure that if your name only is shown on one side all of the other details (including your name again) are clearly listed on the other side.
- Keep consistent. Once you have developed the look of your brand, stick with it and don't try out different approaches for the website, email, and printed material. This will just cause confusion; it's important that everything you send out is clearly from the same place and this will be best tied together by keeping the visual identity coherent across all of your marketing and messaging material.

What are key elements in building a website?

As a voice actor you need a clear easily navigable website. Potential clients don't need to wade through loads of pages to get to your demo area.

The website should be a clear extension of your branding. Everything should look as if it has come from the same place. There's little to be gained in building a show-stopping site that bears no relation to the rest of your marketing material.

A typical voice actor's site map might look like this:

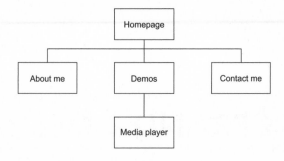

Ideally you will want the content to stream, which means that when a visitor clicks on any content, whether audio or visual, they see or hear the demo immediately. It's a real disincentive to potential clients if they have to download the content and then open it with another application. They just might not be bothered.

Your site should have a password-protected control panel so that you can easily go in and modify the content as necessary. The control panel should be set up in an easy-to-use way, so that it doesn't become a chore for you to keep your site information as up-to-date as possible. Your designer will advise you on the best way to build your site.

And to get you started here's a template for a website home page:

And based on this format, so everything ties together, a template for a postcard (front and back):

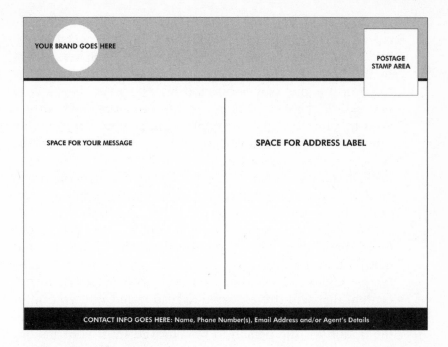

Awareness Campaign

Emails, blogs, postcards, gifts, and promotional giveaways draw awareness and keep you top of mind for auditions and jobs. What works for one actor doesn't necessarily work for the next. It's dependent on that person's track record and personal style. Reminding someone you're still available and would like to work with them again is a whole lot easier than making someone take note of you for the very first time. How do you break into the field or let people know that you want to be hired without being aggressive and a pest?

When you're first starting out or have reinvented yourself with new demos that showcase a more updated style or targeted area of the business, you need to get the word out. The first year is crucial. Here are some suggestions to make producers and casting directors aware of you:

1. **Snail Mail** — Create a series of creative postcards that reflect your personality. It could be a monthly or quarterly comic strip adventure series, weird and unusual photos, adventures your persona has been on, etc. Stay away from pictures of microphones, mouths, and recording equipment. Many peo-

ple do that, so you will blend in and *not* stand out from the crowd. If you've recorded a job that's airing now, let people know it. Listing the jobs you've done is okay as long as you do it in an interesting and unique manner. Keep in mind that some of the jobs you performed may be your client's competitors! So, be careful about what you list and whom you send this information to. People want to hire someone they can trust and have fun working with, not a walking résumé. As a producer and casting director, I'd rather know something about that person, if: they're funny, like to cook, travel, garden, bake, sail, rebuild cars, etc. That personal life story can be intertwined into your marketing materials.

2. **Email** — Using Constant Contact, Vertical Response, Cooler Email, Benchmark Email, or any one of a host of other email distribution sites, you can send and manage monthly or quarterly updates. Once again, you need to provide interesting content that will drive people to read it and hire you rather than delete it or report it as spam. You also need to provide the option for the person to be removed from your mailing list. If people get to know you on a personal level, and you make them laugh or respond in a positive manner, they're more likely to read the email and think of you when jobs come up. Begging for work or bragging about all your jobs quickly moves you into the middle or bottom of the pack of other voice actors looking for work.

3. **Blogs** — If you have something interesting to say, then say it. The majority of the blogs out there are actor-to-actor focused, rather than actor-to-producer. That's because most producers don't have time to check actors' blogs. Once you have worked with a producer and have become a friend, they'll then be more likely to visit and comment on your postings.

4. **Promotions** — Who doesn't like free stuff? Pens, pencils, key chains, mugs, calendars, memory sticks, t-shirts, hats and notepads are just a few items you can use to get your name out there. If your name and logo can fit on it and if it's in your price range, order it. It's the price of doing business. The more unique the promotional product the more it tells about you.

MARKETING STRATEGIES

One of the best voice-over marketers out there is my buddy Harlan Hogan. In fact, we co-teach classes around the country together and he teaches *The Long Haul: Building a Career That Lasts* class at Voice One, my studio in San Francisco.

Harlan Hogan is a voice actor, author of the *Voice Actor's Guide to Recording at Home and on the Road* with Jeffrey Fisher and *VO: Tales and Techniques of a Voice Over Actor*, and creator of the Porta-Booth® audio studios and the Harlan Hogan VO: 1-A micrphone. He can be heard nightly thanking you for "your generous contribution to this PBS station;" in famous slogans "Raid kills bugs fast, kills bugs dead," "When you care enough to send the very best," and "Thick, rich Heinz catsup — good things come to those who wait;" and in political ads that have helped elect thousands of politicians including several presidents.

What's the most common question you get asked by voice talent?
"I'm a voice-over performer — do I really have to market myself?" We all know the answer is yes, but too often we deny the reality of just what that means. Most of us define voice work as the time spent performing in front of a microphone, but that's not the work — that's the reward. The real work of voice-over work is *getting* the work.

Why do you think voice actors are negligent in the marketing and promotion department?
It's understandable that performers would much rather just perform — not — God forbid — sell ourselves. So we ignore, deny, or try to delegate the marketing to others. We *hope* that our performance skills will be enough to sustain our career and keep the work flowing. We sign with an agent and *hope* they'll sell for us. We join on-line casting sites in the *hope* that a constant stream of auditions will keep the doors open. We build hope, not a sustainable business, because we aren't personally and proactively promoting to people who *want* and *do* hire voice talent.

Is marketing the key to success?
My writing partner, Jeffrey Fisher, put it succinctly: "Success as a performer means ruthless and relentless self-promotion." I say, "Talent isn't worth much without a place to use it." We both are saying, "Yes!" you do have to market yourself with advertising, PR, personal websites, sales calls, referrals, developing voice venues, branding, and positioning — aggressive and strategic: Marketing. Marketing. Marketing.

Besides creating the Porta-Booth® and branding your own microphone, what other marketing strategies have you used?
My products for voice-over performers and my work as a voice-over actor share a common branding strategy of absolute quality and exclusiveness. For example, there are hundreds of microphones manufactured but only one specifically designed for voice-over work by a working voice-over performer. Likewise, there are thousands of voice over performers but only one Harlan Hogan. This is a clear-cut strategy that, in both cases, avoids the trap of commoditization. If you allow your product or service to become a commonplace commodity, it is doomed. To make sure that does not happen, I rigorously maintain large customer and prospects lists, have several virtual assistants to design and constantly update three completely different websites for my products and services, and use advertising, public relations, and social media to expand my businesses.

I embrace high-tech but don't ignore the value of a good old-fashioned telephone sales call (even if the "call" is actually over the Internet) and I've made sure my voice customers have something physical that keeps my name on the top of their list. For example, in the last few years I've given away well over 600 Harlan Hogan stopwatches. It's a useful gift and unusual because it's not the commonplace cheap, plastic electronic watch they've become used to (a commodity). Instead, they receive a precision-made, stainless steel wind-up mechanical watch — something many of my younger clients have never seen other than on the opening of *Sixty Minutes*! When they sit at their computer timing a script, every time they look at the face of that stopwatch they can't help but remember: Harlan Hogan - Voice Over.

Websites

First of all, you need your own website. This is your way of hanging up a shingle and saying you're in business. Without having links to hundreds of websites, optimizing your site with key search words, or paying top dollar to GoogleAd Words so your site is in the pay-per-click section, your ranking will not be that high. You have to drive people to your site by adding your link to talent databases and pay-to-play sites.

The largest pay-to-play sites are Voices.com and Voice123.com. For a fee, you become a member and receive email audition notifications. There are several levels to membership and ways you can define the types of jobs you'd like to receive. It's a "beat the clock" type of audition structure. You record from home and upload your mp3s. Within minutes after each posting, dozens of people will have responded. Producers can also listen to your demos and request an audition and job quote. If you book the job, the vast majority of the time you will record it from home and deliver it to the client. Sometimes you get feedback from the producers about your performance, even if you were not selected.

Craigslist is an entry-level way to find voice-over jobs. Type in "voice-over jobs on Craigslist" and several listings should appear from different cities. You can also search a city's listing and mine its site. To do this, go to Craigslist.org, and find the subtitle "gigs" and the "talent" listing. The majorities of the people who post on this site do not understand the value of the performance and often pay extremely low rates.

Voicebank.net is a professional site that talent agencies and producers use. For a fee, talent agencies post their client's demos, receive audition notifications, and upload the auditions. This is an ideal place to post a demo because it is easily accessible to a producer. The majority of the searches are by talent agency, but individuals may post their demos separately.

When you want a place to practice and stay up on the business, try internetvoicecoach.com and voiceoneonline.com. I'm the owner of Voice One and supply written and video content and advice in each.

Building A Client List

While a long, arduous, and never-ending project, developing and maintaining a mailing list is necessary for staying in contact with people who can hire you. Here's a list of resources:

1. **Friends and family** — Let them know what you're doing. If they don't have jobs for you, through six degrees of separation they will help sell you to their friends.
2. **Internet** — Search for advertising agencies and production companies in your city and beyond. Simply type in "production companies" or "advertising agencies." Lots of listings will appear. You can also look in the online yellow pages. Voicebank.net also lists advertising agencies, animation houses, freelance producers, and casting directors. When culling through lists, do your research. Not all of them will be appropriate for your services and talents. Go to that company's website and determine if it is a good fit and who handles voice talent submissions. Large advertising agencies do the majority of their casting through talent agents, so they're a tough sell. Small-to medium-size businesses are better at accepting cold calls.
3. **Resource Guides** — Several websites around the country offer resource information and casting notices. Voiceoverresourceguide.com in Los Angeles and New York, Reel Directory in San Francisco, and the producershandydandy .com in Washington, D.C., are just a few of them.
4. **Talent Agency lists** — If you have agency representation, ask your talent agent if you may use their contact list for a targeted promotion. Many of them will not allow it, but some will if they feel it's a team effort and they approve your materials. Don't expect their list to go out of the office, though. It's proprietary information. If you get responses back, then you can start your own list.
5. **Social Networks** — Yes, you can get work through listings in LinkedIn and Facebook. You're connecting with friends and friends of friends. It's just another approach to the old-fashioned face-to-face time. If you set up groups, remember to be a problem-solver and not a problem.

Whatever promotional ideas you choose, keep them unique and original. Old, rehashed ideas have little or no impact and inspire comparison to the original. Keep your ideas fresh!

Chapter 22

STAYING ON TOP OF THE BUSINESS

Our job as voice actors is to be brilliant. That means honoring the material in a way that motivates the listener to take action and feel. Personality is more important than voice. VO is the only acting business that is precise to the last second and half syllable. It requires building your actor toolkit with technique and acting skills, getting out of your head, and trusting your performance. Clients expect us to be professionals. It's our job to deliver.

Smart voice actors have a gut feeling if they're ready for the business or need more study. Entering the business early should not be financially motivated. The price of success is paid in advance. Study the craft and be ready to be a hero at the job.

The Booking

Whether recording at home or going to a studio, always be professional. Here's a simple checklist:

1. Wear quiet clothing.
2. Don't wear noisy jewelry and take coins out of your pockets.
3. Refrain from wearing perfume or cologne.
4. At least two hours before recording, avoid dairy products and spicy or salty foods.
5. Hydrate. Drink a glass of water at least an hour before recording and bring water to sip on during the session.
6. If recording in an outside studio, arrive fifteen minutes early. [Thirty minutes early is too soon and on time is late.]

7. Bring apple juice, sliced green apples, or vocal sprays and gels to minimize mouth noises and relieve throat irritation like Entertainers Secret throat spray and Oral Balance dry mouth moisturizing gel.

8. Warm up the voice and body so you're mentally and physically prepared.

9. If recording at your own studio and the client is on a phone patch, ISDN line, or Source Connect, test the equipment and allow time for troubleshooting if necessary.

10. Get your questions answered before the recording begins. Then, settle in on a style, attitude, and rhythm.

11. Ask to see video or hear the music bed. Chances are they won't have it, but it's worth a shot.

12. Perform the job with confidence. Never beat yourself up or say you're sorry. When you make an error, stay in the moment and repeat the line again. Know that some jobs are about delivering numerous choices to the client for their approval and some are about getting one good read.

13. If given direction, either verbally or in writing, decipher *what* they want you to do and figure out *how* to do it.

14. When the recording is complete either you or an engineer will edit the file, name it, and normalize it.

15. Delivery will be through email for small files or mp3s and ftp sites for larger files. If neither you nor your client has an ftp site, you can use DropBox, SendThisFile.com, YouSendIt .com or some other Web-based file storage and sharing service.

16. Invoices and payment arrangements can be arranged through check, cash, PayPal, SquareUp.com on your smart phone or iPad if you want to accept credit cards and only pay a one-time transaction fee, or direct deposit. Non-union jobs often take 30–90 days to pay, so try to get the full payment up front, half before the job and half after, or add a percentage to the fee and send a new invoice to the client if it exceeds the 30-day grace period. This should all be on the invoice so you're not surprising them. For union actors, the money portion is all taken care of and the actor just signs the union form and makes sure a copy is sent to the SAG or AFTRA office. Checks usually arrive within two weeks. Non-union actors booked through a talent agent usually receive their payment through the agency.

MOVING FORWARD

Every year, you should write a list of things you wish to accomplish. It doesn't have to be long, maybe five things. Here are some suggestions. Pick and choose what is best for you based on where you are right now. Feel free to add other goals that are not on the list.

1. Buy a microphone or a better microphone.
2. Take a voice-over class.
3. Expand your client list.
4. Get an agent.
5. Define and hone your personal style.
6. Market your talents.
7. Rearrange your recording space so it's more pleasant.
8. Read a VO book.
9. Become a better audio engineer.
10. Join the union.
11. Book a national commercial.
12. Take a singing class.
13. Practice diction and breathing exercises regularly.
14. Join an ongoing improvisation workout group.
15. Take acting classes.
16. Get cast in a play.
17. Add folders in your email to keep track of your auditions and jobs.
18. Book five more jobs than last year.
19. Create a new demo.
20. Assess your pay-to-play site listings and update them.
21. Increase your booking ratio.
22. Respond quicker to auditions.
23. Develop a better system for uploading audio files.
24. Decide how much you realistically think you can make this year.
25. Create a system to achieve your financial and artistic goals.

Saying you want something isn't enough. It takes hard work and dedication. Even though the word "acting" sounds like play, clients take it seriously when they hire voice talent. They've invested their money in you and expect an A+ performance that will support and help build their business.

Decide how you can improve yourself and move forward to achieve your goals.

FOLLOW UP

For first-time employers, it's good to send a thank-you note to the person who hired you. It doesn't need to be long; an email or postcard is fine. Comment on a funny moment, shared hobbies, or cool information you learned. Speak from the heart and don't gush insincere praise. You want to be remembered for additional jobs. But don't tell them that! The note will speak for itself without adding an unnecessary sales pitch.

For steady clients that provide a sizeable amount of work and pay, you might send a gift. It should be something that strikes you when you're walking down the street and see it on sale or you know it's that person's favorite item and you couldn't resist. That gift will send a stronger message of appreciation than a fruit basket.

THE BUSINESS

The primary goal of all actors is to work. Some actors are willing to give away their services for free just for that opportunity. Luckily, the union is there to snap some sense into these people and help them acknowledge their contribution to the business. SAG and AFTRA establish minimum pay rates, referred to as *scale*. If the union actor has been around awhile and the economy is good, the established actor might receive a higher rate: L.A. scale, scale and a half, double scale, triple scale, etc. The talent agent and producer will negotiate that fee on the talent's behalf.

UNION

SAG and AFTRA union performers are considered the top working professionals. In addition to guaranteed decent wages, working conditions, and quick payment schedules, they may also qualify and benefit from union pension plans, health insurance, and dental coverage. While I don't recommend it, anyone can pay the initiation fee and join AFTRA. SAG, on the other hand, does not have an open-door policy. To join SAG, one must first be a principal performer on a SAG job, have three valid union vouchers for three separate days of work as a background performer, or be a member in good standing in an affiliated union for at least one year. The Taft-Hartley Act (a Congressional Act passed in the late 1940s that applies to all union businesses) allows non-union actors under that union's jurisdiction for thirty days without joining. This person's status is referred to as a "must pay." If a person gets union work anytime after that initial thirty-day grace period, he is required to pay the initiation fee and join the union. This principle applies regardless of whether an actor gets another job thirty-one days or several years after the first union job. If the actor does not get union work immediately following the grace period, he has an option to join the union or remain non-union.

Of the union contracts, those for commercials are the most complicated. There is an assortment of categories — wildspots, seasonal spots (spots to run only during holidays), dealer spots, regional or network program spots, local spots, tags, promos, and web. Units and usage dictate how much money an actor gets paid. This system is based on the number of viewing households in an area of dominant influence (ADI). New York, Los Angeles, and Chicago are considered major markets and garner more money for an actor. The word "national," while diluted by the decline of network television, still brings dollar signs to an actor's eyes because of the potential wide scope of unit coverage. The medium on which it airs — network TV, cable, Internet, radio — also has a direct bearing on earnings.

Commercial payments are divided into four categories: session, use, residual, and holding fees.

1. The session fee is based on the actual recording time. The actor is paid for *each* commercial or program regardless of whether it was recorded in less than the allotted time.
2. A SAG use fee is paid when the program airs. Actors who voice national commercials receive additional money every time their commercial airs.
3. Thirteen-week cycles dictate the residual payments. In radio the cycle first starts at the commercial's first airing; in television it begins on the recording session or "use" date. The actor receives a residual payment for radio at the beginning of every thirteen-week cycle in which the spot airs.
4. With SAG commercials, the actor gets the residual payment at the beginning of every thirteen-week cycle and a comparable holding fee every thirteen-weeks that the client elects not to air the commercial continually but holds it for future use.

Tags can bring an actor additional money when they are added onto multiple commercials. Technically, short sentences at the end of a commercial and slogan do not constitute a tag. By union rules, a tag is an incomplete thought or sentence in the body of the spot or at the end, such as, "Today, only $14.95," that signifies a change of name, date, or time. Complete thoughts and slogans are considered commercials. They both generate additional pay for the actor, but on different financial formulas.

The unions have many more complex pay structures that were hammered out in negotiations and approved by the union members. For specific rates in various areas of the business, go to sag.org or aftra.org.

NON-UNION

While not governed by strict union rules and regulations, non-union work offers actors an excellent training ground to learn and master the craft. There is no "magic money." Every non-union job is a buyout. While a few hundred dollars for the job may seem adequate for the time and energy, it can cause hair-pulling and teeth-gnashing if the spot continues to air and preempts a future opportunity for the actor to perform a union job for the competition that could pay thousands of dollars more! The best way for non-union, non-protected actors to not get taken advantage of is to create a contract for the producer to sign. It should state where and for how long the spot can air before additional compensation is due.

Many producers ask non-union actors their fee. This sends actors into a panic. If the actor is new and hungry for work, the rate may be $100, whereas an actor with years of experience might charge $500. With actors lowballing jobs for $50 or less and producers not knowing the difference between a good and bad read, pricing gets difficult. Part of the job of a non-union actor is to educate the buyer. You have to justify the price through:

- Experience
- Recording equipment
- Number of clients or testimonials of satisfied customers
- Interpretation of copy
- Professionalism
- Overall knowledge of the Business

Fi-Core is a fee-paying non-member of the union. That former union actor has approached the union and requested this status in order to take and pursue non-union work. In so doing, they canNOT represent themselves as union members in either written or verbal forms. It is assumed that this resignation is a permanent decision. They are viewed as scabs or anti-union. People who are Fi-Core can book union jobs and get residuals but cannot go to meetings, vote, or take advantage of other member benefits.

As a general note, I suggest that non-union actors use the union rates as their basis for pricing jobs. If you quote a union rate, the producer saves money they would have spent in payroll fees, social security, and allotment due for the actor's pension and welfare on that job. While being hungry for work or doing voice-overs for fun rather than money may be the goal, other people who consider this a business and know how precise and valuable a service it provides should keep the rates at higher industry standards.

EPILOGUE: THE PEP TALK

This book is dense with information for voice actors and speakers of all levels. We all need to communicate clearly, truthfully, and more effectively. We need to make suggestions that someone take action rather than demand results. We must take the two-dimensional words on the page and lift them up so they become three-dimensional, real, and full of life. We need to relax, breathe properly, and allow our personalities to shine through. And, of course, we need to market ourselves, take acting and improv classes, connect and get support from our peers, build a strong client base, become better audio engineers, and ride the highs and lows of this career. It is our job to boldly go where no other voice actor has gone before!

SUMMARY TIPS

1. Pay attention to trends. Watch TV, surf the web, listen to the radio. Are the commonly heard voices quirky, real or announcer-y? Do they have texture, smoothness or crispness? Trust and train your ears; they are your best assets. Use them well so you can continue in this business for a long, long time.
2. Don't let other actors' egos interfere with your confidence or performance. Trust your work and forget comments and posts that get to you.
3. Learn from your mistakes as well as your successes. Personal growth comes through experience. Tough clients make us better performers.
4. Get to know your agent(s) and clients on a personal level, not just as hands that feed you. People like to help friends.

5. Develop a strong stomach. Divorce yourself from any life or client tensions and concentrate on doing the best voice-over job possible.

6. If you're working in a professional recording studio, learn to "read the room." Are you the first to perform or the last actor of the day? You're there to do a job. Don't let your insecurities or need for attention add to the problem. Don't overstay your welcome, either. Be brief, be brilliant, be gone.

7. Use your body rather than your brain. Thinking too much lessens the believability. Trust and commit.

8. Don't get discouraged. It takes time, commitment, marketing, and talent to succeed. Set goals and work toward them.

9. Prepare yourself for lean times. Contracts come and go. You may be a top earner one day and lose the account to a competitor the next. You'll have busy spells and dry spells. That's freelance for you.

10. When you perform, never become less than who you are. Keep your personality alive. Feel the power in the gut. Trust your intuition and creativity. Let your inner child out to play.

11. Strive on a consistent basis to perform at the highest level: unconsciously competent. Creatively, this business isn't that hard. We just make it that way by getting in our own way. Trust, relax, breathe, and believe.

12. Prepare yourself before each meeting, audition, or job. Think and feel first before speaking.

Practice, commitment, and trust are the keys to your success. When you open up your imagination and let the words come alive, the real fun begins! Bank on it.

GLOSSARY

ABC READ Short lines that are repeated three times in the same sound file with different attitudes or inflections to give the editor or client choices. This is used by actors when submitting auditions for 5–10-second TAG commercials. At jobs, it is used to keep track of recordings so that the top of Take 5A can be edited into the bottom of Take 17C.

ADR Automated Dialogue Replacement, used to replace or add spoken word to on-camera actor lip movement.

AFTRA American Federation of Television and Radio Artists. A union for actors, radio personalities, and newscasters.

AIFF Audio Interchange File Format. Professional level audio file format commonly used on Apple computer systems.

ANIMATIC A commercial demo produced by advertising agencies to pitch an account or test a concept. Because the job is not intended for airing, the pay is typically lower.

ANIME Animation style that originated in Japan, with colorful graphics and vibrant characters in action-filled plots that usually have fantastic or futuristic themes.

ANNOUNCER A commercial voice-over performance and style of copywriting. In scripts, it is often abbreviated to ANN, AVO, or ANNCR.

ARTICULATION Clear enunciation necessary for better hearing and comprehension.

BILLBOARD IT A way to slow down or add emphasis to the client's name or key phrases so it stands out from the rest of the copy.

BLEED Sound from the headphones or another actor's mic that gets picked up by the actor's microphone and into the recording.

BODY No, not the person standing in front of the mic. It's the middle section of the script that describes all the wonderful client attributes. It takes the setup information and knocks it down into a solvable client-driven solution.

BOOKING Landing the job through an audition, referral, or demo listen, and having a designated recording time scheduled.

BOOTH The soundproof recording area where the actor enters and speaks into a microphone.

BOUNCE An engineering term used to mix several tracks together and combine them into a single file.

BUTTON Short scripted or improvised personality sound, word, phrase, or sentence at the end of the spot that finishes the scene. It is typically humorous.

CANS Slang for headphones.

CHECK AVAIL Agent's way of checking your availability for a job at a specific date and time. It does not necessarily mean that you have booked the job, only that you are being considered and the client needs confirmation that you are available.

COLOR   The subtle nuances of speech that make the words interesting and meaningful.

CONCATENATION   Recording one part of a sentence with word or phrase variables within that sentence as a means of customizing a response. This is often used in toys, interactive games, and IVR phone systems.

CONTROL ROOM   The recording and mixing room where the director and engineer listen, direct, and record the talent.

COPY POINTS   The essential pieces of information in the script, such as client's name, key words or phrases, slogans, sale items, dates, times, and locations.

DEMO   A voice actor's audio résumé containing an assortment of audio clips that are edited together to show that actor's ability, acting skills and range.

DONUT   A non-fattening announcer segment in the middle of a dialog commercial. The body of the spot "wraps around" the announcer hole.

EDUTAINMENT   Computer games that cleverly blend entertainment and education.

FI-CORE   Dues-paying non-members of SAG and AFTRA.

FILES   The numbers or names of each recording file that is to be delivered to the client.

FPS   First-Person Shooter weapon-based combat gun and projectile weapon-shooting video game that is from the player's perspective.

IMPROV   A commonly used abbreviation for improvisation. It is an important part of voice acting where unscripted and spontaneous sounds, words, or comments are necessary to create a believable story.

INFOMERCIAL   A long commercial structured like an actual television program but is actually a sales pitch.

INTENTION   The tactics or *actions* used by the actor that lead to the end result and character's need getting met.

ISDN   An integration of speech and data used by actors to record their voice in one studio and send it over the phone to another studio.

LEVEL   The recording volume set by the engineer to optimize and capture the actor's voice most effectively.

LIP FLAP   The synchronization of audio to video whereby the voice actor replaces the on-screen actor's dialogue by timing the words to match the lip movement.

LOCALIZATION   Replacing foreign language audio tracks with the language from a new country where the show or product will be distributed.

MILKING   No cow involved in this process. The actor adds as much emphasis as humanly possible while still sounding believable.

MIXING   The engineer's job of combining the actor's recorded voice with the special effects and music to create the finished recording.

M&Es   The audio engineer's music and effects tracks.

MMOG   Massively Multiplayer Online Games that handle hundreds or thousands of video game players.

MMORPG Role-play inside the MMOG where players interact inside a virtual world.

MOTIVATION The prior situation that emotionally connects the actor to read the scripted words in an engaging manner.

MP3 The format used to post demos and email auditions that is typically set at 128 kbit/s. This compressed file is eleven times smaller than the original wav or aiff file. It can also be constructed at higher or lower bit rates for jobs that require a specific size file and sound quality.

NEED The objective or driving force behind the actor's performance that drives the story to its conclusion in an inspiring and meaningful manner.

NORMALIZE A recording tool used to adjust the volume of an audio file to a standard level.

OFF-MIC The area to the sides, front, or back of the microphone where the audio signal is weak because the actor is not speaking directly into the diaphragm.

ON HOLD A talent agency request that you reserve a specific date and time in your calendar for an upcoming job.

OVER THE TOP An instruction given to request the actor's performance be louder, more dynamic, or without constraints.

PAY-TO-PLAY Online voice casting sites such as Voices.com and Voice123, where actors join for a fee, receive audition notices, record and post their audio auditions, and get hired when selected.

PERSONALIZE Speaking into the mic as if talking to a specific, familiar person in order to create an emotional connection and add realism to the written words.

PLOSIVE   The sudden explosion of air as it exits the mouth and hits the microphone. It's also referred to as a "pop."

PLUS 10   A contractual agreement in which the producer agrees to add an additional 10 percent commission to the actor's job payment as compensation for his/her talent agent's time and representation of that actor.

POV   The personal *point of view* of the speaker. It's essential for establishing authority and believability so the listener trusts your client's words.

PRE-LIFE   The history not included in the script that the actor creates and uses in order to enhance the story and have a stronger opinion.

PROMO   A commercial used to promote a movie, TV show, sporting event, musical performance, or theatrical showing.

PSA   Public Service Announcement. Commercials produced to raise the public's awareness of current issues, such as drug abuse, illiteracy and the environment.

RTS   Real-Time Strategy video game that adds positioning and maneuvering capabilities.

REAL PERSON   A popular style of reading copy where it sounds natural, like a real person talking, and not like a professional voice actor.

RESOLVE   The conclusion of a commercial in which all the elements of the copy come together in the final restating of the crucial copy points and suggest that the listener take action: buy, visit, come in, etc.

RESONANCE   The full quality of the voice created by vibrations in resonating chambers, such as the mouth and sinus areas.

RHYTHM The cadence of the words.

SAG Screen Actors Guild. A union for voice-over and on-camera actors.

SCALE The minimum wage a union actor can earn for a particular recording session or job.

SET-UP The attention-getting opening statement(s) that establish the problem.

SFX Abbreviation used for sound effects.

SIBILANCE An unwanted *s* sound that sometimes occurs in speech and often be minimized electronically by the audio engineer.

SLATE Saying your first and last name clearly with an appropriate style, attitude, or emotion that matches the audition that is to follow. The person who receives the audition then has a clear idea about who the actor is and if their personality is a match for that job.

SPECS Descriptive information provided the actor that specifies voice quality, style, and performance desired by the client for that particular script.

SPOKESPERSON A voice actor who is hired on a repeat or contractual basis to represent a company or product. Copy often contains the words: you, us, our, and we.

STAIR STEPPING Having the pitch progressively rise up, down, or zigzag as a means of defining phrases. This technique is especially effective when reading lists.

SUBSTITUTION An acting approach used by the actor to mentally replace a part of the script that they couldn't relate to with a person, place, thing, or real life-event that generates the desired emotional and physical response.

SWEEPS   TV and radio rating periods during which the total viewing or listening audience is estimated. As viewers, we realize this happens when all our favorite programs fall on the same date and time!

TAG   A concise thought or sentence at the end of the commercial that wraps up the story and gives the listener an action or emotional response.

TAKE   The actual recording of copy and the number system assigned to each recording. As in, "Take one, take two, take three…"

TEMPO   The speed at which copy is delivered.

THROW IT AWAY   No, don't put it in the trash! This direction is given when the actor needs to play down and/or speed up unimportant words or phrases.

TRAILER   The voice mixed into a new movie advertisement that plays in the movie theatre before the featured film.

TWITCH GAMES   Video games that require fast finger manipulation of the mouse or joystick.

WARM IT UP   The direction given to smile and lighten up the vocal delivery.

WAV   Waveform Audio File Format (also called WAVE). The industry standard for recording and storing audio files.

WILD LINE   A line of copy that is recorded separately from the rest of the script and then inserted into the original recording. The trick is that it needs to match the attitude, pitch, melody, character, etc.

INDEX

accented speech, 29
acting technique
    attitude choices, 90
    conditioning, 96
    personalization, 50–51, 70
    preparation, 85, 196, 197
    pyramid scheme, 92
ADR (Automated Dialogue
    Replacement), xii, 207, 270
aiff, 9–11, 14, 175, 270, 274
AFTRA (American Federation of
    Television and Radio Artists),
    6, 173, 196, 198, 240, 262, 264,
    266, 270, 272
agent. *See* talent agent
American Federation of Television
    and Radio Artists. *See* AFTRA
American Speech Language and
    Hearing Association, 26, 28
articulation, 17, 19, 25, 26, 36, 208,
    271
audio books, 192–203
    payment, 6, 143, 185–186, 188,
        262, 264–265, 275
    scripts for practice, 198–203
auditions, 5, 10, 29, 64, 88, 92, 162,
    211, 219, 235, 238, 241, 244, 246,
    255, 257, 259, 263, 270, 274
Automated Dialogue Replacement
    (ADR), xii, 207, 270
awareness, 112

Bergen, Bob, xi, 210
Blanc, Mel, 204–205
bleed, 98, 174, 271
board, 248
body, xiii–xiv, 15–17, 49, 90, 96–97,
    262, 269, 271
body of copy, 93, 153, 176, 271–272
bookings, 55, 98, 238
booth, 174, 194, 238, 240–241, 271
branding, 112, 230, 244–249, 253,
    257–258
breathing, 15, 17, 23–27, 47, 263
Butler, Daws, 204–205
button, 42–44, 162, 164, 271

cans, 271
CD. *See* demo
CD-ROM, 206, 213
Churchill, Winston, 30
classes, 7, 24, 29–30, 37, 77, 194, 198,
    211, 230, 238, 241, 256, 263, 268
consonants, 21–22, 131, 192
contracts, 265, 269
copy, 30–46, 272
    adjectives, 38, 45
    comparatives, 43–45
    construction, 42
    copy points, 32–35, 272
    dollars, 36–37
    listener, 31–36, 275, 277
    lists, 31, 37, 39–40, 276

pacing, 38, 174
percentages, 36–37
copywriter, 32, 34, 45, 51, 67, 83, 86
Crane, John, xi, 84
Crawford, John, 89

DAT. *See* demo
demo, 228–232, 272
commercial demo, 228–229, 270
costs, 218
recording, xii, 9–14, 174–175,
193–197
updating, 232
demographics, 45–46
Dewhurst, Colleen, 89
donuts, 100, 106, 124, 272
DVD, 173, 180, 206, 207

Edison, Thomas, 3
emotions, 61, 67–71, 90, 139
Erlendson, John, xi, 96
ethos, 83–84, 87
Evanier, Mark, xi, 213
exercises, 15, 17–20, 22, 48, 92, 263

Frees, Paul, 204–205

Gilbert, Vanessa, xi, 239

headphones, 9–10, 271
Hogan, Harlan, xi, 12, 194, 256–258
holding fee, 265
hook, 66, 79, 191

image, 112, 246
industrial narrations, 6, 46, 230
category I, 172
category II, 172–173
recording, 6, 51
infomercials, xii, 117, 136, 188, 273
intentions, 61, 64–65, 67, 71, 139
Internet, 171, 173, 194, 245, 258, 260,
265
interviews, 171, 235

jobs, 172–173, 263, 270, 274
John Crane Films, 84

layering techniques, 88
logos, 83–84, 87, 231, 245
Look Talent, 241
Lott, Ned, xi, 211

Making it M.I.N.E., 60–71
melody, 8, 22, 30, 72, 76, 81, 277
microphones, 4, 10–14, 89, 255, 258
microphone models for purchase
AKG C414, 13
AKG Perception 120, 11
AT4050, 12
Audio-Technica AT2020, 11
Avant Electronics PS-1, 12
Blue Icicle, 12
Blue Microphones Yeti, 11
C01U, 11
C03U, 11
CEntrance MicPort Pro, 12
Harlan Hogan Signature Series
Voice Over Microphone, 12
JZ BlackHole 1–3 series, 13
JZ Microphone BH-2, 12
JZ Vintage 47, 13
Microtech Gefell MT 71 S, 13
MXL 990, 11
MXL Mic Mate Pro, 12
Neumann TLM 103, 13
Neumann U87, 13
Rode NT1-A, 12
Royer PS-101, 12
Samson G-Track, 11
SE Electronics USB2200a, 12
Sennheiser shotgun MKH-416,
12
Sure KSM32, 12
Telefunken R-F-T AK47, 13
modulation, 75
motivations, 61–62
mp3, 4, 9–11, 14, 175, 235, 237, 240,
259, 262, 274
multiple spots

guidelines for scripts for
practice, 161
Must Pay, 6, 265
narrations, 8, 41, 47, 75, 77, 91, 172,
174–175. *See also* industrial
narrations
needs, 10–11, 13, 182–183, 236
Networking Golden Rules, 5

oral resonance, 29
O'Reilly, Eugene, xi, 24, 29
Orkin, Dick, 77, 89
otolaryngologist, 25, 28

pathos, 83–84, 87
pay-to-play, 4, 6, 53, 231, 236–237,
244, 259, 263, 274
payments, 100, 189, 265
phone patch, 13–14, 205, 262
plosives, 3, 19, 21
Plus 10, 239, 275
pop. *See* plosives
posture, 26, 91
practicing at home, 8
Publicis & Hal Riney, 88
pyramid scheme, 92

radio commercials, 6, 100, 162, 236
recording equipment, 173, 230, 235,
255, 266
recording studio, 5, 9–10, 193, 205,
238, 241, 246, 269
residuals, 6, 196, 239, 267
resolve, 31, 42–45, 60, 70, 80, 93,
102, 105, 107, 115, 119, 136, 275
resonance, 17, 22, 29, 108, 275
rhythm, 8, 17, 22, 48, 72–73, 77, 81,
105, 154, 174, 195, 219, 262, 276
Riney, Hal, 88

SAG (Screen Actor's Guild), 6,
172–173, 233, 240, 262, 264–266,
272, 276
scale, 39–42, 76, 80, 173, 179,
239–240, 264, 276

schedules, 193, 264
Screen Actors Guild. *See* SAG
script. *See* copy
scripts for practice
Anti-Smoking PSA, 142
Baloney's Banquet, 115–116
Brewsky Spud, 144–145
California Tomatoes, 101
Cameo, 167–168
City Fare, 143
Club Sonora, 131
Company Voice Mail, 186
Condor Café, 169
Country Oak, 133
Creamy Delite, 143–144
Creekside Vino, 106–107
Explosion City, 108
Fieldsit Pillow, 153–154
Flowers, 139–140
Fly High Airlines, 130
Funride Cruise Lines, 152
Golden Fields Bread, 102
Good Versus Evil, 219
Google Eyes, 134–135
Happy Homes Realty, 180–182
Heartbeat Way, 128
Illusions, 163–164
Jam Spread, 162–163
Jiffy Lite Dinners, 141
Kitty Menu Cat Food, 103
Lofton's, 132–133
Luggage Rack, 166–167
Math Fun, 220
Minitoys, 107
MovieExpress.com, 132
Nature Series, 190
News Center News Magazine,
104
News Express, 157–158
Peruvian Blend, 125
Precious Darling, 116
Pride Corporation, 182–183
Proposition Q, 142
Quality Hospital, 183–184
Recliner Heaven, 136

ReliableBank.com, 105
Save-a-Dime, 164–165
Skizzer, 117
Sneeze Dust, 151–152
Sofa Connection, 127
Spectacles, 134–135
Splash-O-Rama, 146
Steak Wagon, 127–128
Syber Deluxe 3000, 188–189
Tempting's Morsels, 165–166
Tingle, 155
Train Central, 145–146
Truform Underwire Bras,
    102–103
Tubster, 157
Viberstate Health Insurance, 135
VoiceRecognition, 86
Wonder Insurance, 129
Workerbee Company, 185–186
Zippy Running Shoes, 140
self-promotion, 244, 257
selling, 32, 213, 242
session fee, 100, 265
set-up, 271
SFX (sound effects), 34, 52, 54, 90,
    276
sibilance, 3, 19–21, 276
slate, 235, 276
sound effects (SFX), 34, 52, 54–55,
    75, 77, 90, 115, 120–121, 123,
    133, 146, 193, 209, 211, 229, 245,
    276
Spangler, Joan, xi, 241
station imaging, 112
Stecher, Robyn, xi, 236
storyboard, 52
studio, 9–14, 62, 238, 261–262, 269,
    273
stylized, 111

tags, 100, 265
talent agent, 233–244, 260, 275
    changing agents, 235
    contracts, 234, 264–265
    unions, 236–237

tempo, 72, 77–78, 81, 277
TGMD Talent Agency, 239
Tisherman Agency, 239
toy industry, 209
trailer, xii, 16, 75, 100–101, 228, 236,
    239–240, 277
transitions, 64, 80

undercutting, 78
union work, 6–7, 236–237, 265–266
use fee, 265

Vance, Simon, xi, 193
video games, xiii, 204–206, 207, 277
Voice123, 4, 6, 240, 259, 274
Voices.com, 4, 240, 259, 274
voice-over, xii–xiii, 4–5, 13, 15, 24,
    271, 276
vowels, 22, 72, 131, 192

wav, 9–11, 14, 175, 274, 277
Welles, Orson, 89, 205
word emphasis chart, 81–82

Books from Allworth Press

Voiceovers: Techniques and Tactics for Success
by Janet Wilcox (6 x 9, 208 pages, paperback, $24.95)

VO: Tales and Techniques of a Voice-over Actor
by Harlan Hogan (6 x 9, 256 pages, paperback, $19.95)

Mastering Monologues and Acting Sides
by Janet Wilcox (paperback, 6 x 9, 256 pages, $24.95)

An Actor's Guide: Making It in New York City, Second Edition
by Glenn Alterman (paperback, 6 x 9, 344 pages, $24.95)

The Actor's Other Career Book: Using Your Chops to Survive and Thrive
by Lisa Mulcahy (paperback, 6 x 9, 256 pages, $19.95)

How to Audition for TV Commercials: From the Ad Agency Point of View
by W.L. Jenkins (paperback, 6 x 9, 208 pages, $16.95)

Acting—Advanced Techniques for the Actor, Director, and Teacher
by Terry Schreiber (paperback, 6 x 9, 256 pages, $19.95)

The Art of Auditioning: Techniques for Television
by Rob Decina (paperback, 6 x 9, 224 pages, $19.95)

Promoting Your Acting Career: A Step-by-Step Guide to Opening the Right Doors, Second Edition
by Glenn Alterman (paperback, 6 x 9, 240 pages, $19.95)

The Actor Rehearses: What to Do When and Why
by David Hlavsa (paperback, 6 x 9, 2224 pages, $18.95)

The Actor's Way: A Journey of Self-Discovery in Letters
by Benjamin Lloyd (paperback, 5½ x 8½, 224 pages, $16.95)

Acting Is a Job: Real Life Lessons about the Acting Business
by Jason Pugatch (paperback, 6 x 9, 240 pages, $19.95)

Actor Training the Laban Way: An Integrated Approach to Voice, Speech, and Movement
by Barbara Adrian (paperback, 6 x 9, 256 pages, $24.95)

An Actor's Guide: Your First Year in Hollywood, Third Edition
by Michael Nicholas (paperback, 6 x 9, 272 pages, $19.95)

To see our complete catalog or to order online, please visit *www.allworth.com*.